# ❧ DEFINING ❧ MOMENTS

## BREAKING THROUGH TOUGH TIMES

### Dorothea S. McArthur, PhD ABPP

Cove Press

# DEFINING MOMENTS
## Breaking Through Tough Times
by Dorothea S. McArthur, PhD. ABPP

Published by: Cove Press
Address: 2632 Cove Avenue
Los Angeles, CA 90039-3123
Telephone: 323-666-3598
Fax: 323-666-3598
Website: www.CovePressBooks.com
E-mail: Cove.Books.Publishing@gmail.com

ISBN Softbound: 978-0-9847735-0-3
ISBN Hardbound: 978-0-9847735-1-0

Library of Congress Control Number: 2012932265

First Edition. Printed in the United States of America

10 9 8 7 6 5 4 3 2 1

Photographs by Rob Beckwith.
Author Photograph by Susan Harper Slate
Cover and Page Design by One-On-One Book Production, West Hills, California.

YOU ARE WHAT YOUR DEEP, DRIVING  DESIRE IS.
AS YOUR DESIRE IS, SO IS YOUR WILL.
AS YOUR WILL IS, SO IS YOUR DEED.
AS YOUR DEED IS, SO IS YOUR DESTINY.

Brihadaranyaka Upanishad IV. 4.5
*from The Seven Spiritual Laws of Success,*
by Deepak Chopra

*To my clients for their courage in telling their story*

# TABLE OF CONTENTS

FOREWORD      ix

INTRODUCTION      1

### I. DEFINING MOMENTS
### FROM NATURE

1. If You Are Hit, You Don't Have to Fall      7

2. Two Dirty Ducks      10

3. Brown Leaves and Cactus Bulbs      16

### II. DEFINING MOMENTS
### IN TAKING CARE OF YOUR SELF

4. "To Be or Not to Be ... That is the Question," or "To Thine Own Self Be True"      21

5. Who Do We Need to Please Anyway?      26

6. Building an Introject      28

7. Oh, Please Let Me Sleep      32

8. Don't Put Your Best Friends to Sleep      36

9. I Hate My Feelings ... They Make Me Lose It      43

10. An Anxiety Attack Is Not an Attack      47

11. Integrating Lost Parts of Self      50

12. Fighting Depression the Natural Way      55

13. I Didn't Know I Was an Adult Child of an Alcoholic (ACA)      59

14. The More You Help Yourself, the More Help You Will Get      62

15. Try to Decipher a White Snow TV Screen ... or Decide for Yourself      66

16. So Many Ways to Communicate     70

17. Four Kinds of Workers Interact; Which Are You?     74

18. Life's Two Most Important and Privileged Questions     78

19. Three Most Important Questions for Your
Significant Others     83

20. Our Most Powerful Elixir     86

21. In Memoriam     89

22. A New Way for the Elderly to Grieve     94

23. Warning … Suicide Is First-Degree Murder     99

24. Finding the Right Psychotherapist     101

25. Don't Be Afraid to Ask for a Reduced Fee     104

## III. DEFINING MOMENTS
## WITH FURRY ASSOCIATES

26. How Dogs and Cats Assisted Me in the Psychotherapy
Process Within a Home Private Practice     109

27. Enter Dogs     117

28. New Cats Become Associates     121

29. New Dogs Sign On     124

## IV. DEFINING MOMENTS
## WITH HANDLING LIFE

30. When Greed Takes Away Your Job     133

31. On Birth and War     139

32. When Someone Hurts You … Finding Your Way to
Forgiveness     142

33. A Crisis is Always an Opportunity     146

34. The Backside of an Affair     149

35. It Ain't Changed Since the Cave Man Days     155

36. Protecting Sexual Abuse Victims … From Further
Trauma by Extended Family     160

37. To Punish or Help, That Is the Question          166

38. Three Kinds of Romantic Attraction          171

39. What Makes Romantic Love Last Anyway?          174

40. What Good Friends Can Do but Often Don't          177

41. Artists and Society          181

42. There is a Quiet Way to Be of Service to Others          188

43. Whatever Happened to Right and Wrong?          190

44. What's Happening on My Street?          194

45. Dear CEO/CFO          197

46. A Middleperson Between Low Income and the Wealthy          200

47. It Is Time to Give Artists a Chance to Change the World          204

48. A Plan to Return a Sense of Community, Purpose and Meaning for Sixteen Million Unemployed          210

49. I Wonder What Would Happen If ...          214

50. As a Psychotherapist, I Wish That...          216

## V. DEFINING MOMENTS FOR CHILDREN

51. Anxiety Helps          221

52. Overloaded Report Card Children          224

53. Defeating Bullies Without Getting into Trouble          227

54. How to Help More Difficult Children          232

55. Understanding Adoptee's Loss of Family          237

56. When "I Love You" Means "Please Go Away"          239

57. Adoptee Contradiction          243

58. A Letter of Tribute to Parents of Special Needs Children          248

## VI. MORE DEFINING MOMENTS WITH NATURE

59. Resolve and Staying Power  257

60. Becoming Well  260

61. Depletion Blooms  262

## VII. CLIENTS SPEAK OUT

62. Thirteen Wishes to Rebuild a Nation
From the Clients of a Psychotherapy Practice  269

## VIII. CONCLUSION

63. Japan on March 11, 2011  299

64. When Pain From the Past Becomes a Strength  303

65. So How Do All These Thoughts Add Up Anyway?  305

66. My Personal "Making a Difference"  309

BIBLIOGRAPHY  311

INDEX  314

ACKNOWLEDGMENTS  322

ABOUT THE AUTHOR  323

# FOREWORD

I am pleased to write the foreword for *Defining Moments* because I know this book will be of great help to many people of all ages.

My own family could certainly have benefited from psychotherapy help when I was growing up. Unfortunately, my parents held the all-too-common feeling that you should never talk about your problems to someone outside the family. It was called "airing your dirty linens." I remember hearing my Dad call therapists "shrinks." The look on his face and the tone of his voice told me that he would never consider letting someone get a peek at what was inside him, his feelings about himself and the world. My brother got that message loud and clear. After all, he was raised to be a man, and men took care of business and did it without talking about their feelings.

I remember well sitting across from my brother at his home in Texas as we were discussing the fact that I had started to see a therapist. He admitted that he was having a hard time with personal issues including feelings of being a bad father, wishing he could have a different career, but not knowing how to change work when he had four kids to feed. My brother told me he feared that he was becoming just like our rage-alcoholic Dad, because he found himself screaming at his toddler, and she had started stuttering. He responded, "I can't understand why you think you need therapy? You're the healthiest one in the family." He followed that remark with something I've never forgotten: "If a person can't handle his own problems, he doesn't deserve to be alive." It was one year later that he, a brilliant scientist with a wife and four kids that he adored, took his own life.

I know from personal experience that some problems can't just be handled all by yourself. It was some time after I had begun to see the second in a series of good therapists, that I learned an important piece of wisdom. It takes courage to admit you need help and it's a smart person who seeks it.

Dorothea (known as Dorrie) has deep insightful wisdom that comes from thirty three years as a therapist in full-time private practice. She has gained a lot of experience in compassionate listening, being really present for another human being while setting aside her judgments and expectations. She views each person as her peer, respecting both special qualities and needs. This book is full of kindness, a deep sense of connection coming through each story.

*Defining Moments* does four things. First, it offers real and practical help for people in need. Second, it wakes the reader up to the need, not just for personal support, but for positive transformative change on this planet. Third, she and the clients bring insights about what needs to change within our society now. The final piece that this remarkable book does is to remind us that we can and must place ourselves in direct contact with the intricate and energy filled world of nature; something many of us forget and some of us have never learned.

This morning Dorrie called me while walking four dogs she has taken in as hurt strays. She takes the same walk every morning and today she was excited to tell me that she had just counted seventeen white snowy egrets and thirty-five geese who had flown in and were resting and feeding in a green sanctuary of the Los Angeles River. She told me that one of the geese actually came and sat close to her. I think this bird must have felt the sense of safety that Dorrie's clients feel.

**– Suzanne Arms, Author and Director of the non-profit Birthing the Future, (Birthingthefuture.org), Bayfield, CO**

# INTRODUCTION

I awake in the night and early in the morning with the feeling that we are currently living within an insecure shallow dark world that is hopefully migrating into a harbinger of positive change. This new beginning will be bringing forth greater honesty, integrity, competence, giving, caring, reverence for the protection of our planet, and depth of character within each one of us. I startle as mother nature plunges through the planet, challenging us with earthquakes, tornadoes, tsunamis, fires, storms, oil leaks, floods and dry heat spells, urging us on not to destroy each other and the earth. What can each one of us do to hasten positive change? What can I contribute as an author and Diplomate Clinical Psychologist with thirty three years in private practice?

Arising early, I feed the birds, cats and dogs; take a warm bath to center my thoughts and plans. I walk four dogs off leash by the Los Angeles River where I can marvel at the wild flowers and count the gaggles of beautiful egrets, herons, cormorants, ravens, mallards, stiffs and gaggles of pigeons flying in a large group dance. Finally, I listen to the questions, wisdom and love of my preschool granddaughter on the way to her school, then exercise again with strength training.

Then I am ready to walk into my office to sit quietly and learn from the hours each week dedicated to many different clients. They speak daily acquiring depth in their thinking so that their lives can thrive and they can also contribute to positive change. In the quiet of a therapy hour, we can share thoughts that people don't often say to each other in the real world. Sometimes we share a **"defining moment."** Doing this work is like being in graduate school for life. I've had to write five books to research, integrate and consolidate my thinking regarding their personal and societal issues.

I've always decided to see clients with a wide ranging sliding scale because it does not seem fair that psychotherapy should only be for the upper middle class and the wealthy. However, there are still many people who have decided that they cannot afford therapy at any cost. This is especially true during a prolonged recession for fifteen million unemployed, elderly, disabled, minimum wage workers, struggling artists, families with special needs children, young adults and couples trying to find a place they can afford in an expensive world of college loans, high rents and mortgage payments.

*Defining Moments* is my latest contribution to positive change; making stories, essays, and dialogues available to educated lay public who may be seeking, but are without therapy.

Life can be hard. We all get knocked down, unless we lock ourselves in a room; but then we'd die of boredom. Painful feelings are a rich part of life. The question becomes, "Can I get back up again?" and "What did I learn in the process?" Clients come to me because something is not working well. Together, we look at their life story, discover and honor the knockdowns, articulate unresolved issues, and straighten out any misconceptions. They come to understand how they chose to handle adversity in childhood. Often, the coping skills they needed to survive in their family of origin no longer serve them in the present. Therefore, we discover new ways to handle life and relationships. Finally, they feel sufficiently empowered so that they don't need to talk with me any more.

A "defining moment" is a moment in which something has just been said or demonstrated that is new and "gratefully just right" in helping to solve a problem about living. Some defining moments burst forth suddenly, as represented in some dialogues, while other defining moments come through slowly and are expressed in essay form within this book. Whenever possible, the defining moments have been printed in bold, so that the reader can retrieve them quickly, as needed. Some of the natural defensiveness that we all have to encounter has been eliminated from the dialogues to keep the reader engaged.

I have chosen to write about those defining moments which have occurred in my private life in nature, and during my thirty-three years of practice encompassing some 55,000 therapy hours. These defining moments include issues such as understanding negative feelings, learning from nature, giving support, helping instead of punishing, insomnia, depression, building self-esteem, parenting, adoption, grief, anxiety attacks, male and female work responsibilities, defeating bullies, morality, affairs, friendship, helping others, and recovery from illness, to name just a few. I've stepped way outside of the mainstream, suggesting unique solutions to decrease aggression, and increase compassion.

The recounted dialogues are only a small portion of any therapy hour. However, the knowledge shared between us has seemed meaningful, by itself, to clients in restructuring their lives. Each essay is meant to help people think about their own concerns in a new way, even though it is not a substitute for a therapeutic relationship. For those who feel encouraged to try psychotherapy, there is also an essay on how to pick a competent therapist and acquire a reduced fee, if needed.

In the first section, I've included some defining moments from nature and animals. Some of them have been reconstructed into nonfiction dialogues outside of the therapy hour. The second section is comprised of defining moments that encompass taking full charge of yourself. The third section shares defining moments created by the pets that have been working within my practice. In the fourth section, I consider defining moments about handling life, while the fifth section includes defining moments about children. Finally, a few more defining moments from nature make up Section Six.

Section Seven, entitled *Thirteen Wishes*, encompasses thoughts that my clients and I have shared in regards to larger societal concerns that neither one of us could fix by ourselves in a therapy hour. Together, we have sometimes suggested changes that need to be made within the larger world, and ways that each one of us can contribute. Although essays have been grouped together into sections by topic, each essay can be read independently and randomly.

Most clients choose to talk with me because of debilitating **depression, anger or despair.** We migrate through to **depth** as a result of **understanding.** The depth is richer than material things, and opens the door to **making a difference** which then produces a **satisfactory life.**

I cannot claim that any essay contains an absolute truth. Instead, I describe only the thoughts and feelings that have been shared many times between client and therapist as helpful to others. My conclusions are my own, generated from my experience; they are not necessarily representative of psychotherapists in general. Some readers, I am sure, will disagree, which can be just as useful to them as long as they take the time to discover what they really feel instead. Each dialogue within a therapy hour has had any identifying information completely disguised, or is a recreated collaboration from many dialogues about the same topic. Therefore, any resemblance to any one person can only be coincidental.

I hope that this book will be helpful to students who are in training to become psychotherapists. I suspect that *Defining Moments* may generate lively class discussions about the pros and the cons of what I have decided to say to my clients.

Finally, it is my earnest hope that this book will be available to others, long after I have finished my work as an active therapist, by generating new thoughts, dialogues and resolutions for those who encounter essays related to a particular need. The more each one of us can conduct our lives not only successfully, but also with equanimity, morality and integrity; the greater opportunity we have to peacefully nourish, rather than destroy, both our personal, professional, global and environmental interrelationships.

# I

## DEFINING MOMENTS FROM NATURE

# 1

# IF YOU ARE HIT,
# YOU DON'T HAVE TO FALL

It was dusk on the snow covered roads in the Colorado mountains. Suzanne was driving while enjoying the incredible silence of tall pine trees on either side of the road. Suddenly Suzanne braked as she heard a thunk and watched the vehicle two cars ahead of her swerve, correct and drive on, as if nothing had happened.

The car immediately in front of her pulled to the side of the road. A young couple got out quickly. A deer had been hit while crossing the road. He sat on his crumpled haunches as if dazed by headlights, not yet turned on.

Suzanne pulled over and got out of her car just as the couple was dragging the deer over to the side of the road, clear of any oncoming cars. Suzanne stood in the middle of the road, slowing approaching traffic.

The young deer was wounded but not dead. He sat, frozen like a concrete statue. His eyes gazed nowhere. He was neither dying nor rallying, just stuck in shock. The young couple was also frozen, looking down at him, wringing their hands, dismayed as to how to help further.

No one spoke. The silence was deafening. What to do? How to help? Neither Suzanne nor the young couple had a gun to put the deer out of pain. Suzanne called 911, and asked them to come to put the deer down. Since Suzanne was half way up a steep mountain pass; it would take time for aid to arrive.

It was cold. The couple hugged, reaching for warmth and intuition.

Suzanne walked over to the deer and knelt to be at his eye level. She placed her hand gently on his neck, fearing what he might do since he was a wild animal. The deer did not resist. She gently began to stroke his neck saying quietly, "I'm sorry this happened to you. Somehow it's going to be all right. Take it easy. It's okay if you need to let go. We'll help you and take care of you. I'm so sorry." She kept each movement calm and deliberate to keep the deer from panicking.

The young couple hovered at the edge, nodding slowly as they heard her words. The dusk was turning to dark; the snow continued to fall silently, sticking to the eyelashes of the deer who barely seemed to blink. Occasional cars and trucks drove by, oblivious to the crisis at hand.

The deer stayed a statue; but his body was warm. Time seemed to slow to a snail's pace. Suzanne soon discovered a wound on his left side, however, the bleeding had stopped. Suzanne continued to pat the deer, repeating softly the same reassuring words. She did not want the deer to die alone because she knew aloneness deeply from within her own life story.

Suddenly, life came back into the eyes of the deer. He moved his head, sat up straighter. Suzanne stepped back. The deer got up, gazed directly at Suzanne and then at the couple as if to say, "Thanks, I'll be okay now."

The deer initiated a long shudder that reached into every part of his body. It was as if he was shaking off the trauma completely. He then darted off into the forest, never to be seen again. Would the wound heal? Had his life been saved by kindness, concern, and hope? The shock he had felt only stopped him for several agonizingly long moments.

The deer would go on to fulfill his rightful place in the universe.

The 911 rescue call was cancelled. Suzanne and the couple hugged each other as only strangers can when they have shared a precious moment.

Suzanne climbed back into her car and drove slowly away. The warmth from the car heater made her body shudder from the cold she'd felt standing still, so alone with the deer and the couple.

For Suzanne, when life gets hard, the dark green-brown eyes of the deer come into sharp focus from within her mind. The story of our lives is not about how many times we get knocked down. Rather, it is about whether and how we get back up. Meaning in life comes from helping others get up and learning from them how they do it. **That beautiful deer taught her to take the blow, to accept help from others, to stay with the knockdown until it's understood, then to shake it off completely, letting it go, with forgiveness, and then, to go on, knowing more.**

# 2

# TWO DIRTY DUCKS

O h no! I didn't like what I just noticed.

My husband, David, and I were walking our dogs along the Los Angeles River, watching the mallard ducks bobbing for food in the water with their tails straight up in the air. Young male ducks in their emerald green headdresses flew overhead, swooping and skidding along the top of the water, looking to impress a new female mate. Dragonflies were darting in and out of river flowers. A heron stood watch, silent and still.

Nature seemed peaceful and happy until I noticed two dirty white ducks clinging next to a fence with their backs to the river. They looked grungy, hungry and worried. They clung close to each other. They didn't even know that ample water with their wild feathered friends was only 100 yards away.

A fond memory helped me to notice these two ducks. One Easter, when I was in my early teens, my father brought the same kind of duck home from work. We called him "Jay Robert" This duck survived until Halloween night, then disappeared, probably captured by some Halloween prankster or eaten alive by a fox? I'll never know. I do know that I loved him and cared for him. My parents gave me permission to bring him into the house on occasion. He used to love to drink the leftovers from the glasses left on the lawn after an outdoor cocktail party, then stagger importantly back to his hideout.

It was immediately clear to me that the two dirty ducks, in my present world, had once been owned, caged, and cared for by people. It's likely that they clung to the fence because it most closely resembled the cage they once inhabited. The ducks had apparently been abandoned to fend for themselves like the other wild ducks.

However I knew that these white ducks could not protect themselves because they were unable to fly more than a few feet. They are bred for humans to eat, so they need to be fed. These two dirty birds were literally "sitting ducks" for the band of coyotes roaming around the city looking for food and water.

I was just starting a three-day Fourth of July vacation weekend, overtired from too much clinical work during the last two months of serving a flood of psychotherapy clients. David, was weary, too, from research grant writing at the university. He walked by quickly with the dogs, paying no heed to the ducks. When I brought them to his attention, he responded nonchalantly, "They'll figure out how to get to the river." I heard my own former therapist's voice in my head saying, "It's time for you to rest. You're always helping. Let someone else take care of this one." This voice talks to me when I am too over-compliant in aiding others more than is good for me. Yes, I knew that there were many other people to help who biked and walked each day by the river.

So, with mixed feelings, I made a half-hearted attempt to corral the two dirty ducks towards the river. They clung determinedly to each other and the fence. I gave up on them and went home.

The next day, David and I walked the dogs in the park so I could avoid the dirty little ducks. However, thoughts of them wandered about in my mind. Day three came, and I went back to the river. There they were, still clinging to the fence, even more hungry, filthy and bereft since no one else had apparently taken any action.

I felt bad and ashamed of myself. For the life of me, I could not remember what we fed Jay Robert so I began to ask friends and neighbors. I decided to start with bread and water. Avoiding the ducks was not right, and was disturbing my restful vacation.

Twice a day, I went back to feed my winged friends. Immediately they gulped the bread and most of the water. They used the rest of the water to clean their dirty heads. Their quiet clucking told me just how thrilled they were to be fed. Soon they showed me that they recognized the sound of my car by chortling and running up close to the fence. They became comfortable with my presence. I wanted to take care of them the way I did Jay Robert. However, I did not see how I could bring them home because I had already adopted three abandoned dogs and four cats.

"Soon, those ducks will likely be dinner for a coyote." warned David, "so don't get too attached." I promised to make some calls on their behalf as soon as the holiday weekend ended.

I engaged in an inevitable hour of phone calls with useless prerecorded messages. One overworked Animal Rescue driver said wearily, "I've seven dogs to git to before midnight; we don't do ducks." However, I finally reached a person who directed me to a member of a Wildlife Rescue Organization. She agreed to take them into a flock of three other recently rescued ducks. She would have them transported, by her husband, to a lovely fifteen-acre ranch eighty miles up the coast of Southern California. I felt a burst of joy because this ranch happened to be in the small town where we would retire within the next ten years. We'd purchased a little weekend vacation home there years ago. It was my favorite place to live.

But I had to capture the ducks first and get them to her within twenty-four hours.

It was time to ask David for help. He'd been busy at work, high up in the ivory tower, preoccupied with a major grant deadline. However, he respected my efforts, came home early and agreed to participate in my rescue operation.

David and I asked a neighbor to aid in the capture of the ducks, but he quickly declined to have anything to do with such a project. Instead, he helped us load the car. We gathered two large boxes, pillow cases to put over the ducks' heads, if needed, and some more food and water. David was now actively engaged.

While I fed and played with the ducks, David wandered off down the path alongside the Los Angeles River. Soon, he had persuaded a gaggle of middle school boys, just hanging out with skate boards, to make a quiet circle around the ducks to help us keep them from escaping. Two homeless bearded men who lived by the river watched from a distance with interest.

The ducks had already come to trust me, so I was able to feed them and just pick them up. I even got to hug one briefly. David took them on a two-hour drive in rush hour traffic to their new home, up the coast, while I went back to work for a prescheduled consultation.

I enjoyed speaking several times by telephone with the two ladies who took these two dirty ducks. I thanked them for their warmth and kindness and sent them both a check for duck food and a donation to the Wildlife Rescue Organization. David and I were invited to visit the ducks in their new permanent home any time.

After the ducks were safely delivered, I asked David what he planned to do at work the next day. He responded, "There's plenty to do, but nothing as exciting as those two dirty ducks."

He, too, had caught the spirit and enjoyed our rescue.

David and I did visit the ducks and a lady named Connie who cares for over three hundred wounded or at-risk cats, horses, rabbits, crows, finches, parakeets, pigeons, ducks and gulls independently, and with little apparent outside financial support. She lets recovered birds fly free but many of them prefer to return to her ranch.

The two dirty ducks were fine, living with other birds in a large aviary that protected them from the coyotes. They were dining on lettuce left over from the flea market, dry dog food and water, delightfully clean from swimming in plastic kiddie pools. Maybe I just imagined that they recognized me with their same quiet chortle.

The ducks will fare well, I believe. This is not only a story about the ducks, but also a story about a defining moment for me. It took some time just to watch the now clean and calm birds in comparison to their former dirty worried countenance. **In the process, I gleaned that the only real thing life does is dish out opportunities. I acknowledged, once again, that not helping is painful for me and hurtful to others. Aiding others is not the chore I thought it might be, because the universe will cooperate and respond to the slightest invitation when I play my part with love and honesty.**

As I talked with Connie, I could see what a pleasure it is to interact with an altruistic and generous woman. Difficult situations don't need to be avoided. Rather, they are to be regarded as an opportunity to meet new people and respond in new ways.

My friends are concerned about how to fight back against the dysfunctional and destructive forces of terrorism, corporate greed, scams, inadequate healthcare, and environmental plundering. How do we ensure a stable planet for our children? The problems are so immense, sometimes it seems that the only solution is to "duck and hide." But perhaps it really is as simple as each one of us capturing more giving moments, of not bailing out when there is help to be given.

Each time I go to the river to walk the dogs, I remember the two dirty ducks. They remind me daily to notice opportunities to give to others. Because, as Caroline Myss said in her latest book *Invisible Acts of Power: Personal Choices that Create Miracles:*

*There is no such thing as a simple act of compassion or an inconsequential act of service. Everything we do for another person (or animal) has infinite consequences. Every action gives rise to a ripple effect, just as a pebble that is tossed into a pond sends out wave after wave, widening and covering more and more space. Everything we do and say matters. Period. p.95*

# 3

# BROWN LEAVES AND CACTUS BULBS

Driving out of my driveway to walk four dogs in the park, I noticed a white flower that looked like it was growing out of a cactus. I made a mental note to check it later because I knew that kind of cactus did not bloom in my neighborhood.

Upon my return, I saw clearly that nature was giving me another defining moment. The cactus had hard, stiff leaves culminating in many sharp spikes. Nestled inside this cactus were baby cacti and several white blossoms and blooming flowers tightly clinging together.

The flower did not belong to the cactus. Instead, it was a bulb underneath the cactus that had somehow managed to send a stem and leaf up between the thick, unyielding spiked mother cactus and her babies. The stem had to contort itself, persistently fighting for air and space to accomplish this incredible feat. At the top of the stem were two white flowers and a bud still to unfold. I was amazed because I had never planted a bulb in that location.

**I was quickly reminded that nature does not make excuses. Instead nature makes a plan and tries it out without fear of failure. It either succeeds or fails. We all have good ideas and plans. However, only sometimes, do humans beings follow through into action to succeed, like this bulb.**

More often we have an insight, then we come up with an excuse that makes it impossible to follow through with an otherwise extraordinary plan.

I took a picture of the cactus and the bulb intertwined so I could savor this beautiful message from nature.

Next, I went to the flower store to get some plant food for my garden. After paying, I noticed on the counter a six inch ball of completely brown leaves that looked like they had come from a dead cedar tree. They were selling for $6.00.

I asked the employee, "What is this?"

He directed me, "Take it home and put it in a bowl of water. Within 24-36 hours it will turn green. Keep it in water for two weeks and then plant it in bright light. It will then last forever."

I took it home and did as I was told. The leaves, within 24 hours, unfurled and turned dark green, opening up completely to receive the light. It was beautiful. I put it in the ground and the roots grabbed hold. But the plant faced another crisis when a puppy dug it up. I put it back into water, and again the leaves unfolded in dark green color. It was a reminder that growth can occur even when the situation looks and feels completely hopeless.

I showed both pieces of nature to a couple expecting a child, who had come to visit. They had used drugs. Several friends had helped them to rebuild their lives by providing medical care, shelter, some financial support, a training program, and a job that culminated in a second chance to launch a productive life. This couple accepted and made good use of the help given and were free of illegal drug use for a year. They were building a new life to receive their baby.

I showed the cacti, the bulb and the dead ball of brown cedar leaves to this couple. I offered, "These two plants remind me of you. The cactus is your former difficult life with drugs; the flowers are you pulling away from the drugs to have your own life back again. You have done what the bulb did. Both you and the bulb are miraculous."

The father-to-be responded, "One flower is me, the other flower is the mother of my baby. The baby is represented by the bud."

I added, "The friends who helped you are like the water in the dish where the brown cedar leaves were placed."

"Yeah," he added slowly. "Awesome."

Some of my clients have furled, broken, or undernourished colorless leaves. However, with the right amount of understanding and support that comes from a competent psychotherapy dialogue, they are able to turn green and bloom. That is all it takes.

The bulb bloomed once more a year later, again from underneath and inside the cactus. Another cactus broke through a piece of concrete, reminding me that some of my own excuses are indeed, flimsy.

# DEFINING MOMENTS
# IN TAKING CARE OF YOURSELF

# 4

# "TO BE OR NOT TO BE ...
# THAT IS THE QUESTION."
# OR
# "TO THINE OWN SELF BE TRUE"

## THE UNDERLYING PHILOSOPHY OF THIS
## PSYCHOTHERAPIST

Clients make the first phone call to me for a psychotherapy appointment. Often they say, "I want to come to see you because I'm not **happy** with my life." We make an initial evaluation appointment to speak together to see if I have the expertise they need for me to be of help.

I look for a "successful life" with meaning rather than "being happy" because I see "happy" as only one of many valuable emotions. For example, one day I met with five different clients. At the end of the day, I reviewed my work with them, heard some remarks of appreciation, and decided that it was a "successful" day. I'd helped each one of them in a real way. Out of that experience came many different feelings. I felt enormous frustration and pain as I heard about the cruelty that had happened to one of my clients. I felt a depth of sadness, creativity and insight that led me to write this essay, resulting in a sense of completion and peace. I don't remember actually

21

feeling "happy." However, I appreciated the other emotions because they gave direction and meaning to my life.

We tend to think of "happiness" in relation to "getting what we want." As I observe the clients in my office, I see that "happiness is figuring out who we are."

Everyone is born with both strengths and vulnerabilities. Perfect parenting is not possible. Therefore, every life story has deficits, knockdowns, strengths and growth in recovery. The importance of each experience lies in understanding what knocked us down, and how to get back up again. Every new parent hopes to be the first person to do perfect parenting, yet no one has succeeded. Realistically, we can consider that perfect parenting would leave a child woefully unprepared to handle the knockdowns of real life.

As Mary Pipher said in *Writing to Change the World*, "Darkness is part of the great 'suchness' of the universe." A crisis is not to be avoided because it's an opportunity as well as a danger. Countless times, I have seen that a new opportunity lies waiting behind a client's misfortune. Many of us experience trauma. Our task is to decide whether to live life forever narrowly, as a dysfunctional "victim," or accept the trauma as a learning challenge, mastering it with pride. Trauma presents the opportunity for us to dig down deep below the surface of our awareness where true inner richness lies, and then create the necessary ingredients for renewal. In the process, we become comfortable with fear so that we can handle it next time. Difficulty with life and depth of character go hand in hand; our misfortune and strife often lead us directly towards the very way we are meant to make a viable creative difference in the world. However, it may take many years to assemble all of the pieces that make up the total picture. A life without trauma and difficulty may be a shallow life. When we haven't understood our knockdowns, we can be incredibly cruel to each other by displaying our own unresolved issues with misconceptions, inner pain, despair, violence, and greed. Much of our dysfunctional behavior stems from unsorted previous hurt, denial, ignorance, confusion, loss and distorted memories of experiences, resulting in lack of mastery of life. We owe it to ourselves and others to understand.

As a psychotherapist, I see suffering up close and personal. My office walls are three inches thick with the emotions left behind from the intentional and unintentional hurts heaped upon client after client. Sometimes the only thing I can say that makes any sense is, **"There must be an intelligence to the universe that humans are simply not bright enough to begin to understand in the moment.** Perhaps we are like ants trying to avoid being extinguished under the huge foot of a universal knowledge about the past, present, and future."

Throughout history we have fought wars repeatedly in an attempt to prove that one religion or culture knows more and is better than another. Some seek one religion that explains everything with God in charge "up there," watching us all of the time to make sure that we will be "saved in heaven" if we are good, and "damned to hell" if we fail. Some obey specific rules, hoping to be favored and recognized.

Religion is an attempt to articulate universal truths we can't truly comprehend and is, for me, an artificial oversimplification, at best. However, I do sense an enormous energy and order within the universe. Perhaps there is a plan for all of us individually and collectively that we must ferret out over a life time. It seems as if the universe nudges each one of us at a particular time in a way that comes to light during the psychotherapy hour.

**One of the most magical facts about the universe is that there are no human duplicates. There never has been, nor will there be, another person like myself or any one**

**of my clients.** Therefore, each client has to make a unique decision about what to do with their life and how to make a difference. No one else knows; significant others can only observe and suggest. Sometimes a significant others' threat and jealousy can promote inaccurate advice.

The vast variety of individual strengths and talents on this planet covers every kind of job that needs to be done. Each one of us has the responsibility of figuring out our special talents for the purpose of making our contribution. Every job is of equal value to maintaining the whole universe. Sometimes I indulge in the fantasy of a world in which we all get paid the same salary for whatever job we do.

There are two opposite positive forces within each person that need to be balanced with each other. There is a force to be still, to do nothing except be in the present, rest, relax, sleep, meditate, and rejuvenate. The other force motivates us to do something concrete, to be insightful, creative and effective in contributing something meaningful to someone else or to the survival of the planet. Both forces are necessary to conduct life. If we can keep these two forces balanced with each other, we can be truly effective.

Realistically, we can only make a plan as to what to do with life that encompasses five to seven years because there are so many unexpected turns. As we like to say, "Life happens while we're making other plans." However, we can be guided superbly by reading both our positive and negative feelings. When we ignore our negative feelings with defense or addiction, we lose the power to make effective judgments over time. Unacknowledged emotions fester while weakening us instead of fading away. They leave us, too often, with confusion, and unacceptable plans and behavior toward others.

To mature is to catch the energy that makes plants grow and birds sing. Creativity, as a strength by itself, may appear, but generally it emerges more fully out of a struggle. Only then is there something to say. The universe sends us problems and difficulties so that we can grapple with them and pass on what we have learned to others. Nature also gives much for which to be thankful. Knowing intimately what we have been given helps us decide and commit to what we need to give back to keep the planet flourishing for the next generation. We can have a successful meaningful life that is still open to feeling all kinds of emotions. We can die in peace when we have figured out how we are supposed to make a difference, knowing that we have used our best talents to complete the task. At funerals, the participants address what the deceased have given, not what they have amassed or acquired.

As Mark Morford, *San Francisco Gate Columnist,* wrote on January 3, 2007:

*Our spirits, for whatever unqualified reason, chose to suffer and scream, and pain and joy and come, and lick and try to love because, well, because we have so much to learn. Because this is what we do. Because this planet is one of the most difficult and challenging and brutal schoolrooms in the universe.*

*In fact, the divine (universe) is dirty, beautiful, ugly, sad, tragic, and gorgeous and sticky and mean and deadly and orgasmic and exhausting, all at once.*

# 5

# WHO DO WE NEED TO PLEASE ANYWAY?

## ESPECIALLY FOR PERSONS WITH SEVERELY CRITICAL PARENTS

Sometimes I have a client in my office who feels defeated in terms of receiving approval from others. They believe that there is some way to act that everyone will like. If they can't figure it out, they're "worthless."

We consider together the following story.

I begin by asking, "What do you think would happen if I invited 100 prospective clients to come in and look at the decor of my office and let me know what they think of it?"

Each and every client looks at me blankly, shrugs a shoulder and waits for me to proceed.

I answer, "I believe the following would happen. One third of them would say, 'I like it. I love to look out the window and see the lake with the seagulls sitting on the water. I like the pastel colors, antique furniture, the little miniatures around the room, and the quiet landscape paintings on the wall. I love visiting with the cat and the dogs when they're around, and seeing the plants and bouquet of flowers. I would be happy to do some work with you here.'

"Another third of my visitors would look up blankly and say, 'Ahhh ... to be honest ... I hadn't really noticed one way or the other, but maybe you could be of help to me.'

"The last third would say, 'I don't like your office. I hate the color yellow. I prefer bright colors and modern furniture. It's not professional looking enough for me. I prefer validated parking, separate exit and entrance, elevators, and more of a professional office look. This is not the right place for me to be.' Those clients move on to a therapist in a big office building."

Each client looks surprised and a little relieved as I finish the story.

I add, "I've made this room for me because I'm the person who has to spend the most time here. It's my favorite room, but I don't expect others to agree with me all of the time. If I invited one thousand people to assess the office, the results would still be the same."

I continue, **"We're lucky if we can please, help or aid one third of the people some of the time. The best you can do is to find out who you are, do it and be honest about it. Then, you will attract other people who think, feel, believe and have the same talents and interests you do.** There are enough people out there who like this room and the work I do for me to have a practice for a lifetime."

Finally, I say, "So, how does this story relate to you? You can decide what you want to do with your life, what you prefer in terms of decor. Those who like it will stick around, the others will go away. You don't have to please everyone all of the time; perfection is impossible. You can just be who you really are, even if people who are significant in your life don't like it. You and I can work together to figure out who you want to be."

By this time, the client has relaxed, and is beginning to get that far-a-way look that seems to mean that they're already looking into a future that will become uniquely their own.

I invite them to share their thoughts and we begin our journey together to locate the unique self that only they can be.

# 6

# BUILDING AN INTROJECT

A new psychology intern showed up for the first hour of her training psychotherapy. She is participating in her own personal therapy as one important requirement of her graduate training program. She can choose her own experienced therapist, seeing the therapy process up close and personal, while, at the same time, tackling her own unresolved issues.

She wasted no time in going right to work.

"What does psychotherapy do?"

"Psychotherapy does a lot of things, but one of the most important is slowly and carefully building a new introject."

"So ... what, pray tell, is an introject?"

**"An introject is the compilation of memories that you have acquired from experiencing a significant relationship. It holds the summary messages from that person."**

"So I would be coming in here with an introject from my mother and my father?"

"That's correct. We'll be looking at the positive, negative and confusing messages you may have received from them about living life."

"I already know that stuff. So what will that do for me?"

"We'll see if there are any misconceptions that may need to be cleared up for you; and, at the same time, we'll be building a new introject from me."

"What will that accomplish?"

**"This introject will be thoughtfully built out of the conversations that you and I have together. Each week, in between psychotherapy hours, it will be there more and more clearly for you to check in and read any time you want. If you and I do our job well, this new introject will sit in your head beside the other introjects, holding some new empowering messages to guide you through life."**

"So when I feel lonely, or wish our appointment were sooner, or want to talk with you on the telephone, I could check in with this new introject first and see what you have to say?"

"Precisely. In fact, you can even imagine me two inches high on your left shoulder in the outfit I wear that you like the best. You can have any conversation you want with me privately. If you ask me a question, you will come up with an answer because you've been here for every hour we've done together. If you can't get an answer, and you have to make a decision quickly about something important; you can still call me up because I'm now responsible for your psychological care."

"What does the therapist have to do to build that new introject for me?"

I responded, "All therapists have their own unique process. Personally, I create a positive introject in many different ways. First of all, I try my best at all times to be kind to you. Judging you is off limits. Since I'm always on call for emergencies, I never allow myself to be high on any substance. Therefore, my mind is clear at all times and my judgment is not impaired. I make every effort to be on time and acknowledge your presence when I first see you come in. When and if I make a mistake, we will talk about it together as a means of correcting it, and making amends."

I continued, "In addition, I've created an office with a lake view and lots of warm colors to help both of us feel calm and peaceful. When I sit down to talk with you, I relax completely and let everything else be quiet in my head so that I can listen to you without distraction. Therefore, the hour is entirely yours. I have well-trained cats and dogs who will greet you, treat you with great respect, and be with you if you want to have them around. They understand our feelings more than you can possibly realize. I bring flowers and blooming plants where we can both see their beauty and smell their fragrance. Birds and squirrels are on the office back porch to remind us that nature, filled with the energy of the universe, is there to help us grow. Prisms generate rainbows around the room from the afternoon sunshine while we look together for the understanding and interpretations that will feel like a pot of gold at the end of the rainbow nearest to you. We work together keeping painful feelings in small manageable pieces."

"How do I know what to say to you first?"

"You already knew what question to start with today. It is as if you have brought your life story in a puzzle box of 250 pieces. I help you to put together the unique picture of your life story on the wall. We will only do the parts that you want to fill in. Some days it will feel like we have laid out a bunch of pieces that don't fit together. Other days, they will suddenly attach to each other to make a vivid picture. As an artist, I have some experience with locating the central themes of each picture. We'll look together, with respect, to see how you coped in childhood. We may decide to alter some behaviors for a different present and future. We'll look at the good parts of your life as much as we look at the dark parts, the confusion, and possible misconceptions."

"Is it fun for you to do this work?"

"I enjoy working on our relationship together. When we share the pain, I can bear it because I know that we're both growing. A successful psychotherapy session has learning opportunities for both of us. I look for what you have to teach me so that I will become a better person. Sometimes you may bring me a problem that I'm working on myself. Our dialogue together will be of help. Sometimes I have to listen carefully to what I say to you because it's something that I also need to do for myself."

My new client-in-training sighed. "That seems like a lot of work to me. How can you do all of that all the time? Is it good for you to have so much to do?"

"I believe that it's good for me to be kind and respectful of someone else, to see the energy within the universe through plants, animals and our conversations. Yes, sometimes it is stressful and tiring."

"If I can learn to do all of that too, I know I will become a good therapist."

"As an intern, you'll be watching my work carefully. It's always all right for you to ask any question you want, as you have today. It's up to me to decide how to answer it."

"I have so many questions that I never got to ask my mother before she died. I think I want to talk about her first. My introject from her is too small because she died when I was so young."

"We can get started on that as soon as you want."

# 7

# OH, PLEASE LET ME SLEEP

"I'm having trouble functioning during the day time because I'm not getting enough sleep at night." Stacy dragged her body into my office and lay down on the couch instead of sitting in her usual way.

"Tell me what's happening during the night?" I replied.

"Well, I stay up watching TV until way after my husband goes to bed because I'm afraid that I will toss and turn."

"How much sleep are you getting on average each night?"

"I get about four hours for three to four nights. Then I'm so exhausted I load up with four cups of coffee and am jumpy, cross, and cranky during the day."

"Do you ever nap during the day time?"

"I'm too anxious to fall asleep during the day because it was always light when I got sexually abused by my grandfather." Stacy turned her head away from embarrassment.

"I understand. Until you and I can work on that issue, you need to sleep after dark … **Recent research suggests that adults need eight hours and fifteen minutes of sleep each night. Technology is keeping us up too late. Lack of sleep is cumulative. Therefore, if you're missing four hours of sleep a night, that would mean you are short twenty-eight**

**hours of sleep by the end of the week or 120 hours by the end of the month**. No wonder you feel exhausted!"

"Yikes! … I had no idea." She sat up straight for a minute then, slumped again.

"Therefore, sleep is a very important part of a healthy existence."

"I know … but, what can I do?"

"There are six things you can do that should be helpful. First, get yourself some inexpensive calcium with magnesium. Each one should contain 500 mg of calcium with magnesium and zinc. Calcium will help you to calm down, relax and sleep. It is best to take one fifteen minutes before you go to bed. Health food stores, such as Trader Joe's, will carry them."

"Is that why people were told to drink warm milk before they go to bed?"

"Yes, but these capsules will give you much more calcium than one glass of warm milk.

"Second, you can also take some melatonin. It's the natural substance released by the brain to help you go to sleep. It has no side effects for most people and is not addictive."

"Is that what pilots use to go in and out of different time zones."

"Exactly … and it will help you shift your circadian rhythm to be more like your husband's. Third, you can also shift your circadian rhythm slowly by going to bed ten minutes earlier each night. After you have done this for a week, you will be going to bed an hour earlier."

"Good. My husband is disappointed that we do not go to bed at the same time." She smiled for the first time and winked at me.

"Yes, it must be hard on your sexual relationship. Finally, it's very important to understand that the universe is created for all creatures and plants to rest at night. Flowers fold up, birds stop singing and animals sleep. It's a time for us to rest, not to worry, not to resolve problems, not to work, or venture too far into the virtual world."

Stacy had now gotten out a pad of paper and was jotting down each step.

I persisted, "Once you get into bed, the fourth action you can take is to read a good book until your eyes feel tired. Then, the fifth action is to give yourself ten minutes each night when you turn off the light to think about all of the things for which you are thankful. Don't forget the basics, such as your health, food, shelter, hot water, and significant relationships, pets and friends. Then focus on the smaller things that were said to you, the flowers you saw, birds flying overhead, anything you learned or that happened that made the day worthwhile. Especially honor any creativity that you saw or created yourself. Notice the kindness and compassion that occurred to you or around you. You will naturally become peaceful and you will fall asleep. When you learn to do this every night, you will notice more nature and interactions during the daytime to recall at night. Do not forget that night is not a time to worry or think about problems."

I continued. "The sixth step is very important. If you do not fall asleep within ten minutes, avoid at all costs getting anxious, tossing and turning. Instead, decide what you will get up to do if you do not fall asleep within the next ten minutes. Make it a chore that you like to avoid, such as paying the bills or washing the kitchen floor. You'll likely choose to sleep. Then go deeper into what was positive about your day. If you do not fall off to sleep, get up and do the chore. Go back to bed when you are tired."

"I never thought of any of those things."

"Well, I can assure you that they will be helpful to you.

They're all actions that are good for you. You can use them for the rest of your life ... and none of them are addictive."

"Do you ever have trouble falling asleep?"

"Not when I follow the steps I have just given you. I use them every night."

"Cool ... Thank you so much. I'll stop and get the calcium capsules on the way home."

# 8

# DON'T PUT YOUR BEST FRIENDS
# TO SLEEP

One-half hour into my first meeting with Randy, I looked again at the initial evaluation questionnaire Randy had filled out, and continued on with my next question, "Do you take any drugs?"

Randy answered defensively. "I'm not a drug addict if that's what you want to know."

I persisted, "I don't think you exactly answered my question."

"Well, artists use drugs to generate creativity. You already know that I'm a musician."

"You're very lucky to have inherited some artistic genes. What drugs do you use to generate your creativity?"

"Marijuana mostly. Sometimes I top it all off with some hard liquor."

"How often and how much?"

"No problem, a couple of joints during the morning, sometimes the afternoon when I need a break, and always in the evening," Randy said nonchalantly.

"Does anyone in your family have a problem with addiction?"

"Yeah, my Dad and my Granddad both used to drink too much."

"What do you think would happen if you decided to stop smoking marijuana?"

"My creativity would dry up. I wouldn't write music, I'd stop getting gigs, and I'd have to get a regular stupid job. That would be definitely uncool." Randy's detached demeanor seemed to be fading.

"How has your musical career been going these days?"

"Not so good for the past nine months." Randy shifted uneasily in his chair. "That's one of the reasons I came to talk with you ... I really miss it"

"How long have you been using pot?" I persisted

"Regular use? Probably about a year or maybe two years, I don't know."

"Do you think there could be any relationship between your drug use and your not doing so well in your career?"

"No relationship at all," Randy responded confidently. "Marijuana helps me to be creative, as I've already told you. It's not a hard street drug, you know what I mean."

"How do you feel about your career not going so well?"

"I don't know ... not that good ... I guess."

"Since you've come to consult me about your career, let me tell you something that may surprise you ... You're an artist. Artists present negative and positive thoughts about the world for the rest of us to understand. Right?"

"I guess you could look at it that way. Yeah ... Right!"

"But in order to do that, an artist has to have access to both negative and positive feelings. I'd guess that you have written songs that are both sad and happy."

"Yup."

I moved forward from my relaxed position to sit on the edge of my chair. **"I can see one big problem. You think** that marijuana and alcohol bring out your creativity. I think using any kind of drug, marijuana or alcohol, and any other hard drug actually anesthetizes your negative feelings and tricks you into thinking that you feel good and creative. But in reality, you're putting to sleep the very feelings you need to guide you to be an artist."

"Who the hell wants to feel bad? Then you can't do nothin.' Besides it's not cool for guys to show pain. That means you're doing badly. " Randy got up and began to pace the room.

"Feeling bad or understanding any negative emotion is an important signal that something is going wrong in your life and that a change needs to be made. However, taking drugs makes you feel like nothing is wrong and that no change needs to be made. Drugs give you a dangerously false sense of security."

"That's not my experience. Besides all artists use drugs. Maybe you don't know because you're probably not an artist. You're just a shrink." He stopped his pacing to glare at me.

After some thought I revealed, "Actually I am an artist, but not a musician like you. I'm a published writer, and I draw, sculpt and sing choral music."

I persisted, trying a new approach. "Let's look at this issue another way. Would you ever get on an airplane that is flying from Los Angeles to New York if you were told that the pilot had taken a black cloth and draped it over half of the dials on the left-hand side of the cockpit? Each left-hand dial records the presence and degree of each negative emotion. The black cloth would mean that the pilot couldn't see if any of the needles on the dials were moving upward toward the red zone. He could only see the dials on the right side of the cockpit representing all of the positive feelings. He could probably fly the plane all right for a time, but if his plane began to malfunction, it eventually would crash. Would you put gas, luggage, or yourself on a plane with a pilot who did that?"

"No. What kind of question is that?" Randy paused, stopped in his tracks. "Who would do a such a stupid thing?" He sounded impatient.

"Well that's what a drug addict does. The drug makes it impossible for him to feel and understand his negative feelings. Therefore, he's not able to make the necessary daily corrections for his life to run smoothly. He begins to lose career opportunities and crises begin happening. Everyone has times of pain when life is not going well ... An addict is someone who can't manage pain."

"So I suppose you're trying to say that my artist's career is not going so well because I'm using pot? Lots of my artist friends use, and they seem to be doing just fine, thank you."

"Maybe for now, but not likely in the long run. Your negative feelings are your best friends. You need to sense them; use them to guide you and never be afraid of what they have to say. They're usually right on. No one else has the right to judge them because they are private and a necessary and normal part of life. Could we say that your negative feelings about your career brought you here to talk with me today?"

Randy said nothing, so I tried a different angle. "Did you know that the most severe physical illness is the very rare patient who does not feel any physical pain? They usually die at a young age because they do not know when they are ill or what's wrong, so they cannot take any corrective action."

"Oh God ... I can't tell if my negative feelings right now are telling me you are full of shit, or maybe you're right on and you've made me feel uncomfortable."

"It's important to know the difference, isn't it? Are your feelings hard to reach because you smoked some marijuana this morning before you came here?"

"Well ... ah ... maybe."

My tone and manner stayed very supportive. "A person who takes drugs acts like that pilot, but usually doesn't know it unless someone like me explains it to him."

"I get your drift," Randy conceded reluctantly.

"Well, let's take it just one more step for today. You seem to be saying that you honestly thought that your drug use was fostering your creativity. I suspect that the drugs you've taken have hampered your creativity by taking away your negative feelings. I also think that you may have inherited your father and grandfather's addiction genes. That means that any drug you take will feel ten times better to you than to someone who does not have addiction genes, like me. Therefore, it's a lot harder for you not to use drugs than it is for me. It would take discipline. We can talk more about that later if you decide to return."

"All my friends smoke. Do they all have addiction genes? What would I do for a social life?"

"I don't know how many of your friends have addiction genes or are blocking their negative feelings. You'll have to think that through carefully."

He was pacing his way towards the window overlooking the lake. He wheeled around, "Are you calling me a drug addict?"

"That's an interesting question we would need to consider if you decided to do some further work with me. If you have been smoking up to three times a day, I will just say, at this point, that you may be needing to put to sleep a lot of negative feelings. An addict is usually someone who has the addiction gene and more psychological pain than they feel they can handle on their own. It would be my job to help you to find out what those feelings are so that you could use them instead to guide you. You could also go to a Twelve-Step AA Program, learn more, and find some new friends there who do not use any drugs."

"Okay."

"I'll give you an example of what we've been talking about from my own life. It happened just last weekend. I was sleeping in a hotel. The fire alarm went off at midnight all over the building. Everyone had to come down into the lobby. There were newlyweds, families with infants and children, old ladies, doddering granddads, and everyone else. We all had to wait until the problem was diagnosed and the alarm had been shut off. It took almost two hours. The problem was a bunch of kids smoking pot in room 315. Their smoke set off the smoke alarm system. With negative feelings asleep, they thought they were cool and could stop the alarm by pulling the smoke detector out of the ceiling. Their poor judgment set off all of the alarms throughout the entire hotel and inconvenienced hundreds of people. I suspect the teenagers may be in really big trouble. They were standing in the hallway with not a clue as to what they had done or what to do next."

"Not cool, you bet!" Randy said uneasily.

I looked at the clock and began to conclude Randy's first session. "You'll have to decide if you would like to talk with me further. I would feel uncomfortable taking your fee unless you decide to gradually reduce your drug use and then stop altogether. If you put any feelings to sleep, you will not be able to tell yourself or me about them – a waste of your money, I'd suspect. Think about it and let me know. If you decide not to return to talk with me further, there is no charge for this initial evaluation visit. It's a gift to you. I hope that it's useful, if not now, sometime in the future."

"Thank you for your time. I'll have to think about all of this stuff I've never heard before," said Randy, looking thoughtful and a little dazed.

"You do that, and let me know what you decide. I will be here to help you. Translate all of your feelings about this meeting; and, I promise you, they will guide you as to what you should do with me and your career as a musician. Goodbye for now."

"I think I will be coming back to see you. I'll have to check with my parents first to see if they can help me."

"I'll look forward to speaking with you again, if you decide to return."

# 9

# I HATE MY FEELINGS ... THEY MAKE
# ME LOSE IT

"You don't want to hear what I have to say today." Sandy, the mother of a five year old Ashley, stared at the carpet, refusing to look at me.

"Why would that be?" I encouraged at the beginning of her therapy hour.

"Because ... I was a bad mother last night."

"Do you want to share with me what happened?"

Sandy shifted position uneasily. "No, it makes me hate myself, but I'll tell you. I guess you could say I 'lost it.' Ashley wouldn't settle down last night and go to sleep. She kept bouncing out of bed after I'd tucked her in. I was patient for the first three times, but then something just took over me and I wasn't myself. I pushed her down on the bed too hard and spanked her three times on her pajama bottom. Then, I got up and slammed the door too hard and ... to top it all off, I threw a dish in the kitchen so hard it broke! My husband woke up and was scared of me and mad."

"It sounds like you were really patient for a long time before you lost control? Do you think you hit her hard enough to bruise her?"

"Oh no, I wouldn't do that. It was just a slap, but I never

want to hit a kid. I was … so tired. I didn't have much sleep this week because I had to stay up late to finish a project for work."

"Parenting is the hardest job on the planet, isn't it? No one has done it perfectly yet. Sometimes it's more than we can handle."

"Well, I realized I'd done wrong so I went right back to my kid and told her, 'Moms get mad sometimes, it's not your fault. I'm really sorry. I did wrong to spank you. I hope I didn't hurt you. It won't happen again."

"Wow, you did a rapid and excellent job with that response! What did she do?"

"She rubbed my arm softly and then went to sleep quickly."

"Sounds like she understood."

"Yeah, but I still feel terrible. I told her it won't happen again, but I can't promise that. What can I do so I don't spank her? I don't believe in physical punishment. That's my question."

"There are **four actions** that you can do in the future. **The first is always to trust your negative feelings because they're yelling loudly that something important is wrong. In that way, they are your best friends.** Have a conversation within yourself, by yourself, reading your feelings any way you want. You can have a fantasy about what you might want to do, even an ugly one. Fantasies are free and private; they don't hurt anybody."

"I felt like I was capable of doing anything bad just to make her be perfectly still."

"See, you're already owning your fantasy and learning how badly you needed your daughter to cooperate. Good for you."

Now you can move on to the **second action. Once you figure out what you feel, then try to translate your emotions into reasonable constructive language that's honest and**

**clear.** A negative feeling may direct you to ask someone for help, or set limits, or say 'no' to a request. If it takes a while to figure out what you're thinking, it's always all right to ask for a time-out for yourself. Get away from the source of your frustration until you regain control."

"It was strange, because the feeling was so strong that it almost took over me." Sandy was sitting up straight and looking at me directly, very intently.

"When it feels that strong, there's a very important question to ask yourself."

"What's that?" Sandy looked like she could hardly wait for my answer.

"We're now looking at the **third action** you can take. **You have to ask yourself, 'Does this moment remind me of anything that has happened to me before that also made me unhappy or angry?'** "

"Ohhhhh … now I'm beginning to get it … It did remind me of something that happened before! When I was a kid, I used to be afraid to fall asleep at night, just like my daughter, because … wow! … My parents would take drugs and have fights. Oh my God! … They'd break dishes, just like I did! Whoa! … Back then, I was afraid one of them would be dead or injured in the morning. I wanted to stay up to protect them, but I also hated them for fighting … just like I hated my dear daughter for a minute, when I really love her so much."

"Once again … Good for you to be able to reach back into your life story and discover those feelings. No wonder you spanked her!"

"Yikes!"

"Perhaps you decided to hide your own feelings as a child so they would not make your parents more upset? Perhaps they've been stored inside you all this time."

"That's it! So much anger just came crashing out of me last night."

"Then, lets go back to action two and look at what you need to say, in constructive language, to your husband and your daughter."

"I guess I need to tell my husband what happened in the past. I could tell him that it would help if he could give me a hug instead of being scared and angry. I could tell my daughter that I need to be able to sleep at night so that I can be a patient Mom all day. She can help me by staying in bed. Maybe I need to be firmer with her about that." Sandy looked relieved and thoughtful.

"Now you're understanding your feelings clearly. You can take action on them constructively. I believe your husband and daughter will understand. Your feelings are there to guide you, not to make you feel crazy. Now you'll have a better idea as to what to do with them in the future."

"You're not going to report me to the Department of Child and Family Services?"

"No, there's no need for me to do that. First of all, I know you to be a good and loving parent. You did not physically injure your daughter, and you made amends to her right away to repair any psychological damage. Then you took the **fourth** action we can take when we 'lose it.' You came to talk with someone, in this case me, about what happened in a responsible way, to understand your feelings, so it's less likely to happen again. You may want to talk with me further about your parents' substance abuse and fights whenever you wish to release more of those piled up feelings in small manageable pieces."

"I get it ... I feel better now. I was afraid to come and tell you today."

"You have my respect for doing so."

# 10

# AN ANXIETY ATTACK IS NOT AN ATTACK

An anxiety attack is a wake up call of great importance. Therefore, it is a gift and a blessing from the unconscious, sent in a way that cannot be ignored, at just the right time.

The first anxiety attack feels nothing but scary and can manifest itself in many different ways. When I was in graduate school, studying to be a psychotherapist, and in a training psychotherapy myself, I had an anxiety attack that suddenly threw me, literally, to the ground. I went immediately to the emergency room of the nearest hospital, fearing that something was seriously wrong with my brain. The doctor told me that I had experienced an anxiety attack, and suggested that I think about what was happening to me when it occurred. He did not give me anti-anxiety medication. I recognized that I had suddenly fallen as soon as I heard two words spoken by a friend. These two words described a trauma that had happened to me in early childhood, but I had no conscious memory of it. My anxiety attack was the harbinger of a detailed piece of work I still needed to do to recapture and understand what had happened to me, and how this trauma influenced my responses in the present. It was, indeed, a defining moment of great significance.

Anxiety attacks can be mild or severe. Some are just a vague sense of disequilibrium or dizziness. Other attacks, with heart palpitations, make my clients fear that they're having a heart attack. Most clients are afraid they're going to die. These fears escalate the anxiety making the attack more severe. Emergency care and primary care physicians tend to prescribe Xanax, Valium, or Klonopin which are addictive anti-anxiety drugs, instead of telling their clients to make an appointment with a psychotherapist. Therefore, the client may become dependent upon these highly addictive medications. Anxiety attacks not treated with psychotherapy will tend to continue unabated, leaving the clients feeling increasingly afraid, causing them to withdraw more from the world around them.

I saw two clients recently who were very afraid of the anxiety attacks they were experiencing until they were referred to me. Both clients were in love with someone. The relationship was becoming deeper and more important to them. Both of them had divorce experiences in childhood and messages from parents that made them afraid to continue further with their present intimate relationships. They were stuck between the fear of continuing the relationship and the sorrow of losing it. The anxiety attack about divorce helped them to ferret out the reasons they were afraid. We came to understand the details and memories together. Then they could continue the current relationship without any anxiety attacks.

I have the greatest respect for the unconscious. Its memory is phenomenal, its knowledge superb, and its timing exquisite. That's why, as a therapist, I endeavor only to walk along beside my clients without pushing or pulling, because the unconscious is much wiser than both the client and I can ever be together. **Its "attack" is sent as a gift at the right moment to free each client from past misconceptions so that they may go on with life as a whole integrated person.** As soon as the psychotherapist and client can understand the message being sent by the anxiety attack, the attack then ceases completely because the central issue is addressed and understood.

# 11

# INTEGRATING LOST PARTS OF SELF

I t is not unusual for me to meet and come to understand two parts of a client. The first is the adult presenting the unique life story. The second part emerges later in our dialogue together when the working alliance is strong enough to receive it. It's usually a much younger version of the client. This part has gone into hiding because the child has protected herself by escaping some abuse that happened in the past, and/or blames herself for something that went wrong. Initially, the client may be unaware that this more concealed part exists.

We all know what it is like to get into an argument with a loved one, and behave in an unacceptable manner that appears to "come out of nowhere." Everyone looks puzzled with raised eyebrows, wondering "What just happened to you?" However, it's often the child part of the client, making an unexpected appearance with some important intense feelings that first occurred earlier during childhood. This child's wisdom is suddenly available to help us with the work at hand.

Couples come in for an appointment to report a marital argument. After taking a good history of each person's childhood, we can take it apart, looking at what the adult part of each spouse felt. Then we look at the central issue as expressed through the child part of each spouse. This often allows us to understand and respect feelings in a way that the couple never could before. The child's wisdom is often enormously clarifying, explaining clearly the behavior and the feelings underneath. We can see and appreciate the pain; and, at the same time, even come to have a sense of humor about the uncomfortable interactions that happened. The couple learns to speak and share the dual language of the adult and the child. That is intimacy.

The child shares important pieces of wisdom acquired before psychological defenses came into play to blur painful truth. Next, the adult part of the client begins to talk, to embrace, and protect the child part. As a consequence, childhood misconceptions become erased, leaving instead depth of understanding and feelings. Creative energies become stronger as an integration takes place between the child and the adult parts of the client. Only then can the client take on the full responsibility of maintaining self-esteem.

Within the relationship from the therapist to the client, I provide genuine clarification, reflection, validation, interpretation and encouragement which are all freely given. A strong foundation is being constructed by the therapist and the expanding introject of the therapist to hold together the newly-integrated self of the client.

During one psychotherapy session, a client who had been sexually abused, brought in a journal of the conversations between the adult and child parts of herself. She shared some dialogues so we could see one of many unique ways that the process of integration can happen. Sometimes these dialogues took place within her imaginary larger visual picture.

Adult part to child:

*"Please understand that I'm really working on being able to take you back, to love you, to thank you, to cherish you, to trust you, and to let you guide me with your child wisdom, and*

*to let you be with me for the rest of my life. Then I can do better with my family, friendships, and clients."*

Child to adult:

*"I want you to know that I do know you and everything you have done. You are the only one who has to be introduced to me. After all, I've been locked up inside of you all these years. I knew you when you didn't know me."*

Child to adult:

*"You have been working really hard at this, and I'm proud of you. Remember, you can't push me forward. I will just come on my own, in consultation with your trusty unconscious and your competent therapist. It's not all your responsibility, so don't feel so accountable."*

Child to adult:

*"Look, I took the core of yourself away to save it. I took away the heart of your soul. So you don't have a self to love. I've held onto it, but I've been so battered I can hardly see it myself. You will only be able to have self-love when you integrate me back into your life. Even then, it will be a damaged version. I'm the only one who can see me, your soul and you together. Obviously, I like you better than you do. I see some hope of having a conscious place in your life some day. I just can't wait!"*

Child to adult:

*"How do you think I feel having to go away from you all of these years? I didn't do anything that bad. You think you missed out on being with me! I missed everything, events, being known and respected, and validated. You didn't even know when I guided you. You can't decide what I'm going to do. I'm carrying a bomb so don't mess with me too much or you'll be in big trouble. I hate this whole mess, I hate the damage that has to be revealed. I hate the secrets I hold. I hate that your parents will never be able to validate what happened, and that I hold*

*the sole responsibility of convincing you . . . I may be wise, but I'm just a child. I don't want to make a mistake."*

Child to adult:

*"Well, you had better get used to me, because I'm here to stay. You've gone too far in making contact with me to get away with ever getting rid of me. . . Yeah. . ."*

Adult to child:

*When I didn't understand, I presented myself in a confusing manner. My child responded with confusion. So there have been many years with confusion. That's what has driven the creativity."*

Child to adult:

*"Soo, perhaps there's a chance that you're really going to be able to protect me some more. You're going to be able to give me love, kindness, and safety within your competent mastery. Maybe I won't have to hide much any more.*

This kind of conversation provides richness inside.

Visual picture of integration:

*"The little girl is now a fully grown, replica of me. One day she came toward me out of the waves on the beach. When I reached out to take her hands she was gone. I thought she was bringing me more memories; but no, she appeared to be merging with me to share and survive the despair I'd felt. The little girl is integrated now so that I cannot separate her back out. I miss her because I can no longer speak to this separate piece of strength."*

Visual picture of integration:

*"I was in a forest. I saw myself as if in the shadows of the trees, gray, and transparent. I could almost see through me. I stepped out into the sunshine and saw myself for the first time as the person that I really am. The shadowy person is what I felt*

*as a child. I felt able to tackle my generalized anxiety for the first time because there was a person there of substance whom I could trust to take care of me. I had never felt this integrated presence of the child and adult before, although I somehow knew that she existed."*

The resulting integration is, as anyone can see, worth its weight in gold.

# 12

## FIGHTING DEPRESSION
## THE NATURAL WAY

Tom sat down for his first hour after his initial evaluation. I asked him, "How are you doing today?"

Tom responded slowly, "That's a good question. I know that we met last week and I'm beginning to understand some of the feelings I've had for a really long time. I also feel that it will take quite a few hours for us to settle my particular issues. In the meantime, I do feel mildly depressed some of the time. I don't want to take any medication. I can't afford it because I don't have insurance, and I can't handle the frequent side-effect of weight gain. What can I do to feel less depressed while we're doing this work? I used to drink alcohol, but I don't want to do that any more either."

"Good for you. Your question is important. There are several actions that I can suggest."

"Good, because I need them," he sighed.

**"The first action you can take is to get a half hour of exercise at the same time every day.** If you have a sport you love or want to go to the gym, swim, or do yoga, then be sure to do it seven days a week. If you do not have a sport, find a pleasant area where there is nature near where you live to take a walk. See if you can briskly walk a mile per day."

Tom perked up. "I suppose I could walk near the river, or the park."

"You're getting the idea. **When you walk, do not think about the events that make you depressed. Instead, take long, slow breaths and concentrate on noticing everything you can about the nature around you. Notice the wind in the trees as a model of how to breathe.**"

"Are you talking about a walking meditation?"

"Yes, I walk on the Los Angeles River for thirty minutes every day with four dogs. I've been walking dogs for thirty five years. It adds up to lots of discipline that's good for my overall health. My walk burns two hundred calories a day, and adds up to two hundred and fifty miles a year, for a total of around nine thousand miles over many years. I count the ducks, mallards, herons, geese, cormorants, stiffs and egrets. I watch the baby mallards with their mom, the sixty pigeons swoop and swarm in a graceful dance around the bridge, and the black ravens "caw" to me from the tops of trees. I notice the details of the inside of the wild flowers, watch the hummingbirds feed, and listen to the birds sing. Obsessive, depressed and worried thoughts are chased away by the beauty and magic of the universe. Out of my quieted mind sometimes surfaces a creative idea or an insight without effort."

"Do you do it because you get depressed?"

"Perhaps I would be if I didn't. I take in a lot of psychic pain from the work I do each day. I need some way to settle it in my mind, and let it go. Walking, gardening, writing, and singing with choral groups help me to turn the pain from all of my clients into useful ideas and productive action."

"Cool."

"When you come up with an idea or insight while exercising, don't talk yourself out of it later. Always stay with the thoughts you had while exercising. **When you feel depressed, and want to go to bed, make yourself get up and do something active instead. We have been designed by the universe to move; the more we move the better we feel. Exercise is good for emotional health, increasing neurotransmitters that elevate mood. Exercise reduces stress, oxygenates the brain, relieves muscle tension, and provides a release for pent up anger, irritation and frustration."**

"I think I can make exercise work. I'll have to get up an hour earlier in the morning."

"I get up at six. After my walk with the dogs, I do another half hour of resistance training for the remainder of the hour. I get a little social time then, too."

"Are you tired after exercise?"

"No, I'm energized. Getting exercise allows me to sit quietly for the remainder of the day. A restless therapist is of concern to clients."

"Is there anything else I can do?" Tom persisted.

"Yes, I remember that you're living alone at this time."

"Yup, I get depressed when I have too much time alone."

"Have you thought about **getting a pet?**"

"Yes, but the landlord doesn't want me to have a dog or a cat."

"Yeah, I remember those days. Would you like to have a parakeet? They chirp a beautiful song when you turn on the water, and you can teach them to speak, sit on your shoulder and your finger."

"Wow, that might work! Then I would have someone to talk with me." Tom brightened.

"Precisely … You could also ask a neighbor who might work a long day, if you could take his dog for a walk with you each day. The dog and the owner would probably be delighted.

You could have the companionship with the dog and earn a little extra money to pay for your therapy."

"Awesome … and the bird would not be very expensive."

"There are also a number of foods that contribute mightily to lifting depression. Try fish oil, beans, dark chocolate, saffron, turmeric, walnuts, ginger and sunflower seeds.

"I can do that. I love ginger and walnuts."

"Right … Our talking together each week, and those three ideas should help a lot with your depression. If for any reason, it still persists, then we could look into a consultation with a psychiatrist. But let's try these options first."

"You bet I will … I already feel less depressed."

"You were able to read your discouraged feeling about depression and bring it to me so that we could talk about it and take constructive action. Taking action does a lot to take care of depression."

"Now I'm ready to talk about my relationship with my girlfriend."

# 13

# I DIDN'T KNOW I WAS AN ADULT CHILD OF AN ALCOHOLIC (ACA)

T wo clients came in my office to consult with me in back-to-back hours. Both were adult children of alcoholics (ACA) clients. They did not understand the role alcohol played within their families. They saw themselves simply as available to meet others' needs. They are "givers" to an extreme; they've often hitched up with "takers" who intuitively knew that these two clients would meet their needs.

The first client came in after the Christmas holiday truly bewildered. She had "missed Christmas." She was living with a family from a Middle Eastern culture who did not celebrate this holiday. She had arranged the week before to go to a Christmas evening church service. Her family had offered to do anything she wanted one day last week, but she did not realize that it was Christmas. By the time she looked at her calendar, Christmas had passed unnoticed. She had not decorated a tree or bought any gifts.

The second client was feeling "weird and depressed." It was his birthday. Last year he had not mentioned it to anyone, so nothing happened for his birthday. He had gone on a hike and felt terribly alone. This year he'd told someone at work what had happened last year. They had responded with an elaborate party which made him feel terrible in a different way because he did not know how to handle it.

There was something in common about these two clients. Both of them were truly afraid to express to anyone what they really needed. How does that happen?

I explained to both clients that it takes some time in therapy for an adult child of an alcoholic (ACA) client to understand that **they learned at a very young age to give up childhood and step into a care-taking role for their alcoholic parent. They put aside their own feelings, especially any feeling that might upset the alcoholic parent, in an attempt to keep the parent from drinking.** Children intuitively know that their parents' judgment is impaired because of the substance abuse addiction. They know that their home and their very existence may be severely threatened at any time, especially when the parent is driving. They try to keep their parents on their feet so that the child will have a home with caretaking.

These two clients helped me to understand even more. They told me:

"It feels really dangerous for me to ask for what I need."

"I really can anticipate what others need. If I suggest it before they realize it themselves, they will reject my offer, only to come back and take it later."

"I get my self-esteem needs met entirely by helping others in an exquisite way and having them acknowledge me for what I have done. I have to go on doing that."

"I can meet other's needs for a really long time. I'm doing just fine. But then I suddenly find myself depressed. I stay that way for a while. Then I'm not interested in what anyone else wants. Somebody asks for something and, all of a sudden, I'm mad … I mean really mad. I'm impossible to deal with. I can't help myself. I'm beginning to finally understand why. I guess it's because everyone else is taking me for granted and no one is ever meeting my needs ... I suppose it's the very feeling I must have had so many times with my drunk mother."

"It seems so strange and uncomfortable to put my needs out there. I would rather forget what I want."

"Are you absolutely sure that I won't get into big trouble if I take care of me, too?"

As we work through this pain together, clients are able to try putting out their needs a little bit at a time. They call between hours when they need help and find out that I'm not angry with them and that we still have a relationship. They discover that nothing bad happens. They even begin to have some fun going out into the world to have the kind of goofy fun that belongs with children and the childhood they've lost. They learn that it's appropriate to ask for something that's part way between not mentioning a birthday and coping with a huge party. Instead, they learn to ask for dinner with a friend, lover, or a trip to the store to buy a reasonable present.

I always love the hours in which an Adult Child of an Alcoholic really "gets it." Then they say, "Thank you for explaining it to me so that I could understand. I can now change my behavior in a way that really works and is also fine for others." They've learned that friends want not only to be helped, but want to be invited to give back to each and every one of my clients.

Adult Children of Alcoholics give all of us exceptional care. They fill some of the ranks of our teachers, doctors, and mental health professionals. We have to recognize them, never take them for granted, and help them to attend to their own needs as well as they serve others. Otherwise they may "crash and burn," which would be a tragic result after all the care and concern they have given their alcoholic parents and to all of us.

# 14

## THE MORE YOU HELP YOURSELF, THE MORE HELP YOU WILL GET

A lice looked pale and completely worn out." My husband is still in the process of leaving me. He doesn't see that I'm really upset. He didn't notice that I took too many pills even though he is a dentist. I went to the hospital emergency room to check myself in to the psych ward because I felt so bad, because he wouldn't even drive me there. I don't think he cares if I die. I still love him. I go back and forth between being loving and screaming at him that I'm in really bad shape. Everything I do seems to drive him farther and farther away. We were in love; how can he be so heartless? I don't know what else to do. I feel so hopeless; suicide seems like the only thing left to do. My whole married life has been for him and he doesn't even care."

"I can understand that you're very upset and that this is an extremely difficult time for you. When you're being rejected, it's really hard to remember that you're still a valuable person with your own strengths and talents."

Alice spoke with certainty. "Well, all I know is that I must have done something terribly wrong."

"That's not a foregone conclusion we can make at this time. However, sometimes we learn something new as a result of facing hard times squarely."

"What can I do?"

"Well … let's take a look. Apparently, you're telling him how badly you feel through all of the different ways you've tried to get his attention. It seems that your actions may only be making him pull away more."

"Yup." Alice continued to slump on the couch.

"You have said, 'My whole married life has been for him and he doesn't seem to care.' What would happen if you focused in on what you need to do right now to make your own life feel better for you? … What could you do to help yourself?"

"Well … I think I need to find a new place to live because living with him when he doesn't love me anymore is hell."

"Good thought."

Alice sat up a little more and looked at me for the first time, "A friend mentioned that she has a neighbor who is renting a room in her condo because her husband died. She has a home instead of our tiny apartment, so I could bring my two cats with me. At least I would not have to separate from them too."

"More good thinking … and I wonder if your husband would be more responsive to you if you showed him how you were taking care of yourself."

"When I told him about this possible plan, he spoke to me nicely for the first time."

"There's a principle here that might be of enormous help to you just now, especially when you feel suicidal. Sometimes we ask for help from others by letting them know just how much we've been hurt. In a way, we try to 'go belly up.' We've all tried it from time to time. **I think you're already noticing that the more we can take care of ourselves, the more other people will step forward and give us a hand. When we go 'belly up,' others may get nervous and pull away; not sure what to do or if they can help. However, if we come up with a plan,** take it as far as we can ourselves, then they're more likely to say, 'Sure, I can contribute something.' People like to be asked and like to help, but only when they can figure out what to do and feel as if it's going to be worth their time."

"Maybe you're right ... Three friends have offered to help me with a garage sale and to put some things in storage if I decide to move."

"That's a good example. Have you talked with the person who has the room to rent?"

"Not yet. I fluctuate between wanting to stay in the apartment to piss my husband off, and just getting away from all of his rejection of me. I came here today to ask you what you thought."

"Which one is taking care of you?"

"I guess that leaving would be best for me."

"I agree because **retaliation never really works.**"

"But it's so much work to move. He should have to do it instead of me."

"I get it. Life is not fair sometimes. But, remember that if you have a clear plan to take care of yourself, others have already offered to help. It's a productive plan that moves your life forward and is much better than going to a psychiatric hospital or planning an overdose. You have so much of life ahead of you to enjoy if you take it in hand. I do understand that it's really hard to believe what I just said today. When you take good care of yourself, then you have the most to offer others. I believe there will be another person for you to love, who can love you back fully."

"Sometimes, I wish I could just leave the country for a while and come back later. I need some distance to figure out how I want to earn money. I've been doing whatever job I could get while my husband finished his training to be a dentist."

"Since you're able to tell me what you would really like to do, I can offer you a particular option to look at carefully. You might want to consider the Peace Corps or a program called Teaching English in a Foreign Land (TEFL). They will train you in a hundred hours, place you in a country, pay all of your living and travel expenses, and pay you a salary. Look it up on the internet."

"I'll be sure to do that! ... Well, I do feel more like going on with life now. Thanks for fitting me in at the last minute. Can I see you again towards the end of the week?"

"More good thinking on your part. Yes, of course. Make the rest of your day a good day for you, not a bad day for him. Maybe you can meet with the person who has the room to rent this evening. Before you leave, would you be willing to sign this sentence that you promise not to commit suicide because it's first degree murder and would be treating you unnecessarily badly. Should you change your mind, you will promise to call and talk with me first?"

"Yes, I can do that now."

"Thank you. It's important for you, and would reassure me too."

"Ok."

"I'll see you again for sure on Friday."

"I'll be there."

# 15

# TRY TO DECIPHER A WHITE SNOW TV SCREEN ... OR DECIDE FOR YOURSELF

Mary, age seventeen, sat tentatively on the edge of her chair. "Sooo... It's June. I'm enrolled in Junior College for the fall. My dad expects me to go to Med School and become a surgeon. My mom would be jealous if I did that and needs me to marry, have kids quickly, and live nearby so that she can play grandmother. My friends want me to come back east with them to art school, but I've never lived in the snow. I don't have a clue as to what I want to do. What I **should do** seems very contradictory. Every step I take seems to make someone mad ... so ... I'm not sure what's okay to think about myself."

"You seem to be saying that both your own self-awareness and self-esteem are shaky just now?" I queried.

"Well ... Since I don't know what to do, maybe I'm not worth much."

"I hear your confusion, but I also think that you're selling yourself short."

"One of life's biggest ongoing challenges is holding up your self-esteem. We all struggle to believe in ourselves from time to time, and especially when we're in transition. Sometimes we think too much about what others may want us to do. Then we lose track of our own thoughts."

"Yeah, especially when everyone we ask wants something different."

"Well ... let's take a look. Sometimes it's important to ask the question, 'What would I do if I didn't have to worry about anybody else?' It's only one of many critical questions, and answering it doesn't mean you're being selfish."

Mary sat up straight on the edge of her chair. "Oh God, shall I really tell her?" she whispered to herself. Then her face brightened for a moment. "That's an easy one ... I would take a year away from school and get a job. I want to be on my own, pay my own bills, and decide what to do with my life. I'd like to just take the four courses, this summer on line that I need to be able to work with preschool children. That job would also help me decide whether I want to be a teacher and have kids myself someday."

"So you **do** have a plan for yourself, but you're afraid of disapproval from family and friends. Is that right?"

"Well ... yeah ... since you put it that way." She slumped into the couch again.

"I think that you're on the right track for yourself. What Mom and Dad want you to do, might be right for them, but not necessarily for you"

"You got it!" She looked at me intensely startled.

**"Well, we humans are social beings; and, of course, we want approval and to be liked by others. But no one is really in the position to tell you what to do, because no one knows you as well as you do. There's never going to be, nor has there been, another person like you. Is that right?"**

"Well ... yes. I never thought of it that way."

**"The other problem is everyone is trying to hold up their own self-esteem by doing what they like to do best. It's a full-time job. Therefore, no one really has much time to look at your life, what you're doing, and validate it for you ... Their off-hand advice or criticism may not be very applicable to you. Occasionally, we all get compliments**

and/or criticism. Often, trying to figure out what others think is like reading a TV screen that has mostly white snow or perhaps viewing a show you don't want to watch."

"Maybe I need to get more used to not pleasing family and friends. My mother and father have already decided upon two contradictory TV stories that aren't right for me. That's for sure."

**"Maybe, it's better for you to decide that you're the most qualified authority on what to do with your life. If you're willing to read your own thoughts clearly, make sure that whatever plan you adopt is well suited to your strengths, and is morally correct. Do it well. Then, you can have a feeling of self-worth and peace. It is also a fool-proof way to maintain your self-esteem on your own forever."**

"So, I don't have to hate myself for having a different plan?" Mary cocked her head, looking both puzzled and pleased. Her eyes seemed to sparkle for the first time.

"If you do what's best for you, you'll attract people who like to do the same kind of activities. Then you'll have the companionship of people around you who approve of what you do. You may ask their advice from time to time, but you remain the sole person to decide what's best for you. Do it well, and you will be able to maintain a healthy self-esteem."

"Well, I'm pleased with myself that I told you what I really wanted to do. I thought I didn't know myself. You're the first person to hear it."

"Good for you. I have respect for what you've decided. Your plan sounds sensible to me. Once you decide what to do, you have to evaluate how you're progressing all by yourself. My clients don't tell me how well I did with their psychotherapy hour, unless I did something wrong that made them mad or upset. Therefore, it becomes my responsibility to evaluate each hour myself."

"Now I have to go home and tell my family what I think. I hope they won't be too disappointed."

"If they're upset, that doesn't mean that you're necessarily doing something wrong. Listen to what they have to say. Take it into consideration. We all have to disappoint others from time to time to do what's best for ourselves in the long run. Suppose you apply for a job, there are twenty applicants, and you get the job. You will have to disappoint nineteen people. That doesn't mean you have to turn down the job."

"Yeah ... I get it." I could see the wheels turning in her brain.

"We are really talking about finding your own true self. As you discover it, you will find it to be resilient to criticism, and not afraid of challenge. Your true self does not concern itself with superiority or inferiority. It just knows what is right for you."

"And ... it takes a while to find it?"

"Yes, indeed ... We keep on redefining it throughout a lifetime as we grow and changes happen. Before we finish today, I'd like to offer you one more way to help you build your self-esteem."

"Please ... I have to like myself enough to go ahead with my own plans."

"Right. So ... every day when you wake up in the morning, decide what you wish to do that day that will contribute to your life running well. Then, do as much of it as you can. When you go to bed at night, before you go to sleep, review what you promised yourself you would do. Evaluate how you did. Put items on the list you did not complete for the next day. Give yourself credit for what you accomplished in place of asking someone else for validation. Then review everything you are thankful for. Don't forget what you have already created and have been given. You will fall asleep peacefully knowing where you are with your life."

"Thanks, I never thought about doing that ... instead, I tend to worry."

"That's a mistake we all have to correct many times over."

# 16

# SO MANY WAYS TO COMMUNICATE

Modern technology has given us many new ways to be in touch with each other. Now we can be "plugged in" all of the time, able to receive and send a message by cell phone, e-mail, web sites, texting, tweeting, blogging, looking up each other on FaceBook, MySpace, and events on You Tube. We can find and make new contacts with former friends, adoptees can discover their birth parents, and employers can look up a candidate for a job interview and talk with their previous employers. With FaceBook and MySpace we can see what's happening with our friends each day. We can advertise services and write articles for each other on web sites. We can get information about almost anything, including the news that can be downloaded onto our cell phone. What an advance!

Clients are enjoying the advantages and also noting some of the down sides.

Some teens are basing their popularity and self-esteem on how many contacts they can receive each day. They are texting during class, and keeping their cell phones on by their pillow late into the night so as not to miss any calls. As a result, their learning and sleep are both disrupted.

Children are asking their parents to "Pleeease stop texting" in the middle of a conversation they are trying to complete.

They are tired of hearing, "Just a minute, Dear."

Some clients are forgetting to turn off a cell phone during a psychotherapy hour, and it disrupts our conversation in the middle of strong feelings about something important. Some keep it on because they can't wait to discover who is calling.

**Other clients are noticing that they are spending too much time on FaceBook and MySpace checking in on what other people are doing, comparing their life with others, and hoping for a personal message of some kind from someone as validation to bolster self-esteem. Their self-worth is too much determined by how many "friends" they have acquired and how often they communicate. Some get stuck repeatedly looking at what is happening with a former romantic partner instead of planning and executing the day in a way that would make them feel successful. Living too much in the virtual world keeps them restless, interrupting their own goals. Some clients find that the text message that just came in might be more important than the conversation they are having with someone else at the dinner table.**

Has solitude or time to reflect become a thing of the past? I walk my unleashed big dogs on the LA River each morning as my time to watch nature to see the incredible power of the universe. When people approach, they often cannot hear me say, "Good Morning" and "The dogs are friendly," because they are so plugged into the sound in their ears that they cannot hear my reassurance even when they are fearful of the dogs. I pass feeling disconnected.

Many people have stopped reading books because their reading time has migrated into wandering in the virtual world. They have lost touch with the reality that reading can be a nourishing supportive personal contact with the experience and wisdom of an author.

Some marriage partners are losing important sleep watching addictive porn, or conducting an internet affair late at night when their spouse is asleep.

The legal guidelines to maintain confidentiality in psychology mandate that therapists do not conduct conversations with clients via the internet. Therefore, my clients and I still get to talk with each other by telephone and in person. I remember that e-mail and texting are only 2-5 percent of the total communication, while telephone is 17-22 percent and face-to-face contact is 100 percent. I feel exceptionally privileged to have many meaningful professional 100 percent dialogues each week.

As a result of these concerns, my clients and I have come up with some suggestions to preserve the importance of this advanced technology and to keep it from running their lives in an unproductive way.

1. Make sure to have contact with friends by telephone, arranging for face-to-face visits. Save really important communications for face-to-face contact. Remember that intimacy is two hearts in reasonable physical proximity to each other. Have the courtesy to break up with someone in person, not by text.

2. When on FaceBook, think about the people you would like to reach out to with a message rather than just looking for who might contact you. Then let go and see what happens.

3. Take disciplined responsibility for deciding how many times to "check in" per day.

4. Use the internet wisely for research purposes to learn what you need to know to make your life run smoothly.

5. When you have broken off a relationship, discipline yourself to limit the need to peer into the life of the ex-girlfriend or ex-boyfriend. Move on so that you will be available and have the space to meet someone new.

6. Turn off communication technology when having an important conversation with a loved one, child, or mentor, teacher, doctor or other important relationship.

7. Make sure there is time in the day when you are connected only with yourself, so that you have reflective time to decide how to conduct your own life.

8. Don't put too much of yourself on the internet. Remember that a potential new boss, lover, partner, college or graduate schools might be looking at who you are in the virtual world.

9. Don't cheat your employer by spending too much time socializing on the internet during work hours.

10. Limit your e-mails and texts to useful information. Don't be late meeting others because you can text them saying "I'm late."

11. Save time with a good spam detector and virus control. Be careful what you buy and how much you use your credit card on line.

12. Stay away from porn, especially if you are married. It's very addictive because the hormones released present a feeling of attachment to a virtual character.

13. Don't get too caught up in "Much ado about nothing."

14. Never text while driving. Pull over if a message is urgent.

Otherwise enjoy these beautiful advances.

In the final analysis, it is my hope that we will not lose our cultural and historical heritage by leaving behind only quick superficial bantering communications with each other through e-mail, FaceBook and MySpace. Blogging may be an exception leaving a legacy to read over time equal to such important and informative writings as *The Diary of Anne Frank*.

# 17

# FOUR KINDS OF WORKERS INTERACT; WHICH ARE YOU?

In the work force, we seem to have four basic types of individuals. We can look at the descriptions of two of the types as representing two ends of a continuum. The first we shall call **"Altruistic Work Personality." These individuals appear dedicated to "making a difference." They derive their ultimate satisfaction out of developing and using a natural talent or interest, and doing something lasting that may contribute to the lives of other people or the environment. Secondarily, they desire a sustainable income.** These individuals traditionally are most often seen in the arts, academic world and service professions, and constitute much of our volunteer force. They view the world as an interdependent community and try to contribute what they can. They donate money and effort to worthy causes. They want their inner life to be rich, and are less concerned about external material possessions. If they acquire wealth, they tend to donate a sizable portion of it to others. These individuals are not easily drawn into conflict. They want to live peacefully and use their particular talent to provide a specific service. They are not attracted to large groups and often prefer to work alone or with a small groups of like-minded thinkers. They tend to be naive about the potential for others to be greedy and rip them off.

The second work personality, we call "**Materialistic Work Personality.**" This individual tends to be interested in collecting as much as they can. Perhaps it is wealth, stocks, promotions, land, cars, mansions, antiques, trophies or fame. Materialistic Work Personalities are highly motivated, and are excellent at creating large successful-for-profit businesses or corporations. They are able to use bureaucracy to their advantage — fast tracking to the top as a leader. They produce fantastic products that we can all use and enjoy. They are able to sell themselves well, and drive a hard bargain and close a deal. Conflict is often a positive challenge; competition attracts them. They have little concern for how others are affected while they are obtaining their goal. Ethics, and sharing are frequently compromised in the name of "doing business." Their goal is almost always "to have a little more" of whatever they are collecting, often without the realization that to obtain this hurts other people and doesn't make the Materialistic Work Personality happier.

Materialistic work personality sometimes becomes carried away in reaching their goal, contributing to the imbalance or displacement of the line workers who serve them, their nation and/or the planet. Altruistic work personality takes too long to get concerned about Materialistic work personality behavior, but eventually steps in to try to "make a difference" by attempting to acknowledge the underdog and restore balance. These two work personalities then butt heads often competing and devaluing each other. Materialistic work personality tactics often win because Altruistic work personality may feel intimidated and is unwilling to compromise their ethics; meanwhile, Materialistic work personality is much more comfortable with competing and winning at any cost. Materialistic work personality acquires enormous sums of money while Altruistic work personality struggles, too often, with the proceeds from grants, donations, contributions, fund raising, a bake or community rummage sale.

Both Altruistic and Materialistic work personality individuals are needed to maintain society and each have advantages and disadvantages, strengths and vulnerabilities. How does a Altruistic and Materialistic work personality develop? How can we raise children to have the best qualities of these two work personalities, minimizing the vulnerabilities that might ultimately hurt society or the planet?

It is said that the tallest buildings run the culture. In the eighteenth century, it was the churches. In the nineteenth century, it was the universities. More recently it is the corporate world. Unfortunately the philosophy of the Materialistic personality dominates by telling us all that it is somehow all right to put out addictive or defective products, treat corporate workers with blatant disregard, earn absurdly large bonuses, bailouts, lower taxes, golden parachutes, and intimidate each other with lobbyists, law suits and buyouts solely for the purpose of increasing profits. The movie, *Insider*, is a testament to the degree that such a philosophy can be carried out. When we behave this way, what kind of message do we give to our children? How can we expect our kids to be considerate, ethical and caring in the face of such blatant hurtful ways. We seem to be at a loss as to how to handle this ongoing problem, even in the face of a recession.

There are two other kinds of workers. **The third kind is the person who says, "I want to make this amount of money in my pay check. I don't care what kind of job I do as long as I reliably get the money. Life, for me, begins after work.** These kind of workers frequently do a somewhat repetitive job cheerfully and responsibly. After work, they do what they want with their free time utilizing sports, hobbies and parties.

The fourth kind of worker is an artist. They want time to be creative with what ever form of art they practice. They are persistent in their creative endeavors, although they sometimes have to fight discouragement and frustration in gaining acceptance for their work. They need four hours a day to do their creative work. In the remaining time, they may also choose to have a more routine job that pays the food and rent and keeps them out in the world where they can interact with others for the purpose of generating further creativity.

Artists have to work with Materialistic Work Personality in Hollywood's entertainment industry even when their styles of functioning and overall goals are so very different.

Which kind of worker are you? How are you interacting with other kinds of workers? Are you presently the kind of work personality you want to be? If you are not, go directly to the essay entitled "Life's Two Most Important and Privileged Questions" for further help.

# 18

# LIFE'S TWO MOST IMPORTANT AND PRIVILEGED QUESTIONS

My thirty-year-old male client sat down and looked at me blankly. After a time, Ken spoke. "My life sucks."

I asked gently, "Why do you say that?"

He responded, "That's the problem, I don't know … I do all the things everyone else does … I'm bored and lonely … what can I say?"

"How are you bored?"

"I hate work because I do the same thing over and over every day … after work it's bad because I don't have anyone to do something with at home. My parents and family live far away. How did my life get this way anyway?"

"Let's take a look together. It seems to me that the people who have a life worth living have been able to ask and answer two questions positively."

Tom looked at me directly. "Soooo … what, pray tell, would be the questions?" Ken said intensely, with a seeming combination of curiosity and impatient irritation.

**"The first question has three parts. 1. What do you like to do best? 2. What are your strengths and talents, because you generally like to do what you know how to do easily and well? And … 3. How can you get paid for what you like to do best?"**

"My talents don't have nothin' to do with making bucks. Soooo ... what's the other question?"

"The second questions is: "Have you been able to find a loving, supportive relationship that could grow and last for fifty years?"

"Zero on that one, too. No wonder I hate life."

"I think you're being very hard on yourself. Let's go back and work with the questions. What do you like to do best? Don't worry about whether you get paid for it or not."

There was a long silence while I watched a squirrel walk along the telephone wire outside my window. Then suddenly he sat up straight and took a deep breath. "I love to organize and arrange things. I like putting colors and shapes together."

"Those are important and interesting artistic skills. What kind of jobs utilize those skills?"

"Well ... now that you ask, I have thought about it. I think interior design, fashion design, or landscaping are jobs that use those skills, but they require education. I didn't like goin' to school."

"If you take the time to sit down and write down on a piece of paper all of the things you love to do, with or without pay, and all of the things you hate to do, you will begin to see a picture of who you really are. Out of that list emerges a number of jobs that would likely make you happy while at work. And ... there are all kinds of ways to learn on-line these days."

"I never thought of looking at my work that way. Someone I knew offered me my current job. I didn't have to interview, I just took it and assumed I'd solved my career problem."

"You did succeed in earning money." I supported, then continued, "I can think of three basic kinds of workers you and I might talk about to help you out. The first kind chooses any job, and does it faithfully; life starts every day after the job ends. Then they do the activities, hobby or socializing that truly interests them after hours"

"That's been me." Tom acknowledged.

"The second type of person insists that he train and take on a job that is of real interest and taps his talent in some explicit way. Secondarily, he would like a sustaining salary. Work is his life. He relaxes with time for family after hours."

"That's what you're suggesting I consider?"

"Perhaps … The third type is an artist. Artists feel compelled to create, using their artistic genes. Often they don't have a choice. They work hard, but sometimes there is creative work to do and sometimes there isn't. Therefore, many artists decide to have another job to make ends meet so that worry about lack of funds won't hamper their creativity. I affectionately call this work a 'job-job.' Sometimes, it's a job that uses their creativity, too. Other artists may need a mindless 'job-job' so they have the time left to let the creativity percolate. Artists may also need a 'job-job' to keep them in contact with the community so that new creative ideas can be generated."

Tom brightened, "I used to like to draw and paint when I was a kid. But I stopped because my parents weren't impressed and didn't pay for any art lessons. I thought that meant I wasn't good enough so I stopped. Maybe they just didn't have enough money."

"Your parents' lack of interest or resources should not be a deciding factor for you now. It's your decision, and yours alone."

"I see what you mean."

"It seems that you're telling us both that perhaps you're an artist?" I encouraged.

"I guess maybe I'm an artist without support."

"Artists often have had a struggle that compels their artistic genes to create. Sounds like you have both art genes and a struggle in childhood. Congratulations!"

"Thanks," Tom uttered quietly as he looked up and smiled for the first time.

"Before we stop today, let's look at the second question. **Can you find a loving and supportive relationship that can grow and last for the next fifty years? This question gets easier when you've found out who you are and what you really love to do. While you're out there doing it, you're likely to meet someone who has similar talents and interests. That person will understand and therefore can be supportive. When you're ready for her and believe that you deserve her, she'll arrive. I've seen that happen so many times before with previous clients.**"

He brightened again, "That sounds like a miracle." He looked alone and thoughtful for a time. "Maybe I don't get very far with dating because I don't know what to say about who I am."

"If you find a job that you really like and it challenges you, then you will naturally feel a pride and confidence that is easy to share with an interested woman."

"Yeah, who wants to hear about my boring job?"

"You only need to discover one woman in a city of 13 million."

"You've made sense of my feelings. I do feel better, but how can I be sure to succeed?"

"You have to make a plan, and then be willing to work on it. Most important is the belief that what you want is really going to occur. What happens tends to be what we believe will happen. Hopefully this hour has strengthened your belief that you can consider carefully what you need in terms of work and a relationship for the purpose of making it your reality."

"You've given me a lot to think about." Tom looked relieved and tired. "I'll make that list and see what develops from my thinking. I guess I have a ways to go, but I'll get started on the first of two questions you've given me before our next meeting. If you can go on helping me, maybe I'll get where I need to go."

"We all try to figure who we are and what we need throughout a lifetime. It's an ongoing process. Sometimes we're encouraged, and other times we feel disheartened."

"Thank you." He got up and went to the door with an energized step. He turned on his way out to say, "I wish I'd come to see you ten years ago." He waved a goodbye.

"I can already see that you can read your feelings. Enjoy making your list. I'll look forward to our meeting again next week."

# 19

# THREE MOST IMPORTANT QUESTIONS FOR YOUR SIGNIFICANT OTHERS

A mother, father and teenage daughter came in to my office as a family for psychotherapy. They sat down on the waiting room couch wearily. The daughter pretended to doze off on a pillow. They sat in silence with nothing to say to each other. I wondered why they had come to see me. They did not look at each other. No one wanted to open the conversation once we moved to my consulting room.

We began to look at the particular problems that were fueling their silence, not relevant to this essay. In the process of their discussion, the mother asked me. "How do we get a conversation going at home? We sit down for dinner and have nothing to say to each other. I don't know where to start. It feels so awkward."

I responded, "There are three questions that have been extremely helpful for many families."

"Please go ahead, I need to know." Dad prompted.

"The first question to ask is, '**How was your day today ... really?**' This question allows you to find out what has happened that is significant for each person. Don't interrupt, just listen."

"OK?"… Dad looked at me for the first time. His daughter yawned and seemed to wake up.

I continued, "The second question is very important. Ask, **'What are your needs? Is there something I can do for you, or that we need to do together?'** Again, do not interrupt."

Dad chimed in, "We seem to get into a disagreement quickly because my wife is very critical of our daughter."

That brings me to my third question. Ask, **'Do you want to know what I'm thinking about what you've said?'** If the answer is 'no.' do not say anything further. If you feel a need to confront, find something supportive to say first. If you're just disapproving, the other person will shut down or start an argument. If they don't want to hear what you think, just reflect back what you heard from them. That way you can find out whether you heard it correctly."

"I don't care any more," said Mom, sounding distant and discouraged.

"Are you sure that's what you feel?" I asked.

"Well, maybe what I really feel is that I'm a failure as a mother."

"Why?" asked Dad.

"Because my daughter does not behave the way I want her to."

"Keep on asking her the first two questions. She will tell you. Maybe she has some really good reasons that you can respect."

Dad chimed in, looking directly at the mother, "Thank you for telling us instead of being shut down. I don't think you're a failure as a parent. I just think you expect too much. Your daughter is quiet because she fears that what she has done will disappoint you."

Their daughter responded for the first time as she moved to the edge of her seat. "Yeah, Dad's right. Whatever I do with my day is not enough for you so I don't bother to tell you anything any more."

I concluded, "What you've already told me leads me to believe that your daughter is doing extremely well. There's much for which to be proud, and you have given her the genes, basic skills and financial support to be successful. I wonder if she's asking for more psychological support in terms of validation."

I turned to the daughter, "Did I hear you correctly?"

"Yes," as she relaxed back into the chair, "Mom, if I could get more support for what I do right, I would feel safe enough to tell you more. I don't want any information from you if it's only critical. If you cannot understand that I'm already doing well, there's nothing for us to talk about."

"I think your Mom is also saying that she needs some validation as a mom in terms of what she has given to you ... that you appreciate it."

"O...kay," daughter agreed, reluctantly.

"You've managed to start talking with each other. You've heard what each one has to say. Use the information you've received, try what I have suggested, see if it works, laugh a little bit; then come back again next time to tell me what happened."

# 20

# OUR MOST POWERFUL ELIXIR

Everyone who finds the courage to start some psychotherapy tells me that they have been injured in some way. They share their selective perceptions and childhood misconceptions about why this betrayal happened. They generally take more of the blame for what happened than they deserve. In a nutshell, they hurt. They're afraid, due to feelings of low self-esteem, to do what they really want.

There are many ways for me to help. **However, the single most important interaction I have to offer is support.** Support builds self-esteem, an essential component for conducting a successful life. Through trial and lots of error, I have come to understand that support is:

- ❂ being consistently available on time

- ❂ holding an unwavering belief in someone else

- ❂ showing perseverance in helping others reach their own goals

- ❂ genuine caring

- ❂ careful listening

- ❂ accurately reflecting

- ❂ asking constructive, respectful, open-ended questions

❈ noticing what is right by looking at the glass of water as half-full rather than half-empty

❈ showing pleasure and giving genuine congratulations when progress is accomplished

❈ interacting creatively, thoughtfully and uniquely with each individual

❈ sharing a related personal story only when it contributes to clients' comprehension about their life situation.

❈ setting appropriate limits

❈ noticing logical consequences

❈ being humorous in a positive way

Confrontation is the highest form of support. It is an interaction that asks another person if they can be better than they are now, and encouragingly asserts the belief that they can. However, confrontation holds risk in terms of losing the relationship if the person feels too vulnerable to receive it constructively. The danger of losing the relationship is minimized if the confrontation can be sandwiched between two valid and genuinely positive statements.

Giving support is like watering and feeding the soil around a plant that is beginning to droop. Support is not:

❈ advising

❈ lecturing

❈ judging

❈ teasing

❈ using sarcasm

❈ being arrogant

❖ making demeaning remarks

❖ punishing

❖ manipulating

❖ controlling

❖ insisting

❖ convincing another person to do something because it is really better for you, or enhances your own self-esteem.

Some persons believe and masquerade these actions as support. However, they are the opposite of support. They are like taking water and good soil away from a plant. These actions lower the self-esteem of both the person who is giving the action and the person receiving it. The biggest gift we can give is to steadfastly believe that others can do whatever they need to do to survive and thrive, especially when the chips are down. Support offered is given in private moments; it's not for bragging or for someone else to hear. It is sustaining truth, delivered with perspective from someone who cares and knows. Support is gentle, providing a sense of safety that can go a long way to heal past wounds and allow bruises to disappear. There's nothing stronger than gentleness, working so much better than manipulating, controlling or pushing others to change in the way we might need them to be.

When I give support, I earn the trust to hear what it is really like to walk in someone else's shoes. From that experience, I gain the wisdom needed to support myself and the next person who walks across my path. Both the trust and learning are sufficient rewards.

# 21

# IN MEMORIAM

Alison sat slumped in her big overstuffed chair in the dark living room. It was gloomy due to early morning fog off the Atlantic Maine coast. No lights were on. Alison's brother, Dan, came into the room, looking frustrated with his hands on his hips. The room was cluttered with papers and dishes. Alison's startled expression told him she had just come out of a daze. He waited.

She began slowly. "It's November 13. It was one year ago today, you know, that my daughter died in the car accident. I feel so empty. I'm lost in a room so dark that I cannot see the furniture. I feel so angry I could scream. The tears have been leaking out everywhere for days. Somehow, it must have been my fault. I should have done something to prevent it. I should have made her take driver's training. I'm hopeless because I don't know what to do with myself. These feeling have plagued me now for one whole year."

"Yes, you're right. It's the 13th. I've tried to be your best brother for the past year, but I must admit I'm beginning to burn out on grieving. I wonder if we can ever make the 13th of a month just a regular day. I've had people die that I cared about, but I don't grieve for a whole year. Something seems wrong here."

"I know but I want to do something special today because it's the anniversary of her death," Alison whispered softly.

"I don't really know what to do. I already have some plans for today. I just don't think she would want you to act this way, a whole year later."

"Some people have told me that the anniversary is when feelings come up, and the second year is harder than the first year."

"Yikes! ... Damn ... I suppose you could make it that way if you want grieving to be your life-long profession," Daniel snapped back.

"Never mind. I'll do something by myself."

Dan walked out to his garage and slammed the back door.

Alison slowly dumped her large frame out of the chair and limped across the room. She went out the front door and shuffled her way down the street to the village dock. She clutched a box in one hand that she pulled out of a deep apron pocket.

The ferry sounded its horn to announce its departure in five minutes. Alison found enough money in another pocket to climb on the boat just as they were pulling up the gangplank.

It was cool but the fog was lifting, giving way to a golden sun reflected by the ocean. Alison found a deck chair and slumped in the same position she'd taken in her living room. She didn't even notice that she was sitting next to a soldier in uniform. The soldier watched her discreetly in silence for a time while the boat pulled away from the dock. Then gently, he asked, "You look uncomfortable. Is there anything I can do for you?"

Alison stared straight ahead, acting as if she did not hear him. Instead, she watched a seagull circle and land on the flag pole of the ferry.

He waited patiently.

She said, "It's the anniversary of my daughter's death. I'm still devastated"

He responded carefully, "I can relate to that. My best friend died in the Afghanistan war a little more than a year ago. I was afraid that I would never stop missing him."

"How did you handle it?"

"Well, let's see … **I grieved for a long time. When the anniversary came around, I decided that it was time to turn my sadness into a memorial. That is … I guess I decided to give up all of the sad, angry, bad and bitter feelings that engulfed me. I felt like they were draining me of life and making me feel dead. So … instead, I decided to make a memorial to him that celebrated all of the good feelings we had together …** Enough about me. Tell me, how old was your daughter? Were you and your daughter close?"

"Yes, I think we were. She was twenty. We struggled when she was a teen, but we both always knew that we loved each other and were there for each other."

"Well, I decided on the anniversary to celebrate my wonderful friend's relationship for as long as I was privileged to have it. I remembered all of the best things about my friend and us. I cherished the fact that he saved my life more than once … What part of nature did your daughter like the best?"

"The water … the ocean right here."

"My friend liked gardens. So … I made a special garden for him with his name on it. I chose flowers that represented his favorite colors. I took the little bit of his ashes his parents gave me out of the box and put them in the garden to nourish the plants … Did you talk easily with your daughter?"

"Yes, most of the time. We argued some."

"After I finished the garden, I sat down right there and talked to him. I told him what I was planning to do next with my life. I talked to him just the way I always did. I swear I heard his voice say, 'Thank you, buddy, go for it. I'll be with you. You can talk to me any time."

"I see," said Alison slowly.

"What did your daughter like to do best?" this stranger soldier coaxed.

"She loved to come out on the water in a canoe and watch the baby seals."

"If she were to speak to you now, what do you think she would say?"

"She would tell me to knock off the crying and throw her ashes in the water so that they would float over the rocks to the seals and dolphins. Then she would tell me to get my ass in gear and go to art school, so I could be an art teacher. I'd just started school before she died. but I dropped out with the grief."

"Can you grant her wish?"

"Yes ... I have the ashes with me ... and I could sign up for a course in January."

The ferry pulled into the next harbor, passing the rocks where the seals lay guarding their young. Alison thought for some time, then slowly pulled the box from her pocket and scattered a few ashes on the water from the boat. She watched them drift toward the rocks and the seals.

There were no tears; instead she was almost smiling.

She turned to the soldier and said, "Thank you." He nodded quietly, and got off the boat. She returned to her deck chair to make the journey back home. This time she sat up straight. She was filled with feelings that made her strong: willingness, reason, trust, love, and even joy and peace. The boat docked near her home.

She walked briskly back to the house. She heard the leaves rustling in the trees for the first time in a year. Dan looked surprised. "What happened to you?" he blurted awkwardly.

"I met a soldier on the ferry who taught me a thing or two. I'll be better now," Alison said as she started to cook a late breakfast. "Want some?"

"Well, I guess so … sure … You're different. What happened to you? I don't get it." Dan mumbled through a mouthful of scrambled eggs.

"I'm learning to let my daughter go and to remember the good times we had together. I'm taking back my own life, to do what I know she would want me to do. That's enough for one day, don't you think?"

"Yeah … you bet. Good for you." Dan got up, took his dishes to the sink, came back and hugged her awkwardly. "So what are you going to do?"

"Get my ass back to art school in January."

"Go for it." Dan slipped quietly out the back door to the garage.

# 22

# A NEW WAY FOR THE ELDERLY
# TO GRIEVE

"I came to see you because I feel so lost. I don't know where to go or what to do with myself. My wife died six months ago. We were married for 50 years. She was my lover, my friend, my mentor. We worked together in the same business; I had a landscaping firm and she owned a nursery. Therefore, on a daily basis, we had eight more hours together than most married couples ever do. She was a very intelligent lady, far brighter than me. I looked up to her." He sat on the edge of the couch, glancing uneasily around the room, not sure that he should be talking with a therapist.

"It sounds like you had a very good relationship with your wife for a long time. You're a very lucky man. However, I bet it does not feel like that now because you miss her so much." I responded.

"I hadn't thought of it that way. I suppose that's true. It just feels so difficult now. I don't know what to do with the grief. I drive up and down the coast, thinking about her. Sometimes, I don't even know where I am."

"Psychology is a young profession. We're still learning a lot. We originally thought that everyone who lost someone had to go through the same stages of grief: shock, sadness, anger and guilt, denial, bargaining, and finally integration. For a much younger person, this may be still true." I continued, watching him carefully to see if he was following me. "Have you been to a grief support group?"

"Yes," he said warily, " I suppose it helped some … I know all of those words you just spoke."

I continued cautiously, "I think that we're rethinking how an older person who has been married happily for a very long time, might better manage the loss of a loved one."

"There has to be another way."

"Well, let's look at it. You must have had thousands and thousands of conversations with her."

"Yes, indeed! We worked together like two bodies and one mind."

"So if you asked her a question now, you might have a very good idea about what she would say if she were still here today?"

"Oh, yes! I knew her very well."

"And your memory has stored everything she has said to you, either consciously, subconsciously or unconsciously."

"Yes … Is that really true?"

**In psychology, the compilation of memories of your interactions with her is called an "*introject*." It's inside you. You can reach out to it at any time. That is, you can ask her a question and she will answer you."**

"I talked to her like that until about three months ago."

"What happened to make you stop?" I queried, puzzled.

"My brain told me to stop eating. I was not hungry any more. Then I didn't want to see anyone and I didn't want to talk. I went to the doctor and he told me that all of my tests came out normal. There was nothing wrong with my body. I guess I just didn't want to live any more."

"Were you waiting to die so that you could be with your wife?"

"The doctor told me that sometimes people want to do that when they've known somebody really well who died."

"He's right. Some people decide to end their lives on this planet because it's so hard to be without the person they've loved."

"The doctor took the time to talk with me. He told me to get some exercise and listen to music I love. He gave me some medication for depression, but I did not like how it made me feel. I felt flat."

"So you almost decided to die, but you're here still coming to talk with me."

"Well I tried alcohol and decided I would become homeless if I kept that up. I returned to smoking and decided that was also a bad idea and stopped that. Then I tried a legal prescription of marijuana and realized that was stupid, so now I'm completely clean."

"That must have taken a lot of discipline. Good for you."

"Now I've nothing left but to come and see you."

"What made you decide to go on living?"

"I think it was the conversation with the doctor. I also think that I would like to write a book about my wife because she has an interesting story. But I'm not sure."

"Maybe it's time to start talking with her again and ask her what she thinks." I encouraged.

"Yes, I could do that, but I think I'd already decided that I want to live some more."

"How old are you?" I asked.

"I'm almost 72. I was able to set up my new apartment, so I figured I was doing something right."

"You're right. Do you like to read?

"Yes, I read a lot."

"Then you're a good candidate to read Gail Sheehy's book called *New Passages*. It's all about a 'second adulthood' because so many of us now have good health due to modern medicine. We are able to live longer. She'll tell you that it's completely normal for you to feel confused at this time in your life. You'll need to go through a 'second adolescence' to figure out what skills you would like to take on with you into your 'second adulthood.' You may find something completely new to do that will give you pleasure and uses skills you have already acquired. You may become a different person and find a new person to spend time with."

"I think I definitely want to keep on living. You've given me a lot of new ideas. I'll be in contact with my wife again through the intro…? What did you call it? Yes, introject? I will ask her what she thinks about writing the story of her life. I know she'll talk with me now."

"Do you want to tell me how she died?"

"She had a sudden heart attack. By the time I called 911, she was already dead."

"So you had no warning that this was going to happen?"

"No, we were working together as usual. She was in the car sitting next to me. All of a sudden she slumped over and was dead before I could pull over to the side of the freeway. I was totally unprepared."

"No wonder this has been such a hard six months for you!"

"Well, I'm glad I came to talk with you. I visit my daughters often, and I'm going back to my home country in Sweden to visit all of my relatives. Then I'll decide whether to go back to work and where to live. Some friends have offered me some part-time jobs. Maybe I'll be ready for that soon."

"Don't forget to talk with the introject that is your wife. From what you have told me, she will give you the very best advice because she knows you better than anyone else. Make sure you're looking at your favorite photograph of her while you talk with her. You have every right to keep the relationship inside of you alive as long as you are on this planet. No one can take it away from you; it's yours forever and you've honestly earned every minute of your time with her introject. Writing her story may be a real help to your readers. Perhaps that is what the universe is offering you to do with her death. Good luck, and let me know if I can be of further help to you."

"Thank you. I'll probably come back to see you so you can help me stay on course and make it all happen."

"We can complete your initial evaluation at that time. Then I will know your whole life story better. I am glad we've had a chance to talk."

# 23

# WARNING ... SUICIDE IS FIRST-DEGREE MURDER

Sometimes we human beings reach a point in life in which we feel so discouraged or in so much psychic or physical pain that we decide it would be better if we were simply dead.

**If you have felt suicidal for some time, and you have already made a plan as to how to kill yourself, you would be most wise to put down this book and call for an immediate appointment with a psychotherapist, or your local mental health clinic.** Should these feelings be strongly present after working hours, reach out to a friend, and go to an emergency room or urgent care. Be honest about your suicidal plan. Some of the other essays in this book might comfort you and give you hope while you are waiting for your appointment.

**Ninety-five percent of clients who have come to see me with suicidal thoughts are making a valid cry for help rather than wishing to end life.** The suicidal thoughts make it abundantly clear that **their despair is extremely serious.** We have always been able to take a thorough history to figure out the specific problems. Understanding is a critically important response and form of caring. We read the negative feelings we find carefully, in small manageable pieces, especially when they are acutely painful. The relationship between us deepens, gives meaning, respect and support. Then, as we are able to look at some solutions to the problems, the suicidal ideation recedes.

Some people suffer dark depressions for physiological reasons. They may be lacking sufficient serotonin, have a bipolar depression, have a bad reaction to antidepressant, or become overwhelmed because they are a Highly Sensitive Person (HSP). These people can be helped enormously with the right kind of psychiatric medication, natural medication from a holistic doctor, and/or a change in diet, and psychotherapy.. The correct medication often works within forty-eight to seventy-two hours, giving the client a whole new perspective on life.

Persons who have faced a very difficult life may contemplate suicide at some point. However, when they reach out for help, they become empowered to make a conscious existential decision to go on living that remains permanent.

**I have never met a client who deserved to die. I have seen many clients over the years who mistakenly thought that they should leave the planet. Once we go to work together to make living worthwhile, each and every client over the past forty-one years has decided to continue with life, and has figured out a way to make it better than it ever was before.**

**So ... take heart and reach out for the help you need and resist the urge, no matter how strong, to ever treat yourself cruelly in a manner that could cause death, physical harm or psychological pain while you are alive, or prematurely rob you of your deserved existence.**

# 24

# FINDING THE RIGHT
# PSYCHOTHERAPIST

Everyone thinks a long time before they make their first appointment with a psychotherapist. They have already tried to fix the problem one more time themselves. It is a big step to pick up the telephone and to make the first call. I have high respect for anyone who contacts me since it's a major responsibility to have an hour each week to exclusively talk about the self.

Because it's such a big step, I always make time to talk with any new client by telephone. I want each person to have a sense of who I am before they come into the office. I usually ask what happened that made them decide to "contact me today as opposed to last month or next month." They will often respond in a way that gives me a preliminary sense of the presenting problem.

When my clients arrive, I give them a brief form to fill out and then we sit down to talk for one and one half hours.

**Each one of us has a job to accomplish during that initial meeting. First, I outline the client's responsibility. I generally will say, "I'm going to be asking you a lot of questions. You can answer any question you want, or pass on any question since you are still trying to get to know me. Your job today is to sense how it feels to be saying**

more personal kinds of things to me. If I have any habits, looks, behavior, or mannerism that reminds you of someone who has had a particularly negative impact on your life, I might not be the right therapist for you to see. If this meeting is uncomfortable for you in that way, please let me know, and I will refer you on to someone else. I have a rich referral source."

Then I outline my responsibility. "My job today is to see if I can understand the presenting problem and what might have already happened in your life to aggravate that problem. If I figure it out correctly, I should be able to say something to you that you may not have ever heard before, but it sounds just right. If I can do that, it usually means that I have located the correct central issue. I can generally get to it within the first two hours."

I also add, "I would encourage you to see more than one therapist for your initial consultation. If another therapist comes up with the same central issue, then you know you are on the right track. Each therapist will have a unique way of working and there are many different theoretical orientations. I will charge you for this meeting only if you go on to make a contract for psychotherapy with me. Then I will charge you the same fee we decide upon for your ongoing work. If you do not return, this hour is a gift to you so that you can afford to move on to someone else."

At the end of the hour, I ask, "How did it feel to do the initial evaluation with me?" I also give each client the option to think about it and get back to me by phone. I feel that it is very important not to attempt to "close the deal" with a new client. The material we talk about and the nature of the relationship is tender and does not lend itself to any kind of manipulation.

Finally, I encourage my clients to ask me any questions they might have about my training, education, and the process of therapy. I also provide each one with a statement about my professional background along with my office procedures, rules of confidentiality, and recommendations as to their options if there is any difficulty with the therapeutic relationship.

It is important to me that all clients leave the initial evaluation feeling respected, supported, encouraged, and comfortable with their first psychotherapy hour. Only then will they have the courage to return to say more and more about what is really on their minds. I will be a special private intimate coworker in a truly professional way until their work is done.

Then I must open the door for each client to leave, no matter how much I might miss them. A good therapist must be an expert at handling loss. I will not see most clients again. However, our meeting will hopefully have made a critical difference in a very positive way. **They will leave with the thoughts and feelings, unique to their situation, which we've shared together, now tucked away in their souls. Their work with me will serve as a reminder to them anytime of their right to live a decent, successful life with compassion for themselves and others.**

# 25

# DON'T BE AFRAID TO ASK FOR
# A REDUCED FEE

If you have finished reading this book and have become interested in doing some psychotherapy yourself, but have limited funds; don't give up.

**The ethics of the profession of psychology ask that professionals give some portion of their work to clients without charge.** In 1994, I founded and am president of a group of fifteen psychotherapists, THE INDEPENDENT PSY-CHOTHERAPY NETWORK (www.therapyinla.com). We all work with some form of sliding fee scale. Many other therapists carry one or more clients pro bono or with minimum charge especially when there is a special need. I charge for the initial evaluation only if the client goes on to make a contract with me.

**It is always a right to request a reduced fee.** Since the therapy process involves regular meetings across time, many therapists will consider a financial arrangement that allows you to afford treatment without interruption. Some therapists will suggest that you can come in for a half hour, or on an "as needed basis" after you have completed some work.

I remember my first meeting with my first therapist in 1971. Full fee was, at that time, $35 per hour. I was in graduate school so I could only work part time.

At the end of the hour, I asked, "Would you work with me for a reduced fee?"

He responded, "Yes, 1 would."

I took a deep breath and then offered, "I could afford to see you once a week for $15 per hour or twice a week for $10 per hour."

I waited.

He thought for a very long minute and then responded, "I will see you twice a week for $10.00 per hour."

That was a defining moment for me. His response validated my interest and motivation to understand myself as a client in training to be a psychotherapist. This meant a lot to me. At that moment, I made the existential decision to pass the same gift on to those clients with similar need, and passion to understand themselves. The universe keeps sending me some clients who have quickly earned my highest respect and admiration.

Go for it, and, if there is a valid need for a reduced fee, don't forget to ask.

# III
## DEFINING MOMENTS
## WITH FURRY ASSOCIATES

MY FURRY
ASSOCIATES

# 26

## HOW DOGS AND CATS ASSISTED ME IN THE PSYCHOTHERAPY PROCESS WITHIN A HOME PRIVATE PRACTICE

As a clinical psychologist, trained in the 1970s, I was taught to be very sure that my office was quiet, that there would be no distractions to disturb clients from the process of sharing feelings without resistance. It was my job to provide that atmosphere. And for many years, I did just that. I didn't even display any pictures of my family. My office, although warmly decorated with miniature artifacts from museum collections, was a blank screen in terms of information about my family life.

I am writing this essay because so many therapists are moving to home practices. Some are confronting, for the first time, the presence of family pets. The Psychology Examining Committee is sanctioning continuing education regarding Pet Assisted Therapy. Do these therapists allow their animals any contact with their clients?

After my adopted daughter arrived, I decided to move my practice to an unusual colonial house in Los Angeles built in 1937. This duplex residence became my solution to the super-mom quandary. We lived downstairs, and my office was upstairs. Each unit had a completely separate entrance. Therefore, my commute to work was just fifteen steps, which gave me more time to spend with my daughter. If she needed special care during the week because she was sick, I could more easily provide it for her. In the evening, I could slip upstairs to finish my "homework," which modeled a good example for her. My husband could help me with the computer billing and formatting of my manuscripts, while my daughter helped me, over the years, with some secretarial tasks.

Fellow clinicians raised their eyebrows when I first moved home. Wouldn't my clients see too much of my personal life? Might they "hang" around when they weren't supposed to and find out about my family in a way that might interfere with the psychotherapy process? My husband and daughter were careful not to be in the driveway while clients were coming and going. Therefore, rarely did they intersect. The therapy seemed to progress well. Clients either asked or figured out that I lived downstairs. Occasionally we would discuss who knew me better, those who came upstairs or those that visited me downstairs? We came to understand that both relationships were special in different ways. My clients never hung around when they weren't supposed to be there.

My daughter benefited from knowing that I was "nearby" even though she understood that there was a strict rule that she could never enter my office when there was "a car in the driveway," unless she had an emergency. Only once did she break this rule. At a young age she got away from her father and gently knocked on my closed office door. When I opened it, she just stared. I asked why she'd knocked. She answered calmly, "I just wanted to see what a client looks like." The client laughed, Dad reclaimed her quickly, and my client and I went back to work on the therapy issues at hand.

On another occasion, I slipped out to the store for a few minutes because a client had cancelled. I made the mistake of not informing my family downstairs. When I returned, I had a determined daughter sitting on the porch step. She admonished me in no uncertain terms. "Don't you **ever** go away without telling me. I thought you were upstairs working." She helped me to understand how important it was to her that I worked nearby.

Our family has always loved animals. Since I married forty three years ago, we've rescued ten dogs and six cats. We've loved them all equally. They have been free to roam indoors or out with the aid of dog doors and an enclosed yard. I write this essay to share with my readers the warm wisdom, companionship and intimacy that is possible between pets and humans.

Now there are certain hazards that have to be overcome if you have a home practice and animals. At a prior residence near a fire station, the three dogs liked to go out on the back porch and howl whenever the sirens blared. The porch was directly above my home office window. Therefore, I had to either lock them inside during client hours or move. I chose to move.

Eventually, the animals began in small ways to interact with the clients outside of the office. The cats liked to climb on the hoods of clients' cars and soak up the warmth from the engine, especially on windy days. Gradually each animal realized that they were missing time with me and they'd better figure out a way to get in on some of the good warm intimate conversation going on upstairs.

The first one to figure this out was Nicholas. He was a large, totally black cat who walked like a panther. He was known affectionately in the neighborhood as "THE KING" because he acted like one. He patrolled the street making sure that we were protected from all of the fierce furry things, especially other cats. Any cat who did not defer to him had to face a fight. There were very few challenges.

Nicholas made his entrance gradually into my office. At first, he slipped through the dog door and curled up in a corner. He convinced me that he would not bother anybody, so I let him stay. He moved into my lap one evening when I was especially tired because there were several emergencies to handle that day. I noted that his purring gave me energy and made me feel calm and confident.

Then he made his debut. A client had just arrived. She came up the stairs three at a time, with Nicholas tailing her. Instead of quietly sitting in the waiting room, as is customary, she bounded into my office and sat in the client's chair. She was sobbing. Before I could move to my chair and ask, "What's the matter?" Nicholas had already climbed onto her lap and was licking her chin. She sputtered. "I'm so sorry I barged in. I just discovered that my cat had been killed on the highway." It was utterly clear that Nicholas already knew what had happened and was comforting her before I could figure out how to help. She hugged him, appreciating his attention. I was utterly amazed in this defining moment. She grieved the loss over time and acquired two new black cats.

Nicholas began to show up more and more. Often he would sit on my lap. It was the day before Christmas Eve. Another client was examining the merits of getting herself a pet for Christmas. She was unsure about her ability to be a responsible pet owner. Toward the end of the hour, Nicholas hopped off of my lap and climbed into hers. He reached up and licked her on the cheek. It was as if he had been listening and understood. She took his gesture to mean that she could have her long-awaited pet. I got a card in the mail two days later from this person. She said, "I went to the pound that afternoon and picked out a small black dog. I named him Nicholas because he reminds me of "St. Nick." I hadn't told her the name of my cat, because I was still feeling ambivalent about allowing the animals to be present.

I pondered these two defining events. Did this animal know thoughts and feelings that I didn't? Could he actually be helpful? Was I crazy and just rationalizing his presence because I loved my pets? What about clients who were allergic?

Well, I would soon find out.

A client walked into the office for her initial evaluation and discovered that I had a cat. She was immediately perturbed but wanted to stay because I had been "highly recommended." She feared that she would have a strong allergic reaction necessitating a call to 911. I asked her if she would prefer a referral. She somewhat fearfully decided to stay to see what would happen, because I explained that I had a very good air filter. She was surprised to discover that she did not have any allergic reaction. Therefore, she concluded her hour by making a contract with me. I kept Nicholas out of my office during her appointed hour. However, it soon became evident that Nicholas had a plan of his own. He would show up in the waiting room every week for her hour. At first he sat in the doorway and just stared at her with an unending look that said, "Go ahead, see if you can sneeze." Each week he would sit six inches closer to where she was waiting on the couch. As the weeks went on, and she had no adverse reaction, he ventured into the office during her hour. I stayed out of this contest between the two of them, leaving the decision as to whether Nicholas came into the hour completely up to my client. She invited him to come into her session. Just before she concluded her work with me, he managed to hop into her lap. She never sneezed once. I dealt with her other unresolved issues, while noticing that Nicholas appeared to have taken care of her cat allergy completely by himself.

This was another astonishing defining moment. I could only articulate Nicholas's cure as introducing her very slowly, carefully and kindly to the source of her allergy. Since this defining moment, many clients have been cured of allergies to dogs and cats, and fear of animals by the gentle presence of my pets in this office. It makes me wonder about allergies. I used to be allergic to cats myself.

It had been widely misconstrued that animals do not have a good sense of time. Therefore, one might ask how Nicholas could possibly keep track of my client's regular appointment time each week? Is his behavior merely a coincidence? Yet recent studies on dogs say that these animals know when their owners are returning home from wherever they went. The animal will get up and stir or walk over to the window, at that very moment, even if their owner is hundreds of miles away. How do they know? What wisdom do they have that is inaccessible to humans?

I have always perceived all of my animals as having a very good sense of time. For instance, Nicholas waited in the bushes for me every morning. When I returned from taking the dogs for a walk in the park, he greeted the dogs by walking between their legs. I'd pick him up and he pressed his head into my cheek on the way to the front door while purring vigorously. This happens every morning. My dogs always knew when it was time to be fed. They barked at my daughter if she had not fed them. If I see clients past 6:00 p.m. the animals will sit in front of me and stare until I acknowledge and explain my transgression of overworking.

Was there a wisdom here that could actually help my practice?

The next animal to arrive was Heather. She is a small black and white feral cat with yellow eyes, chubby cheeks, and long white whiskers. She was found in a very poor section of the city, badly dehydrated and very hungry. My daughter, Kendall, was home from school, sick with a sore throat. Heather climbed onto her chest while she was lying down on the bed, and settled in for the weekend by lying across her throat. Kendall and Heather proceeded to provide warmth and healing for each other while forming a lasting attachment.

How did Heather know that Kendall had a sore throat? I'm rarely sick, but on the few occasions when this has happened, one of my animals will intuit the place on my body that hurts and will stay with me until I feel better. A client called to cancel her hour with me because she had injured her ankle. She was on crutches. She noted, with some interest, that her dog followed her everywhere she went, even to get a drink of water. He was obviously taking care of her, ready to be of assistance if she fell. It is also well known that dogs know, before humans, when their owner is about to have a seizure, and are also able to detect and bring attention to a melanoma by repeatedly sniffing the area where the melanoma is located.

An award was given to a dog by the Los Angeles Humane Society. This animal accompanied his owner on a walk in Griffith Park every day. The owner noted that the dog turned back and started going home just as they were about to climb a sizable hill. The owner had no choice but to follow him, puzzled. When the owner got back home, he collapsed on the floor with a heart attack. The dog knocked the telephone off the counter onto the floor where his owner was able to reach it and dial 911. How did the dog know that his owner needed to go home to get medical attention? What signal do they get that is not available to humans? Thanks to the dog, the owner lived to tell the story.

Heather and Nicholas showed up at the end of a client hour together just outside my office entrance. Nicholas had ripped the pad on his paw and was holding it up to show me.

Heather sat right beside him beseeching me with her eyes to take him to the vet.

Heather was not initially as strong a participant in the psychotherapy process as some of my other animal associates. Instead, she would sit on the steps outside of my office. She was the most feral of the cats. Therefore, she really did not like to be picked up or held. She preferred a secret ear and chin scratch in the middle of the dark night. I think that she was less able to pick up signals from clients because she remained afraid of people.

# 27

# ENTER DOGS

The same friend who brought me Heather, also introduced me to Sasha, a middle-aged Samoyed. We know little about her history. Apparently Sasha walked into a grade school classroom one day. A parent brought her home, but traveled a lot, leaving Sasha alone in the backyard with only dry food and water for up to five days. Sasha had some allergies and a thyroid problem. My friend persuaded this lady to give Sasha to us.

We drove to the owner's house on Memorial Day. Her daughter let us in. Sasha was in the backyard. Her back was bleeding and she was so dirty and matted that it took two baths to discover that she was really a white dog. We played with her for a few minutes and found her to be docile and friendly. We had left the door to the backyard and the front door of the house ajar. Suddenly Sasha got up and ran outside to our car. She played briefly with our other two dogs and then jumped into the car. Nothing we could do would get her out. She had made up our minds for us about taking her. The lady who had owned her and a neighbor who had walked her from time to time both cared enough to come to visit us once. They seemed satisfied that she was in good hands, and we never heard from them again.

We brought Sasha back to good health quickly. However, she was apparently used to being abandoned. Whenever we took her out for a walk or to the beach, she would find a new family to whom she could "belong." She would lie down next to them, just in case we should leave without her.

I had always kept my dogs downstairs when clients were in the office. The cats were the only ones to gain entrance through their own persistence. However, Sasha picked up a fox tail. It penetrated her thigh and worked its way below her skin underneath her thick coat. She had to have a surgery to remove it and then wear the inevitable plastic Elizabethan collar to keep her from licking the wound. Because Sasha was miserable with her collar, I let her come into the office one day so that I could take the plastic collar off and keep an eye on her bandages. She was overjoyed to be with my clients and me, lying on the cool hearth near my chair. She remained quiet throughout five therapy hours.

The wound healed quickly but not before she'd decided that she always wanted to be in my office. Any time she saw me leave for the upstairs to go to work she would come to my side with her tail wagging and her brown eyes staring me down with the question, "May I come too?" If I hesitated, she would dance a little dance in which she waved her head from side to side. Perhaps she was making up for the hours of loneliness in the previous owner's backyard.

Sasha knew that she had to be quiet in order to stay. She could do that for a whole day as long as I took her for a walk each morning. My clients seemed to enjoy her presence. Many of them would stop to pat her briefly on their way to sit down. If clients arrived when I was down the hall or downstairs,

Sasha would get up to greet them. She would stay with them until I arrived. I was surprised and appreciative of this sweet courtesy. Although she appeared to be sleeping most of the time, she was obviously listening and completely aware of what was going on.

I had one couple visit me with infertility problems. They had tried many different ways to be parents and were obviously getting discouraged. Sasha would get up every time they came into the waiting room. She would wag her tail and sidle up to them as if to say. "You'll be good parents, don't give up, I'll come and live with you."

Whoops! Now I had two cats and one dog who interacted with clients at will. Sasha was always there, Nicholas was in and out, while Heather greeted clients on the porch. I went on with my work.

I always let my clients decide what kind of involvement, if any, they would have with the animals. I ran an excellent quiet air filter in my consulting room. It kept the air clean for all of us and warded off any allergy problems. Only one client, in three years of work, asked that the animals be removed. Each client was given full permission not to engage with any animal. Most wanted to have a brief interaction with a dog or cat, even if it was just a nonverbal pat. The animals rarely approached anyone formally dressed in a three piece suit. They instinctively knew that animal hair was not allowed. Occasionally a cat was dumped off a lap, but the cat was not perturbed, nor was the flow of our dialogue disrupted.

I periodically did an evaluation of my practice, specifically asking about the animals. No one complained.

Many of my clients were talented, hard-working, responsible people who had lives that were frequently short on un-adulterated genuine support and love. Their parents had died, divorced, disappeared, or were too preoccupied with some form of addiction to hold themselves together. Other clients had parents who had, out of psychological need, inadvertently sabotaged my clients' attempts at success and independence. All of these clients were under-served in terms of unconditional positive regard. First, the positive regard that I gave to the animals was evident. I would sometimes engage in a brief dialogue with each animal with such phrases as, "You know the rules, settle down or go downstairs." "Are you going to let me sit in that chair or not?" "Wow, you look beautiful today." "Your fur is so soft." "Are you thirsty?" "Do you need to go out?" Clients seemed encouraged by the kindness between us all. Often when they heard the gentle scratch on the door from a pet, they jumped up to let the animal in before I could. They felt included in "my family of associates" rather than separated as a "client" who "did not belong downstairs." It appeared that the therapy process took a shorter time to reach a satisfying conclusion because of the animals. Many clients, who did not have pets, decided to acquire one for themselves.

Apparently, the oxytocin released by the brain when in the presence of the animals made it easier for clients to talk openly. As one lady said, "I felt so angry when I first came in today. I could not have told you if Nicholas had not climbed in my lap." Another said, "These animals are special. They really help us. When a cat gets on my lap and purrs, my voice just takes over." Other clients would walk into my office and see which animals were present. A few, especially children, did not wish to have a psychotherapy hour without their chosen creature. A fourth client said, "You should charge extra for the animals; they have something special to add." A fifth client suggested that I change my sign at the bottom of the stairs to read, "McArthur and Associates."

# 28

# NEW CATS BECOME ASSOCIATES

My adopted daughter's birth grandmother was dying of cancer. We went to see her to say our farewell. We had visited her many times over a decade and never knew that she owned two cats. They were apparently afraid of strangers, so they hid under the bed any time company came. On this day, there were many relatives and friends wandering in and out of her apartment, coming to say a final good bye.

I was sitting next to Nanna when two large orange cats arrived. They climbed onto my lap. I thought they were try-ing to visit her so I placed one on her lap, but she was in too much pain to receive them. It became clear that they had come to see me. Were they looking for a new home?

Squeaker and Rascals were brothers who had never been separated from each other. They were very large, long-haired, orange marmalade cats. Squeaker was twenty five pounds while Rascals weighed seventeen.

In Nanna's last con-versation with me, she informed me that she did not have any relative or friend who wanted to take in the cats. I told her that I would receive them and either keep them, if they fit into our family, or find a suitable home for them. Since I had already adopted her granddaughter, she seemed to trust me and appeared relieved.

Several days later the cats were delivered to our home. We already had Nicholas and Heather downstairs where we lived, so I decided to start Rascals and Squeaker upstairs in the computer room in my office. After a few days of watching them settle in nicely, I was encouraged to leave the door open. Gradually, over a few weeks, the cats began to migrate slowly down the hall. Clients would stop to pet them briefly. They quickly overcame their fear of strangers.

Nicholas and Rascals had one serious fight. Therefore, Nicholas had to stay downstairs, unfortunately ending his "associate" status in my office. I don't think he ever forgave Rascals for taking away his job.

Within three weeks, both Squeaker and Rascals had decided, without any input from me, to go to work as my assistants. They created their own job descriptions. Squeaker chose to reside in the waiting room and greet the clients while he lay on the couch purring loudly. He was especially warm to any new anxious client, as if to say, "Don't worry, just tell her what you really feel and everything will come out all right." Squeaker assigned himself one additional job. When he perceived me to be tired or stressed out by all the psychic pain I'd taken in that day, he came off his place on the waiting room couch and climbed onto my lap in the consulting room. He'd purr loudly and deeply so that I felt energized and massaged by his love.

Rascals has assigned himself a completely different job. He'd hide in the book closet in my consulting room and come out quietly when he perceived that a client might need the comfort he had to offer. He'd always show up when clients were dealing with loss, showing tears, anger or confusion. He'd sit at their feet, asking if they'd like his company. If they didn't want him on their lap, he'd go under the couch, directly below where they were sitting, If the client was allergic and wanted him to leave, he'd do so without a hint of feeling rejected.

Rascals has provided significant clinical support many times over. For instance, one day a client was considering the question of whether he should sell his gun to pay another month's rent, or return to using the gun to play Russian Roulette, flirting dangerously with killing himself. Rascals appeared and offered his opinion in another defining moment. The client was sitting with his hands on the arm rest, fingers hanging limply over the edge of the chair. Rascals climbed upon his lap and put his paw next to the client's fingers. The client clasped his paw, held it lovingly for a moment and said, "I'll sell the gun." This client also entered the Twelve-Step program and has gone on to have a productive life.

Daily these two new dear animals wandered in and out of the office, doing their assigned jobs to earn their keep. Their presence provided a sense of peace, calm, respect, unconditional love and intuition that was magical for me and all who come through my door to talk. I've watched Rascals and Squeaker carefully because they often gave me clues as to what to say or do next.

Squeaker died after years of work in my office. He was buried in the back yard under a flourishing pink geranium plant. Rascals grieved the loss deeply by refusing to eat. I had to ask him directly to stay on and work with me without his brother. He accepted. I've wondered whether to get him a companion or whether any animal could really replace his brother.

# 29

# NEW DOGS SIGN ON

asha, the Samoyed, reached old age and died peacefully one day. I was surprised to find out that my clients were deeply impacted. We had to take some time out of each client hour to grieve her loss.

After several months, I found another Samoyed in the pound to take Sasha's place. Angel has a soft seal face with big brown eyes, black eyelids, and white eye lashes. There's not a mean bone in her

body. She lies next to me on the brick hearth, trying to feel the cool through her thick white coat.

Two other dogs have also become part of the practice. Teddy is a black Labrador-Great Dane combination. We have speculated that he was likely thrown out of a car on a boulevard and was rescued as he tried to make it across the street when the light turned red. He wanted to be with me so much that, as a puppy, he learned to lie quietly by my side. He never entered a room without greeting the

client. Teddy is happiest when he can follow me wherever I go. He's a natural protector and faithful guardian. If a client appears depressed, Teddy will go downstairs and bring up a stuffed toy mallard duck that squeaks and place it at the client's feet, inviting him to play and laugh with him.

A client who was physically abused as a child reported a dream in which Teddy came and nuzzeled his hand. As he spoke tearfully, Teddy got up, came over to this client and demonstrated the identical behavior being articulated within the dream. The client cried about Teddy's implied understanding. How did Teddy know?

Chelsey is a Korean Jindo, abandoned in a local park. She looks much like a coyote. She's the watch dog over my practice with an unlocked door during office hours. She's learned the sound of each client's car and step on the stairway as they approach the office. If the client is new, she will briefly bark. She seems to be checking to see if the client really has an appointment or is, indeed, an intruder. Otherwise, she lies right next to me always.

As I was completing this manuscript, Luke arrived just one month after Angel reached the end of her life. I was walk-

ing the dogs near the the L.A. River when I saw a rust colored Great Dane, Ridge Back mix, loping with great speed and the utmost grace of a deer or horse near the water. He climbed the river bank and began to run with my dogs. Teddy took immediate notice, ran with him, and put his head on his shoulder every time this new dog stopped. It was as if he was bringing my attention to this animal. Teddy and Luke continued their play and running together for twenty minutes. This new dog followed us to our car. I wondered what I was going to do. My own dogs decided for me. They climbed into the third seat in my minivan, leaving the second seat completely open for this new huge arrival. I hesitated but invited him into the van. I had to ask three times while Luke looked at the river, at me, at my dogs, trying to believe that he was going to be rescued. He jumped into the car. None of my dogs growled while I drove home. Luke was very thirsty and hungry.

A trip to the vet revealed that he had sustained a back injury, and was micro-chipped to an animal shelter miles away. That meant that he may well have traveled many miles up the river to find me and my dogs. We provided our contact information to the micro-chip company, and checked the internet daily, but no owner ever contacted us. Luke is very intelligent, well trained, friendly, and wonderful with children. He had obviously been owned, but was also abused.

We could only conclude that he may have been part of the foreclosure tragedy. Perhaps his owner was unable to find an apartment that accepted animals, while the animal shelters were overflowing. Therefore, foreclosed pet owners were dropping their animals along the river where dog owners walked their dogs. Perhaps their dog would be claimed. Another example of the pain the brokers have caused while collecting their fees from owners who could not afford homes.

By default, this intelligent sweet dog became ours. We named him Luke.

Within days, Luke had discovered my office on the second floor. He proceeded gradually to become involved with the clients. He, too, designed his own job description. He would stand at the door and greet the client. Next he would walk with the client to the waiting room. Then, he lay down next to the file cabinet where I stored the current files and reviewed each file before the client's hour. When I invited a client into my office, Luke would escort each one in then, sometimes lean into them for a minute to warm their legs. Finally, he would follow the office rule of lying quietly on his dog bed throughout the hour. At the end of the session, he would escort the client to the door. Some clients loved him enough to sit on the floor next to him. Teddy and Luke, both half Great Danes, quickly became fast friends. Luke and Teddy were proud working dogs; never missing a client hour even if it meant delaying their dinner.

Teddy came to the end of his life at age fourteen (105 years in people age). I saw thirty-one clients that week, and was, once again, surprised at the impact he had. All but two patients noticed immediately, asking where Teddy was. Some clients cried and gave extra support to Luke, who missed his buddy sorely, while continuing to work in my office.

Rascals died of old age. I then brought into the office, Rachael, an abused, new female cat. Before she could take up her job, Heather showed up saying, "I'll do it" After years of being a feral cat, mostly outside greeting clients on the porch, she moved into the office waiting room, and then into my office to sit on my lap and occasionally visit clients. Rachael remained shy, so she mostly stays in the computer room to keep me company while I write.

Clients frequently commented that they enjoyed and respected the warm and orderly relationship that I have with each animal. It made them feel safe that I would be able to help each client bring some order and limits into their own lives. Since all of these animals have been abandoned in some way, they know what it is like to feel lost, to want to be loved. Perhaps that's why each animal intuitively appears to understand many of my clients' needs. Their presence makes all of us feel safe when the office door to the outside world is unlocked during office hours.

**Each animal has served my clients extremely well over many years. In the final analysis, I've allowed them in the office because I can now see clearly what they have provided. Our human brains are condemned to repeat what we don't understand. Therefore, each client and I have to battle our way through the pain of unresolved issues to reach an understanding that frees each person from the dysfunctional repetition of a past hurt with a significant other. The animals are important to have around because their simpler brains do not hold unresolved issues with the same complexity. Therefore, I conclude that they are freer simply to provide the unconditional love and validation needed to accomplish the difficult work of psychotherapy. Finally, scientific experiments reveal that the presence of animals encourage our brains to release oxytocin, which promotes health and increases positive social interaction with people. I can no longer imagine my practice without these animals.**

Many of my clients have added a pet to their lives as a result of knowing my animals. It is a well known fact that our blood pressure goes down when we interact with animals and goes up when we talk with people. Do you have a pet to provide the same for you?

A friend sent me an e-mail from a six-year-old boy (author unknown) entitled, *A Dog's Purpose*. This six-year-old watched his family dog being put to sleep. The parents and vet commented upon the sorrow that dogs do not live as long as people. The boy piped up. "People are born so that they can learn how to live a good life – like loving everybody all the time and being nice, right?" he then added, "Dogs already know how to do that, so they don't have to stay as long."

The e-mail continues; "If a dog was a teacher, we would learn things like:

- *When loved ones come home, always run to greet them. Never pass up the opportunity to go for a joyride.*
- *Allow the experience of fresh air and the wind in your face to be pure ecstasy.*
- *Take naps.*
- *Stretch before rising.*
- *Run, romp, and play daily.*
- *Thrive on attention. Let people touch you.*
- *Avoid biting when a simple growl will do.*
- *On warm days, stop to lie on your back on the grass.*
- *On hot days, drink lots of water and lie under a shady tree. When you're happy, dance around and wag your entire body. Delight in the simple joy of a long walk.*
- *Be loyal.*
- *Never pretend to be something you're not.*
- *If what you want lies buried, dig until you find it.*
- *When someone is having a bad day, be silent, sit close by, and nuzzle them gently.*
- *Live simply.*
- *Love generously.*
- *Care deeply.*
- *Speak kindly.*
- *ENJOY EVERY MOMENT OF EVERY DAY!"*

# IV

## DEFINING MOMENTS
## WITH HANDLING LIFE

# 30

# WHEN GREED TAKES AWAY YOUR JOB

Ruth came up the stairs two at a time. I could hear the anger in her pounding footsteps, and her hard breathing. She'd called for an appointment "as soon as possible." I ushered her into my office. I knew her to be an excellent legal secretary for the past 20 years and a highly ethical person at work and with her family.

She was so anxious to talk, she began before we had a chance to sit down. "I got laid off, no warning, only a little severance and medical insurance, no explanation, no appreciation, no caring, no letter of recommendation, just a walk to my car. Computer locked up with all my important phone numbers and twenty minutes to pack up my personal things." She paused to take some huge breaths …"**and** … this lay off has **nothing** to do with the recession. This firm has **tons** of money; my salary is just a tiny drop in their humongous bucket. I know because I saw the budget last week. The recession is just their excuse to make more money for themselves at my expense … All the big firms are doing it, getting rid of whomever they don't want anymore, Damn, I'm so mad."

I managed, "I'll bet you are," so as not to disturb the flow of her emotional outburst.

"My boss knows that I have one special needs kid in a private school and one kid in college and a mortgage. How in the hell am I supposed to pay that out of unemployment? So, just another foreclosure, who cares? That's the problem, nobody cares where I used to work ... there aren't any jobs left out there for me."

I added, "It sounds like it's all about more money for your boss, and that won't really make her happier."

"I'm glad you understand, because most people don't get it. They think I did something wrong and have been fired. But I've done my work well. I just had an evaluation two months ago. They didn't have **any** complaints."

Ruth paused to let some of her anger and sadness drain slowly out of her. She looked like a deer in the headlights, forlorn, weary and frightened.

She then continued, "And ... I learned the other day who my boss really is. She gets a free cell phone from her firm. She doesn't have to pay a dime for it, but she charges her clients fifty cents a minute for calls while she spends hours on her cell phone ... just another way to rake in money while she screws other people. She and the other lawyers pride themselves on being successful. I think they're "fat cats" or "greedy bastards"... Tell me, am I crazy? Are you going to lock me up? Bring on the guys with white coats. I'll fight back. I'm so pissed ... and scared ..."

"No way are you crazy; you're reading your negative feelings well and making a lot of sense."

Ruth bursts in quiet sobs. "What am I going to tell my two daughters? Go ahead and drop out of school? Jesus. They've worked hard to get to this place. Back to junior college? What kind of jobs can they get?"

Ruth paused only for a moment, "And get this one. I have a friend who was working for the government. She got laid off. She talked with her landlord and got an adjustment in her rent, while he went behind her back and got a judgment against her in court. My friend has to leave by Sunday. with two young boys. No place to go but a motel. She's a bright lady who won't be able to get another apartment or a job with the government because she now has a judgment against her. They may have to move home with her parents back in Florida."

"That's not right either."

Ruth then screamed, **"Tell me please. What the hell has happened to morality, to integrity, to what my parents used to call right and wrong? I've tried to be responsible, and this is what I get for it?"**

"Yes, I've known you to be very responsible."

She had not finished ranting. "Why do the "fat cats" always win, and those of us who are responsible get screwed as if we are the ones who did something wrong? This is happening to **sooo** many people unemployed like me."

"If I had to choose whether to be you or your boss; I'd choose to be you, even though I know that you are in a terribly awkward position right now."

"Why?"

"You have something very valuable that the "fat cats" may well not have."

"What, pray tell, could that be?" Ruth queried with irritation.

"You have integrity and you know how to act in an honorable way."

"Yeah, a lot of good it seems to do me."

"Let's take a look. Integrity and honor are most important in maintaining your self esteem, and peace of mind. These are the cornerstones of your reputation. It's your reputation that will get you a positive response from other persons of integrity."

"Maybe," she relented a bit.

"I believe that the 'fat cats' think they need more money because often they don't have integrity, and they are not honorable. I don't believe they have any peace of mind because the more they have the more they want to feed their ego. No one can really trust them. They think 'a little more money' will finally give them an image that displays a good self-esteem, but it doesn't. They believe they need to have way more money than is 'sufficient to survive.' "

Ruth sat quietly, thoughtful.

I continued. "You're quite right to spend this hour looking at the difference between success and greed. Success is doing well financially but in a way that helps other people proactively advance their lives psychologically and/or physically at the same time. Greed is taking what you can get for yourself with no regard to how your gain may involve stealing from, being destructive towards, or psychologically detrimental to others. There is a huge difference between success and greed. Success is to be praised, while greed often involves other illegal actions such as lying, fraud and scams. Greed needs to be punished; at the very least, with a loss of title or position. Greed eventually fails; you can see how many businesses are in trouble right now. When that happens there needs to be consequences for the 'fat cats' who hurt people like you."

"So I'm not crazy after all?"

"No, you are richer than your boss because you know about integrity and morality. I think it impossible to have a happy life without compassion, caring, and concern for others. Your boss's absence of caring leaves her very deprived."

"Thank you."

"Furthermore, I believe that you and I can work together in a way that will help you to go on and do something even more meaningful and financially adequate than working for a boss who doesn't care. Out of this crisis will emerge a new plan for you and your grown children." I paused again as I watched Ruth look up and smile at me for the first time.

I concluded, "We will think creatively together and discover some people of integrity who can truly help. I know that you have the capacity to come out ahead in all of this. In the meantime, I'm sorry that you've had such a rotten lousy day. I'm glad that you could come in and talk about it right away. I have respect for the way you have thought it through."

"Well, maybe I can go to work on some of my old dreams I'd hoped to do once the kids were on their own. I'll just have to figure out a way to bring them about sooner. Maybe I can now take some time to do a badly needed surgery before my insurance runs out. "

"There you go. Good thinking. You're on the right track. You will be able to do this new work sooner than you would have otherwise because this crisis happened today."

"Well, I'm beginning to feel better now. I'm glad that you could see me through the anger before it ate me alive."

"There's one more important thing to say to you. One of my supervisors in my training internship told me something that I will never forget. It has guided me in maintaining my private practice."

"What did he say?"

"He said, **'There is always, always, room for quality on this planet.'** If your work is of quality, you will not have to advertise. Work will come to you by word of mouth. It will be enough. I have found that to be true for me also. Quality work brings in money and makes a demonstrable difference for others. If there is lots of money, some people like Bill and Melinda Gates and Bill Clinton donate it towards worthy causes. Other people use the money to show their worth and make extravagant luxury for a few. You can tell the difference and choose with whom you wish to work."

"Good thoughts to hang onto. Thanks for the extra time. I'll see you later this week at our regular time."

"Go for it."

As she left, this time going down the stairs, two at a time, with a ring to her step, I was reminded of a passage from Deepak Chopra's *The Seven Spiritual Laws of Success: A Practical Guide to the Fulfillment of Your Dreams:* (p.29) I wished that I could share it with her boss.

> *"If we stop the circulation of money—if our only intention is to hold onto our money and hoard it—since it is life energy, we will stop its circulation back into our lives as well. In order to keep that energy coming to us, we have to keep the energy circulating. Like a river, money must keep flowing, otherwise it begins to stagnate, to clog, to suffocate and strangle its very own life force. Circulation keeps it alive and vital."*

# 31

# ON BIRTH AND WAR

I arrived for the Lamaze class in the early evening, and looked around for the birth mother of the infant my husband and I hoped to adopt in another six weeks. She stood out from the other couples because she was sitting in the corner looking shy and alone. We were the only female pair. All of the women in the room were with husbands, and showed the gentle curve of pregnancy. I walked over to her feeling awkward and stupidly slender.

The teacher moved to the front of the room and began to organize the class. Each couple introduced themselves. She came to us last. Everyone stared. Our birth mother spoke first, and only gave her name. I did not wish to be mistaken for a lesbian couple, so I gave my name and explained that I was a prospective adoptive mother in class willing to learn so that I would be able to help my birth mother during delivery.

The Lamaze coach proceeded to teach the class. During break, all of the other couples shared an obvious intimacy we could not possibly have. We had known each other only for a few months.

Towards the end of the class, the men were asked to give a massage to the pregnant women. I felt even more out of place. However, somehow I managed to accomplish the task.

Despite my discomfort, reserve, and shyness in this situation, it was also a very strong defining moment. I had the unusual opportunity to walk in the shoes of a man. I realized just how "not included" I felt in this process of pregnancy. Birth belongs only to a lady. Sometimes marital problems emerge because the woman feels involved in her new role, and the husband begins to drift away, feeling excluded. The class was intended to help the father of the fetus have something useful to do to help the mother during the often difficult and painful delivery process. It seemed to me that his assignments were downright insignificant in relation to the job the woman does. My husband was not even invited to attend this class.

How did the universe give pregnancy and birth to a woman when a man is supposed to be the strong, brave one, taking on the pain and injury needed to protect a family? Is it possible that many men might just feel left out and downright jealous? My father was a physician. He told me that some of the longest and bravest moments he ever saw in the hospital were women giving birth to their infants. However, he was not present for the birth of any of his own three children.

**Pregnancy and childbirth are difficult and dangerous for women. It is a rite of passage into adulthood that involves risking death while completing the journey. Young men may have a separate need to risk a life threatening situation.**

**What does a man do with these feelings? Suddenly, the defining moment happened inside of my head. I heard the crying out in pain of a woman in labor; and, simultaneously, a man on the battlefield. The sounds seemed exactly the same. I wondered if men solved this conflict over and over again through war, because it was what they needed to do to honor their warrior spirit and feel as brave as women.**

Men are supposed to be the brave ones. However, war is so much more traumatic and painful than giving birth; resulting in death, injury, amputation, grief, guilt, loneliness, depression, Post Traumatic Stress Disorder, and recurring nightmares too awful to reveal. There must be a way for men to be brave in a more useful and less painful way.

Cable television's History Channel began to play significant battles every day, all day long. I hoped that if men could watch these shows, they would see how repetitive, useless it is, and how many people suffer and die. Would they conclude that we might need to negotiate verbally to wage less physical battles in the future? But no such luck.

If my thinking had some merit, I was left with a few questions. Would war stop if men could become pregnant and deliver babies themselves? If women ran the world, would we talk instead of fight? Have we reached a point in civilization where we could marshal the warrior spirit of men to encompass protectiveness, and negotiation rather than brute force? Would acknowledging the different and competing roles between men and women help us to live more peacefully with each other, with fewer wars?

## 32

# WHEN SOMEONE HURTS YOU

### FINDING YOUR WAY TO FORGIVENESS

**W**e are condemned to repeat what we don't understand. If someone did something bad, we may decide to replay it with another person of similar characteristics hoping to understand "where we left off and the other person began." In the process, we can hurt other people, both purposefully and unintentionally. Other people can hurt us for the same reasons. Acting on feelings about past hurts displays what is called an "unresolved conflict."

So ... here you are. Someone has hurt you. It really hurts. Perhaps it was sexual, physical or verbal abuse. Maybe it was neglect, abandonment, sabotage, poverty, addiction, a serious illness or accident. What are you going to do about it? You do not have to feel afraid; you will find the right time to deal with it.

You may seek psychotherapy if you feel hit, hurt, demeaned, rejected, angered, guilted, embarrassed, confused, anxious, panicked, lost and/or shamed. Misconceptions can fuel these feelings, leaving a sense of disintegration, desperation and failure. The initial psychotherapy hours are often challenging ones.

If you decide to come and talk with a therapist, I can suggest the following journey although it would need to be individually tailored for your particular needs and your own unique life story. You may be able to take parts of this journey on your own by reading about your conflict and writing in a journal.

First, we'll look at what you're feeling and find the words to describe it. We will honor your feelings since they will guide us through your past experience.

Second, we will go on a search through your memory of the past, your bad dreams and nightmares and your insights, to recover as completely as possible just what happened that was hurtful to you. Repressed memories may surface suddenly as your unconscious mind listens and cooperates with us. We may be able to talk to the hidden younger person inside you who was hurt, but didn't dare say anything back then, so that we can really understand. In the process, that younger person will not feel so alone, will be cared for and will begin to integrate back into your adult self.

Third, we will look for information about the unique life story of the person(s) who hurt you. We'll try to understand who these persons were, and why they did what they did to you. We'll likely see that your perpetrators were also suffering in pain from unresolved conflicts. We tend to hurt others when we're doing poorly ourselves. Your actions may have innocently triggered their problem causing them to lash out. You are often not the problem; instead they are acting out on their own problem with you.

Fourth, we will come to understand the ways in which you survived this event, the courage that it took to do so, and the ways you tried to protect yourself from its happening again. We'll clarify the ways in which it was not your fault. Then we are ready to replace the old behaviors with new behaviors for the present and future.

Fifth, in talking about what happened, we will realize that all of the thoughts, feelings, resentments, bitterness and actions you have previously experienced cannot change the fact that this wrongdoing happened. It will always be with you in your memory.

Sixth, out of all of these dialogues, you will come to see that you have love for yourself, rather than shame about the events that happened. You will become a stronger and deeper person if you are also able to muster some compassion for the person who hurt you. You will know "where you left off and the other person began." You will accept that you cannot change the past. It will be clear. Your understanding will likely have brought you towards some degree of forgiveness.

Seventh, the events that hurt you in the past will no longer hold center stage in your life. You will not forget, but you will be able to "put it on the back burner," and make new, healthy goals a priority for yourself. Therefore, you and other people may eventually benefit from the wrongdoing that has happened to you. Because, out of the pain unfolds, like a miracle:

- ❀ a foundation of strength and respect for yourself

- ❀ a new integrated character that understands both past and future survival

- ❀ a new known purpose in how to lead your life.

- ❀ a sense of confidence, security, and protection about how to handle inevitable future knockdowns.

- ❀ When you have "got it," you will earn respect from others because you have a depth of character that recognizes and articulates compassion for others' adversity. As May Sarton was quoted in Julia Cameron's *Walking in this World:* (p.123)
  *It always comes down to the same necessity; go deep enough, and there is a bedrock of truth, however hard."*

You are entitled to some help with your psychological

work and the dialogues and essays within *Defining Moments*. can assist you. If you have an "unresolved conflict," and are ready for some psychotherapeutic help, read the essay in this book entitled, *How to Find the Right Therapist*, and maybe the essay entitled, *Don't Be Afraid to Ask for a Reduced Fee.*

Never give up the right to take good care of yourself and to make a unique difference with your own special talents. You will add substantially to the quality of your life, with a "ripple effect" to others' lives as well. You will come out ahead of where you were before.

# 33

# A CRISIS IS ALWAYS AN
# OPPORTUNITY

It is September of 2008, and my heart will not stop hurting. It is flooded with stories of people in fear because several natural and manmade crises have happened. Hurricane Hanna and Hurricane Ike have swept away countless homes. I see a photograph of a man searching through the outside rubble looking for the neighbor's cat. Lehman Brothers' workers have suddenly lost their jobs. They are leaving the building with their belongings packed in cardboard boxes. A father, on the way to see his son get married, was supposedly killed instantly by the Metrolink Freight train crash in Los Angeles, but his cell phone kept sending a signal all night even though he was unable to utter a word and finally expired. If the engineer on Metrolink who made the mistake of text messaging on the job hadn't been killed instantly, how would he live with the fact that twenty-five people died and one hundred and thirty-five were wounded, many in critical condition? My heart goes out to the families still checking at hospitals and morgues to track down a relative on that Metro link ride. And the stock market is down 1400 points in the last three days, stripping away college funds and retirement dollars from innocent people who have worked hard and now will be in need.

As this was happening, the Santa Ana winds fueled fires

raging in Southern California. Horses were trapped in ranches their owners couldn't reach while hundreds of homes burned to the ground. While 45,000 people were in Red Cross Shelters with no homes and no income, CEOs continued to destroy homeowners with unaffordable loans resulting in foreclosures while taking bonuses and salaries in the multi-millions. These images swirled in my mind, churning up fear and anger for all of us. In all of these instances the pain for people directly hit was so enormous. How will these people cope?

**A crisis can be a danger resulting in a slip on the mental health continuum down into further disaster.** During these difficult times, I will, of course, help anyone who calls, regardless of ability to pay, to avert such a collapse.

**However, every crisis also carries an opportunity to climb up on the mental health continuum; to do something completely new, something that each person might never have fully thought out before if life had gone on in the usual way. It's a time to get back up again to start afresh.** A quote on my refrigerator says, "Barns burnt; now I can see the moon." When a home is destroyed, valuable items are painfully lost; but also, the junk, excess, and responsibility for both are irrevocably cleared away. In one of the greatest bestsellers of all times, the 1966 version of *Think and Grow Rich*, Napoleon Hill tells us:

> *Remember all (people) that succeed in life get off to a bad start, and pass through many heartbreaking struggles before they arrive. The turning point in the lives of those who succeed usually comes at the moment of some crisis, through which they are introduced to their "other selves." (p. 40)*

**Remember your health, your strengths, and all of your dreams that may have been forgotten for a long time, because of the daily routine of your present life. Perhaps one**

of them can now be brought forward to become fulfilled. It may make up for the loss you have suffered and perhaps give you even more. Have faith and the belief that you can do it. An ending is also always the beginning of something new. Take this knockdown as an opportunity to get there.

A huge crisis forces an existential moment for society as a whole. We have to make a clear choice. As a culture, it's an opportunity to look closely at the ways in which we can increase our morality, integrity, compassion, cultivating the ability to acknowledge and help others. It's a time to give, to be honest with ourselves and others, to create together something new that is better than it ever was before, casting away, once and for all, what really doesn't work anymore. The freshness of a new beginning has the same magnitude as these painful losses.

I ask any of you who have been knocked down by recent events, are you in crisis? Which way are you going to go? Can you pull out of your confusion, shock, helplessness, irritability, and sleepless state to begin to reach out and talk with others, to volunteer, donate, remembering what you still have to build upon? Can you reach out to children and animals, to listen, offer answers to questions and keep them safe?

Remember that the universe is watching, perhaps yearning for all of us to emerge as better people. Can we, this time, turn old greed, corruption, scams, fraud and aggression into caring? Don't get left behind. Instead believe the familiar saying:

*"Ask and you shall receive*

*Seek and you shall find*

*Knock and the door will open"*

"Every adversity carries with it the seeds of a greater benefit." (Hill, p.81) Maybe our collective seeds of corrective actions will stop the next natural, human and economic disasters from being so severe.

# 34

# THE BACKSIDE OF AN AFFAIR

A young couple came to my office for an initial evaluation for conjoint psychotherapy.

Both were casually but neatly dressed and looked stiffly uncomfortable. They sat on opposite ends of the couch. They did not look at each other. Instead, both gazed apprehensively at me. After I had introduced the process of an initial evaluation, they wasted no time in getting started.

Linda opened the conversation saying in a negative monotone, "We're here because my husband has had two affairs."

Dan interrupted defensively, "Wait a minute. They were a long time ago and didn't last that long. They were no big deal."

"Oh **yes**, they were! The first one started five years after we married and lasted for several months. The second one lasted for longer than that and took place one year ago ... **Supposedly,** it ended, but I personally believe that it's still going on."

**"Noooo it's not.** Why do you think that? I've told you it's **over**." Dan interrupted sternly.

"Because your cell phone bill still has her number on it from time to time. I check it every day on the computer. And two nights ago, you came home an hour late for dinner. I don't think you were hungry ... I'll bet you had dinner with what's-her-face." Linda raised her voice to score her definitive point.

Dan leaned towards me and started to explain. "She always thinks I'm doing something bad. Therefore, she gets resentful easily. She's forever watching me. When I make a mistake, she never forgets. Everything I do goes into the computer file in her head as a wrongdoing ... It's hard to love anyone who treats me like that."

I'd now heard enough to be able to respond. I broke into the first brief silence.

"Let me see if I can help you both a little bit. First of all, the latest statistics suggest that over fifty percent of men have affairs. Twenty-five percent of women used to have affairs, but this percentage has increased to about forty percent. That's just to remind you that you are not the first or the last with this problem. First, let's look at what an affair is."

Linda jumped in, "Duh! ... It's when a guy cheats on his wife. Everyone knows that. But the statistics say I could do that to you, too, buddy. Get it?" She punctuated her thoughts by lightly slapping his knee.

I continued, "Actually that's not the definition I had in mind. **An affair is a relationship that occurs for the purpose of plugging a hole that exists within the marriage so that the marriage can survive.**" I responded.

"Interesting. I can relate to that." Dan perked up.

"What do you mean by a hole?" queried Linda as she suddenly looked caught off guard and confused.

"Good question," I responded. "Usually there's a problem within the marriage. The couple wants to keep the relationship, but doesn't know how to deal with the problem. The solution is to go outside the marriage to fulfill some need not being met within the relationship. Then the marriage can go on. Often the spouse left out never finds out."

"But I didn't think we had a problem," denied Linda. She looked at her husband for the first time.

"Would you like to ask him?" I suggested

"Well?" She looked at him and waited.

"You don't seem to want to sleep with me any more. You were too busy breast feeding the baby. I feel like you don't have time for me."

"Yes, I do ... I didn't know you felt that way. I thought you didn't want to make love to me any more after I had the kid because I was still overweight from the pregnancy."

"No, it's not that." Dan took a deep breath. "Whatever free time you have, you spend checking up on where I am and what I'm doing. You keep asking me about the affair, over and over, every day. I can't stand it. I wish it had never happened ... I promise you, I've ended the affair. You are the one who is keeping it going by talking about it all the time. How do you think that makes me feel?"

I helped again, "This is tough to talk about, and you're both doing a good job. I think that your husband has a point worth understanding here. **It's my experience that there are two parts to an affair. One person goes out and has the affair. That's what Dan did. The person left behind finds out about it and keeps the affair in the middle of the marriage long after the extramarital relationship has stopped. The person left behind watches to see if it's still going on and demands every detail about what happened. Therefore, both people hold equal responsibility for their part. It's my experience that the aftermath of the affair often lasts as long or even longer than the affair itself. It poisons the marital relationship. The person who strayed finally says, 'Well, if she thinks I'm still doing it, even when I'm not, then I guess I might as well just go on doing it. After all, I'm already guilty as charged.' "**

"Yup." Dan confirmed with a nod of his head and a stomp of his foot.

"So you did the first part and I'm guilty of the second part?" Linda questioned thoughtfully.

"Yeah," he said again.

"Ohhhh," she conceded quietly.

I continued to encourage them both. "The good news is that Dan didn't leave you to be with this other lady. You see, **affairs rarely turn into marriages. That's because they're only a piece of a total relationship. If the marriage breaks up for the affair, the affair almost always falls apart because its limited function is to help preserve the marriage.**"

"The affair lady doesn't get a very good deal then?" Linda inquired.

"That's correct. They come to see me too. They're furious."

The wife turned to the husband with tears in her eyes. He reached over and took her hand. She tried to gulp away the lump in her throat, saying haltingly, "Does she mean that there's a chance that you still love me? You might really want to be with me?"

"Of course, if you can stop thinking I'm cheating on you. You have to believe that I love you."

"So I'm responsible for my part of the hole in the marriage?" Linda asked again for reassurance.

"I guess that's one way to say it," Dan admitted. "But we all know my part, too."

They both moved closer to each other. He put his arm around her shoulder. She buried her face in his armpit and sobbed. He comforted her silently. I waited quietly. Then they sat back up and she asked, "Can we come and talk with you more about the hole in the marriage?"

"Yes, I would be glad to help you with that. Psychotherapy is a good way to talk together about problems that surface for all of us from time to time. I will ask you both about the story of your lives, and we'll see if there are unresolved issues from the past that might be causing some trouble within your relationship. When those issues are understood by both of you and subsequently resolved, the problem usually falls away naturally. There's always a reason for a problem. We come to understand that here by using respect instead of judgment and fear. That really helps. And, by the way, talking about it openly is intimacy."

"Can we go ahead and tell you our life stories today?" said Linda, eagerly reaching for more closure.

"Yes, we can get started in the time that we have left and finish it next time you come in to see me."

"We should have come here sooner. I didn't know that therapy could help." Linda wiped away her tears, brightened some and then offered, "I just had an idea."

"What's that?" Dan queried.

"Might it be important to share with Dr. McArthur that both of our parents have had a lot of conflict, have gotten divorced and remarried?"

I responded, "Good for you. You're already thinking about your own unresolved issues. We can look into that question much further. The short answer is that many kids who grew up in a home with a divorce are scared that they, too, will get divorced when they grow up."

Linda added, "Ahhhh ... and my Dad had three affairs and then my mother left him. I guess they never understood about the hole in the marriage ... and he never married any of the affair ladies. Interesting! My Mom was really hurt though ... I guess I've just been afraid that the same thing would happen to us," she said, looking at Dan.

"And how did you feel when your Dad left?" I questioned.

"I was ten, almost eleven. I've never felt so scared in my life. It felt like I no longer had a roof over my head. I knew I wouldn't feel safe anymore. I never want my child to feel that way."

"So you've been checking up on Dan partly as a way of trying to protect your kid from a divorce?" I offered.

"I guess so," Linda was thoughtful again.

"Do you understand better, Dan, why Linda became so anxious about your actions?"

"I never really thought about it that way." Dan placed his head in one hand and then reached out an arm to offer his other hand to her.

"My guess is that we have done enough for your first time here," I said. "I think you have a new way to process what's happened. Perhaps you would do well to think about this hour separately and then share your thoughts with each other at the end of the day. I'll be glad to work with you further if you decide to return. This relationship sounds important to both of you and your child."

Linda got up, pulling Dan by his arm because they were still holding hands. "I'll talk with him, but I hope that we'll be coming back. Thank you for your clarifications."

"Thanks and goodbye for now," Dan smiled.

Remember, understanding is one way to love. Enjoy the rest of your day," I concluded.

# 35

# IT AIN'T CHANGED SINCE THE CAVE MAN DAYS

Lois, an exasperated female client, sank down on my couch with her husband and launched right into her session. "Okay, soooo ... Both my husband and I work. Actually, I work a few more hours than he does **and** I have a longer commute because I pick up the two kids. How, in God's name, can he come home and calmly sit down to read the newspaper or *Newsweek* while I can't even think about plopping anywhere. I have hungry, tired kids, dinner to get on the stove, children's homework to get started, pets that need petting and feeding, and God only knows what else. I get so mad because he can relax, and I go crazy keeping on working. I'm lucky if I'm done by 9 pm, and then the kids still need to be put into bed. He'll do some things to help, but I have to ask and define it clearly or his head is back in the newspaper. Are all men like that, or am I just a glutton for punishment? I don't mean to start the hour bitching, but this is the only place I have some time to say what I feel."

I settled in to help. "Your life sounds like lots of other females' lives. A number of statistics for dual-working couples suggests that women work an average of sixty-plus hours a week while men work about forty-seven."

"Whhhyyy???" Lois shifted position on the couch angrily. Her husband appeared lost in other thoughts as he looked out the window at the sunset reflected on the lake.

I began, "Every married female client has said basically the same thing. I think that it goes back to the basic difference between males and females. Nothing has changed since the days of the cave man."

"Explain ... pleeease ..." my client responded with a touch of annoyance.

**"Well, the cave man's job is to go out into the wilderness, whatever the weather, find the bear, kill the bear and drag it back home to the cave. When he gets home, his job is done and he can rest on the floor of the cave. He's tired, and some of the time he has risked his life."**

"Yeah?" Lois responds. Her husband is suddenly paying attention.

**"And the women's job is to cook the bear, make clothes out of the bear's skin, sweep the cave, gather other kinds of food, and take care of the kids."**

"Sooo ..."

"So that formula worked basically until we decided that many women want to go out and hunt for a bear, too ... or maybe a goat, or a deer, or some sheep. Thus was born the *super-mom*."

"And maybe the *super-mom* is also a necessity financially?" she added emphatically.

"Yes, that is increasingly true with the high cost of living in this city. **However, *super-mom* comes about, her genetics tell her that she can go out and get a bear, or a deer; but her "real job" doesn't go away. She still has to cook, clean, and take care of the kids. The man gets to rest because he has done his job. We can try to train him to do more, but it does not really fit naturally into his genetic job description. Women want to be out in the workplace; but unfortunately most men don't want the women's job."**

She added tentatively, "I'm one of those women who enjoys the stimulation of the workplace."

"The *super-mom* is working sixty hours a week and that's too much; but we haven't figured out what else to do. Men are helping at home, but only when specifically asked. When they don't initiate help, that does not mean that they don't love you or respect what you do."

"Yeah," piped up her husband named Ken.

Lois turned towards him. "It sure feels like you don't care some of the time. Maybe I could stand it if you would acknowledge my double role by doing something special such as bringing me some flowers ... just every once in a while or for Valentine's Day."

I continued, "It's my experience that husbands do their special thing. Back to the cave man. Some husbands bring home buttercups, some bring home wild blackberries, some bring home ladybugs. Each one has their special gift, but it's not always the one his wife had in mind."

"Are you telling me that this is ok for men to be like this? Are you letting them off the hook?" Lois stared directly at me.

Ken had been listening and watching her intently. He finally spoke. "I think what she's saying is right, although I never really thought of it that way before."

I added, **"I think this is the way men are, and that such basic differences are not subject to a lot of change. If we women understand that, we don't have to feel so resentful, so frustrated, and so hurt as you seem to feel today. We can go on giving them the directions they may need to help us out with our job at home after work. We women can share how we feel clearly, in a way that husbands can understand somewhat. Otherwise, husbands feel like they're doing their job in terms of bringing home the bear and the buttercups."**

"Well, what you've said, does make me feel better. I guess I was taking it all too personally. Still, it's frustrating." Lois relaxed into the couch. " I think men have got the easier deal."

"Maybe so."... I've heard too many men say, 'I looked at her job and decided I did not want it.' Pregnancy, giving birth, and being a super-mom is, in my opinion, a harder job. Perhaps that's our secret and ... when the cave man understands how warm and cozy the cave is, it becomes easier for him to bring home something special, without being asked."

"Got it," smiled Ken, as he moved closer to his wife on the couch.

She looked at him and smiled. "Do you understand what she said? Can you remember? I don't always like my cave-man-job in the home either. Do you think we could split up some of those chores?"

Ken was now fully engaged. He sat up straight and said, "I was just going to suggest that ... now that I 'get it' better. What if I helped the kids get a snack and do their homework while you start the supper? I think I'd rather do that than have you mad at me."

"You've got a deal. That would be really helpful. Besides the kids prefer to ask you when they have homework questions, anyway."

I encouraged, "Good for you both. Understanding can facilitate negotiation. You're already doing it. Many dual-working couples agree that the chores at home need to be split equally between the two spouses. Each one takes the chores they can do the most easily. Once they decide, they don't need to talk about it anymore. The feeling of conflict slips away."

"Then there might be some time for us to talk, and even fool around once the kids go to bed, before I'm completely exhausted." Lois added.

"I could go for that result." Husband slipped one more step closer to her on the couch, and rubbed her knee.

" I know, Mr. Testosterone." Lois winked at him. "Let's give it a try."

# 36

# PROTECTING SEXUAL ABUSE VICTIMS

## ... FROM FURTHER TRAUMA BY
## EXTENDED FAMILY

Sometimes psychotherapists have to learn a lot suddenly, even after many years in private practice. Three clients, who had been sexually abused, took actions that reinforced what I suspected about sexual abuse victims, their family's and society's reactions to their abuse. Family's response of disbelief and rejection, in each case, created a second trauma resulting in rage turned inward for each client. This result suggests that the psychotherapist has a special responsibility to understand, warn, and then validate the client in preparation for this likely second trauma.

During this same week, the magazine *Psychotherapy Networker* (January/February 2004) article by Bessel Van Der Kolk entitled "In the Eye of the Storm" arrived in the mail. From the article I learned why sexual abuse victims are very easy to dismiss or abuse again. They have a hard time protecting themselves from further abuse for two reasons. They were put into a traumatic situation where escape was impossible. Their body may have been frozen in time with an active response that could not be completed. Therefore, when the stress level gets high, they may again feel the same kind of physical freeze. Secondly, the traumatic event is stored in the lower parts of the brain (limbic system) and is not easily transferred to the frontal lobes where speech and reason take place. Therefore, it is often very difficult for the victim to articulate what happened in a believable way. This is especially true if the abuse occurred before the time of language development. Therefore, in the real world, their stories do not ring true. Someone can say, "I don't believe you." The victims do not know how to fight back to defend themselves. In the last analysis, without support for the client from a psychologically sophisticated knowledgeable outside party, the perpetrators, who are used to deception, easily win once again.

It appears that the secondary disregard of sexual abuse from family is almost as damaging as the abuse itself. It is one thing to have something bad happen sexually. It is another for a family member to be a perpetrator. When there is no one else in the family to understand or take appropriate action at the moment or in the future, the victim's unresolved rage, disappointment and devastation may get turned outwards towards anyone who acts like the perpetrator and/or inwards to become serious suicidal risk.

I have always been validating and supportive of clients who have been sexually abused. Most of these past adult clients have never told their families because their intuitions warned them clearly that there would be no support. The clients who have other family members currently at risk for sexual abuse are generally the ones who are forced, by the laws of mandatory reporting, to share these details with family.

**I have learned that it is essential for me to tell my clients that sexual abuse appears too difficult for the vast majority of family members and society to contemplate or imagine, let alone live through. When the client understands this important information, they can avoid feeling traumatized once again, get back on their feet to finish their own work on this issue, and go on with life.**

It is now understood that Freud believed his female patients when they explained that they had been sexually abused. However, he sensed that society was unable to hear this information. He therefore minimized what he revealed to society by using the label "Hysterical Personality." How far has society come in being able to accept sexual abuse now? The evidence suggests that we still have a very long way to go. In the meantime, appropriate therapeutic support, in place of family, can be life saving. In summary, I can now answer three questions with renewed clarity.

1. How does the victim respond to sexual abuse and telling the family?

    There are some common responses that are characteristic of most victims. If the abuse occurred before the age of six, there may well be confusion as to the identity of the perpetrator and the nature of the sexual intrusion.

    Victims are often confused about what it means to tell the truth because the perpetrator has taught them to lie. Most victims fervently hope that what happened was not really abuse or that they are remembering something that actually did not happen. They worry excessively about misrepresenting themselves or their perpetrators. Some victims experience a somatic response as the body's way of communicating that the abuse really happened. This pain can be every bit as painful as the original sexual abuse encounter. I have seen the longing to be believed and understood by family and also the power that therapeutic understanding and even minimal family support brings to return victims to fuller functioning.

    Under pressure, the victim can dissociate or psychologically leave their bodies because that is the coping behavior they learned while experiencing the abuse. They feel worse than a "dirty dishrag" because they were abused. Since a perpetrator tends to look "through" them rather than "at" them while the abuse is happening, victims tend to feel that their existence and feelings are completely unimportant. In addition, the immature child's brain views grownups as all powerful and perfect, leaving the child totally to blame.

There is hurt and rage when the family members support the persecutor and deny the victim equal rights. There can be confusion about enjoying or hating sexual relations, especially if their current sexual partner does something that reminds them of the former abuse, even if it is gentle and kind. Rage can turn inwards as suicidal ideation.

2. How does family and society respond to a sexually abused victim who tries to address what happened in the past?

Perpetrators tend to deny, disappear and quietly go on acting like perpetrators. Someone who is falsely accused, in marked contrast, tends to engage easily and responds with compassion, concern, sadness, and caring. In most cases they stay with the issue until resolution is achieved.

**Sexually abusive behavior appears to be so unacceptable that some family members prefer to immediately reject it. They act incapable of considering that it might have happened and imagining what it must have been like. Some knew that the abuse was happening at the time but systematically ignored the signals. Sometimes, they are completely unable to respond to this shocking information. It is therefore predictable that they should become defensive by turning a blind eye. It is far easier to respond with hostility, rejection and direct punishment while the victim is too immobilized to resist. Silence from a family member may mean**

that person has also been sexually abused. The victim faces new trauma by this kind of family response and is, once again, devastated by the dismissal of information and lack of support.

3. What are the therapist's responsibilities?

It is imperative to avoid new trauma caused by the family's defensive hostility whenever possible. The therapist must provide the belief, respect and support that are missing from the family. It makes sense to believe the client because the details of the sexual abuse are too unpleasant and unique to make up.

It is important to consider very carefully with the client whether to tell the family if the statute of limitations has expired, and if there is good reason to believe that the abuse is not continuing with any other victim. The therapist and the client must weigh carefully the advantages and disadvantages of revealing the abuse to the family. The client's opinion is very important since the client knows the family members better than the therapist.

When the case requires mandatory reporting, the client needs to be fully informed ahead of time that the family is not likely to be responsive in a positive way. The family's behavior does not mean that the client is bad or is lying. The client needs a clear explanation that s/he is never to blame for the abuse or the reporting because the victim's immature, underdeveloped childhood brain can only misconstrue that it was the child's fault.

If the abuse is confronted, or the abuse is reported to the Department of Child and Family Protective Services, the therapist has to be available to help the family through their defenses to their own underlying horrified feelings. Revealing abuse always constitutes a family crisis. This is often difficult, if not impossible, when the family doesn't want to be involved or lives far away. Therefore, the decision to report is often fraught with deep conflict for the therapist.

The therapist needs to be available on a long-term basis to help the family or effectively refer the family to another therapist. Families of my clients need the information about psychological and physical reactions to abuse so that the family can stop viewing the victim's minimal response as "incompetence" or "lying." The goal in such long-term work is to help any family member willing to believe the victim, and to understand that their support is critical in the healing process. We can actively celebrate and compliment any family member who is able to understand and be supportive.

We can also help families, inasmuch as possible, not to fragment by taking sides and rejecting anyone. This is especially important for family events such as holidays, decade birthdays, births, weddings, anniversaries, and funerals. The July/August 2003 *Psychotherapy Network* magazine has a specific article on how to bring a family disrupted by sexual abuse allegations together for weddings and funerals without fragmenting further by arguing about the abuse.

The therapist can always hold on to the hope that the family will, in time, come to a more understanding position. To promote this, the therapist's door needs to remain open, especially for other members of the family that may have been abused.

# 37

# TO PUNISH OR HELP,
# THAT IS THE QUESTION

I started a consultation with an adult client, Ann, and her mother, father and brother. "We are here today to talk about how to handle the knowledge we now have that Ann appears to have been sexually abused by her cousin, Alan, over twenty years ago, when she was a child. Her Aunt Betty was taking care of your children, Mom and Dad, while both of you worked a second job. Ann has now told all of you. Is that correct?"

"Yes,"

"So we're meeting to understand how you all feel about this news, and to decide how to handle this information with Alan and Aunt Betty. A holiday season is fast approaching when all of the family gets together."

Mom chimed in, "We haven't seen or spoken to either one of them for a month since we learned about the abuse. I don't care if I never see them again."

"And Alan should suffer some consequence for what he did. People go to jail for stuff like that. I can't pretend that nothing happened," added brother knowingly.

Dad was very quiet. 'What do you think?" I asked gently.

"I would have to talk with Alan first before I made any judgment. I have no idea what to do just now. You got to understand; he hurt my baby."

"I do understand," I reflected.

"We have to do something … if we see Alan and Aunt Betty at Easter dinner, one of us will surely slip and say something that would give away what we know." suggested the brother.

Everyone turned to Ann to say, "What do you think?"

"I've had a lot of time to work on the issue of abuse here with Dr. McArthur. Believe me, I've been mad and sad. But I have come through the anger at Alan pretty much. You have to remember that he and I were also friends for most of my childhood. We did lots of good things together, too. I was able to talk with him on the phone the other day. However, I haven't seen him. I think, for right now, I just want to finish up with my own psychological work."

"But what he did was really bad." Mom emphasized.

"You're right and entitled to your feelings, especially as the mother of Ann. Does doing something bad make him a bad person?" I queried.

"Yes, I think so," Everyone nodded concurrently.

"How about describing him as 'troubled?'" I suggested.

"Yes, we agree that he has been troubled for a really long time." nodded everyone in agreement. "There's ample evidence about that. He's really difficult and angry much of the time, especially with Aunt Betty."

"How do you want to respond to someone who's troubled?" I nudged.

"You mean we should be helping him?" Everyone looked surprised and irritated.

"Perpetrators of sexual abuse and those with deviant sexual fantasies tend to be people who feel extremely lonely and have a very low self-esteem. They tend to think that if they can create sexual arousal they will feel better about themselves and more powerful, at least for as long as it lasts. I wonder if Alan felt the same way?"

"But he hurt Ann," Brother reminded me.

"That's indeed true. But are you just going to hurt him back? What would that accomplish?"

Mom chimed in. "When people hurt me, I just cut them out of my life. Then they're gone. I've been doing that all of my life. It works well in the sense that I don't get hurt anymore by that person."

**"When something bad happens, that is often the easiest time to learn to cope in a new way."** I encouraged.

"I hadn't thought of it that way." Mother drew back in her chair.

"What about Aunt Betty. She's just as much at fault; she should have known that sexual abuse was going on," added Brother.

"But, she's very old and tired now. It would just kill her to find out what had happened. It was a long time ago," reminded Dad.

"It's also possible that she really didn't know any more than you did," I suggested.

Mom tried again, "I guess I need somebody to blame so I don't have to feel so guilty that this all happened. Ann wanted to know why we left her with her aunts and Alan. We had to earn extra money. I had no idea that this was going on. It never happened when I was a kid, and I played with cousins my age throughout my childhood."

"Alan is not a stranger, but a family member. Perhaps we could say that love is the only response that's never wrong. We are taught as doctors to 'Do No Harm.' Someone in your family has already been hurt. Do we want to add to the hurt, or try to help so that it won't happen again with anyone else? Could we use that principle here?" I questioned her.

"It's hard to love when I feel angry and guilty. " said Mother.

"You bet it is. The trouble is that retaliation never works. It only weakens. It hurts you as much as the person you retaliate against ... You are the only ones who can decide, because you know the people involved. I can only suggest the following: **What if you were to write a letter to Alan from all of you? You could let him know that you are aware of the abuse accusation. You would be confronting him, which is an interaction that is a high form of caring. You could tell him that Ann has gotten some help in the form of psychotherapy, and that she's doing well. You could offer him some referrals for psychotherapy also. The psychotherapist could then evaluate him in regard to his present behavior, and decide about treatment, and reporting options. That would be a gift that provides structure and control. Maybe it would help him rather than hurt him, making everyone feel better. Then you could start talking to each other again. Ignoring Alan and Aunt Betty makes everyone lonely and is a dysfunctional response. They must feel very rejected and without knowing why."**

Ann had been twirling an elastic band around her fingers. She stopped, looked up and said, "I like that idea. He'll hurt in therapy like I did, but it would be a good kind of hurt. It would make him better if he could stand it. If he doesn't follow through, and tries to abuse someone else, we know enough now to report him to the Department of Child and Family Protective Services. There isn't anyone around for him to abuse now."

I offered, "Perhaps we are not ready decide today. You all have time to think about it before the holiday. If you decide to write a letter, you could fax it to me to review, if you want. We can also meet again to work through your feelings before you decide. It's difficult because the Easter holiday is coming up in just ten days. You may have to go with another temporary solution just to manage this upcoming event. Anger and guilt take time to process."

"We have a lot to think about," admitted Dad.

I concluded, "I appreciate all of the feelings that you have shared today. You have gone further than many families in your discussion. I've seen families who simply reject the victim because they cannot cope with the truth. You have shared normal feelings most people feel when they hear about any kind of abuse. As a family, you may be able to go beyond these expected feelings to a solution that will make you all feel that you have grown instead of feeling weakened. Please let me know if I can be of further help."

"Thank you for talking with us all today, and for your ideas, " Ann concluded, while everyone nodded.

# 38

## THREE KINDS OF ROMANTIC ATTRACTION

Carol looked bright and cheerful. This was a pleasure to see because she has been dealing with a separation from her husband. She began our psychotherapy hour right away.

"I went out to a party with a friend last week. I met a man. His name is Alex. I don't really know how it happened, but, I guess you could say, we were both attracted to each other. He noticed me, I watched him, he followed me around, I knew where he was all the time. We talked together really easily."

"Sounds like fun for you after a long time of sadness."

"I think so too, but I was also puzzled. As you know, I have been dating two other guys who are really nice to me. However, I found myself thinking about Alex much more even though I do not know him as well. I'm not sure why, or whether my thinking is right. I'm not sure what attraction is or means."

"I have heard clients talk with me about three different kinds of attraction. Perhaps you are asking which kind of attraction you were feeling."

"What are the three kinds?"

**"The first kind of attraction, I call a physical one. Your body, and his body say, 'It would be so nice and feel so good if we could get together physically."**

"Yah,"

"**The second kind of attraction is an attraction of mutual strengths. You are both interested in the same kinds of things, have some similar and some complimentary talents, and are at the same level of psychological maturity.**"

"That feels more like what we felt."

"**The third kind of attraction occurs between your unconscious and his unconscious. You are attracted to each other because he reminds you of someone significant in your life story who disappointed or hurt you in some way. In a like manner, you remind him of someone in his life that represents his unresolved issue with someone in his past. In other words, two unresolved issues hook up in a mysterious magnetic way. They are replayed and intertwine in a way that usually disappoints both of you a second time. The magnetic attraction can feel instantaneous and really strong.**"

"Well … that sounds like a possibility too."

"Most relationships are a combination of all three. If the second kind of attraction is strongest, the relationship thrives, and often deals with smaller unresolved issues over time. If the third kind of attraction is the strongest, the relationship generally ends up with a separation."

"So, you must be saying that it is important to figure out which ones are driving the coming together."

"Good for you to see that … Tell me, what did you find out about Alex?"

"I kept thinking about him because I wanted him to call me. I found out that he is very busy. He is working in a job full time, going to graduate school to get a PhD in conducting, and he plays organ for church jobs. So he really doesn't have much time for a relationship."

"Does that remind you of anyone important in your own unique life story?"

"Dahhh! … My Dad and my first husband. Both were pilots and had hardly any time for me."

"Sooo … which kind of attraction do you feel you have with Alex?"

"I guess I have mostly the third kind of attraction. Maybe I was feeling like a middle aged divorcee and wanted him to call, and then, I would feel okay about myself again."

"You are figuring all of this out really well … You can take some time to see what is going to happen from here. Validate yourself by realizing what you have done right, and that three men are clearly interested in who you are. Go enjoy and see what your unconscious and present feelings tell you to do from here. The right answers will emerge."

# 39

## WHAT MAKES ROMANTIC LOVE LAST ANYWAY?

*Don't you want somebody to love?*
*Don't you need somebody to love?*
*Wouldn't you love to love somebody to love?*
*You'd better go find somebody to love.*
### The Jefferson Airplane

Many clients ask what makes romantic love last at some point within the psychotherapy relationship. Artists, poets, psychotherapists, philosophers, writers, teenagers, and parents have sought the ultimate answer to this puzzling question. Many clients feel that they have not experienced romantic love, or saw it modeled by their parents.

I have an answer that comes from my own marriage of 43 years and my experience with clients' life stories. It is only my answer; I cannot claim it as a universal truth. First, it is important to say that I believe we humans are inherently social beings. We want an intimate relationship with each other.

How do we find such a relationship? Dating is very hard. The entertainment industry likes to portray in the movies a loving relationship as easy and effortless, leaving all of us feeling a little bit inadequate. However, in the movies, actors and actresses get to use as many 'takes' and 'cuts' as it takes. In real life, we have to make instant decisions about what to say, how much to tell, when to touch, when to "have sex," or when to "make love" after the relationship is developed enough to talk about STDs and other personal private matters. Healthy relationships that last forty to fifty years are made slowly, deliberately and carefully with thought and verbal sharing, resulting in a common consensus. Forging the beginning of a romantic relationship can feel as difficult and intrusive as taking the SAT or GRE, going for a job interview, and enduring a physical examination.

Two people come together, "attracted to each other." This attraction is an arrangement of sorts, impossible to describe because it is different for each couple. There is a magic to it; perhaps the intelligence of the universe is the only one to truly understand. There is already obvious chemistry. However, I believe two people have to build and then tend an underlying foundation that turns a meeting of attraction into a long-term monogamous love relationship that will last for 40 years? This requires that both husband and wife:

1. **have enough respect and love for themselves to dare to be intimate verbally and physically with each other.**

2. **take responsible care of themselves physically and mentally so they can be fully present for each other.**

3. **are able to share and validate the individual growth steps they themselves need to take to continue to make life successful.**

4. **are able to understand and support the growth steps their partner needs to take to have a successful and meaningful life.**

5. **are increasingly able to articulate their own and their spouse's life story, and the resulting strengths and vulnerabilities. Often, their strengths and vulnerabilities are complimentary. They are able to utilize their strengths and minimize the vulnerabilities through**

verbal exploration and help from within the relationship. The goal is a sense of wholeness for both individuals and the relationship.

6. are able to compromise because the survival of the relationship is more important than the individual wishes of each partner.

7. are able to realize that the growth of a deep friendship is an essential, large component of a romantic love relationship.

Engagement to the right person is a lovely and joyful experience. It is both a commitment to the long term future, and simultaneously an enormous relief that the complex dating game has concluded. As we recognize just how difficult dating is, we can then "cut ourselves some slack" as the normal mistakes occur when we only have one "take." The long-term relationship takes many years to mature, starting with the "honeymoon period" in which we put only "our best foot forward." As the love and respect is earned, we dare to admit more about the questions, vulnerabilities and the growth that is still needed to mitigate problem areas. Two people grow together, with tolerance for each other's mistakes, and pride in the progress made. No one can or has to be perfect.

# 40

# WHAT GOOD FRIENDS CAN DO
# BUT OFTEN DON'T

Family relationships are very important, but often have long-term conflict embedded within them. Perhaps we could say that one of the reasons we have friends is because family relationships can be so complex. Friendships are often easier because they are less complicated, less loaded, and more straight-forward. They can be nourishing, supportive, long-term and deep. Other friendships come and go, as the goals, passions, and needs of each individual moves in different directions. Over the years, I've helped many clients process relationships not only with family, but also with important friends. We are inherently social beings, enjoying contact with each other.

I hear over and over again from clients that there are four actions friends can take that contribute markedly to the intimacy and long-term survival of the relationship. Unfortunately, these actions are sometimes absent or incomplete.

**The first action is to get to know your friend by asking questions that would help you to understand what it feels like to walk in their shoes.** We can do this with interest, rather than being superficially cheerful, pretending with a false self to be a different person than you really are, being demanding, controlling or over adaptive to a fault.

**The second action is to share with a friend out loud what we admire about them.** Often we notice, but fail to share this valuable information. We all need to be told when we're looking nice and doing well. It helps immensely to contribute to an optimal internal level of self-esteem that encourages and sustains relationships.

**The third action is to first recognize our feelings and then verbalize honestly out loud when a friend has taken an action or acquired something that makes us feel threatened, jealous or envious.** Such feelings can happen normally when a friend purchases the home we've always wanted to live in, buys the sports car we've longed to drive, gets the job, degree, or award we've coveted, or produces something artistic in the field of music, drama, dance, visual arts or literature. During these times, friends sometimes give a dysfunctional response of sarcasm, gossiping, going silent or retreating. They don't show up for the house-warming party, or the book signing, gallery opening, or award ceremony. The person who has acquired something suffers from feelings of rejection and aloneness. My clients learn to read their friends' behavior as a "backwards compliment" which means that the client has indeed created or done something significant and worthwhile.

Many people believe that jealousy is a dysfunctional feeling. Instead, I see it as merely one of many negative emotions that tells us clearly that we want something that someone else has. Therefore, it is preferable and acceptable to maintain the relationship by saying out loud that we're feeling a longing or a jealousy to have the same thing a friend has just acquired. By admitting these feelings out loud, we acquire the chance to understand what we want and can begin to move into a position to acquire it. The friend can often be of help and will understand. This action, then, strengthens the relationship.

**The fourth action would be to come forward and address any problems within the relationship in a constructive way.** It takes courage to address a concern, and insight to resolve it.

When we have outgrown teachers and parents, we learn most things, as an adult, by trying something. In the process, it's human to make mistakes, to say or do something that is inadvertently or intentionally hurtful in a way that gets us into trouble with a friend. When that happens, some friends silently pull away instead of addressing the problem constructively. If a confrontation is in order, it can be sandwiched between two positive statements. My clients always appreciate it when a friend takes the courage to address the problem at hand. Clients bring the information back to me so that we can figure out what change needs to take place. Sometimes the friend may feel insecure about continuing the relationship. In that case, the client enjoys responding with support and validation. Once again, meaningful help is often exchanged to deepen the relationship.

Technology has given us a new form of communication. We are talking with each other about important emotions and plans through e-mail, textings, blogging, and instant messaging. The younger generation now has internet MySpace and FaceBook in which they can suddenly silently be eliminated by an angry friend without explanation. Those who work in cubicles are said to be distracted from work every three minutes by communications from others that takes up twenty-eight percent of work time. Perhaps it's a way to measure how many friends we have and who cares. However, this form of communication only uses two-to-five percent of the total interaction with each other. Telephone brings it up to twenty percent, while a face-to-face contact is one hundred percent. Important conversations are easy to misinterpret by these newer forms of technology. Hopefully, we are not missing out on getting together where we can see important information presented through facial expressions, tone of voice, and other nonverbal communications.

Occasionally one of my clients takes the courage to call a friend who has slipped away, and ask what went wrong. If it's really important, we may invite the friend to come into a portion of a therapy hour, as a significant other to the client, so that we can constructively figure it out without judgment. We use reflective listening together until we can shape a solution that represents a constructive integration of feelings.

I've spent hours with my clients, on their dime, trying to figure out or guess what a client did that made a friend pull away. Did we come up with the right answer? **When a friend does speak truthfully, it may well become a defining moment for all of us.**

# 41

# ARTISTS AND SOCIETY

I have seen many artists over the years as clients in my private practice. They walk into my office with a humble quietness. They see the world deeply through an exquisite lens and can feel sadness, concern, disgust, and triumph about civilization and joy about nature easily. Many artists have a need to understand and are deeply impacted by the poignancy of their own life story. They often experience themselves on the outside of the "in" crowd in childhood, and can be bored in school. Some have become accustomed to putting themselves down because it's commonplace for artists to have doubts about the validity of their creative endeavors.

Many of these clients have silently discounted their creative genes because their parents did not acknowledge or encourage them to actualize their particular talent. Instead, family responded cautiously because they were afraid that their artist child would not be able to make a sufficient living by practicing their art. Parents may encourage a degree in business, or law instead of a degree in fine arts. As a result, many artistic clients view their opportunity to create as an "extravagance" they should not bother to indulge.

Being an artist is one way to make sense of and express feelings about living life on this planet. An artistic piece of writing, exhibition, or performance can bring forth and regroup feelings we didn't know we had buried deeply inside us. Art can reach out and aid a viewer the way a therapist helps each person reach a resolution. When an audience gathers to watch a movie, play, concert, poetry reading, or dance performance, they mutually agree to study together whatever the artist has decided to say.

However, clients come to realize they are artists when they use their particular talent in a way that feels effortless, and brings contentment with results that make them feel proud. A few are so passionate and compelled that they do not have the choice not to be artistic. Some feel their creative expression comes "through" them from the outside world, while others feel it is generated from "within" themselves and their life experience. Still others feel their creative expression comes from both sources. Whichever way it happens, the creative work of an artist has to be a solo journey until the creation is completed. It is important to suspend judgment and detach from the outcome to let the creative idea unfold. Sometimes that journey leaves the artist feeling isolated, different, alone and afraid. When the creativity is completed, others may become involved in getting it out into the world.

Throughout my own life as an artist and psychotherapist, and many hours with clients, I've come to understand that society and the world in general often does not treat our artists well.

I believe that most people are jealous of artists, especially the ones who get to perform in public. Probably everyone has had dreams of being in the "limelight" with that wonderful high moment when artists are performing and their creativity is appreciated. Many get to hear the clapping and to feel that they have done something truly meaningful and important. Artists tend not to be interested in riches or fame. Instead, they just want enough support to go on doing their creative work. Many famous artists have lived in poverty. What are the words that the culture so frequently articulates just before the word artist? The answer is, of course, "struggling" and "starving."

Perhaps, because society is jealous, they make artists create and complete most of their projects with no financial compensation. Maybe they'll look at their work after it's done, and maybe they'll respect it, and maybe they won't. Often they don't even bother to look carefully or even respond. In the meantime, they give artists little hope. They think nothing about discounting them and their creative endeavors. Especially, actors and authors have to be experts at handling rejection after rejection as an expected and normal part of the process. Artistic clients come to me to quell their fear, acquire a strong enough self-esteem to survive society's tentative response.

It would be outstanding if society could take a step forward and treat our artists with the utmost respect. That support starts right in my office. Many of these clients are often Highly Sensitive Persons (HSP) with an overly tuned response to one or more of the five senses. Artists are our deep thinkers with acute intuition; our quiet and honest leaders, observing, creating and commenting on what we most need to hear as a society and as individuals. Artists risk saying something really important, even if they get rejected. They tend not to stay on the well-worn path, but to carve new trails.

But often, society is reluctant to hear what artists have to say, because maybe they will have to alter the way they do things as a result of artists' input. Therefore, they shut artists up with lack of support, ignore them, or criticize them. Many famous artists have become known only after they've died.

In writer's workshops, authors are often encouraged not to write unless they absolutely can't live without putting words together in that effortless way that brings contentment. After the first draft, there is a lot of editing to finish each piece of writing. Success is difficult and often elusive.

There are two conditions that contribute to becoming a successful artist. First, the person has to be born with creative genes. The second condition is always a surprise to my artistic clients. Artists are often involved in a struggle, such as a difficult childhood, that becomes well understood by the client in terms of emotions and misconceptions. The resolution of this conflict often gives shape to the particular subject and expression of their creativity, while lack of resolution may block expression. As the clients and I work on their unresolved issues, their creativity is able to flow freely again. Their resolution shapes an important creative endeavor that can make a difference for those who may suffer in a similar way.

My clients and I have been trying to find or create a word that explains the quiet joy that is happening when an artist is in the act of being truly creative. Clients have been using such words as "surrender," "something bigger than yourself that teaches something about yourself," "abandon," "lost in an energy of potential," " connected so that nothing else is in focus or matters," and "solitary." "Being creative presents the only time I can truly love myself." "Creativity is like a cat, it comes out when it wants to."

As pianist, Karl Paulnack said, on March 2, 2009, in his welcome address to the freshman class at Boston Conservatory,

*"Music allows us to move around those big invisible pieces of ourselves and rearrange our insides so that we can express what we feel even when we can't talk about it."*

Deepak Chopra in *The Seven Spiritual Laws of Success: A Practical Guide to Fulfillment of Your Dreams* explains it, but is also unable to do it with a single word:

*This exquisite combination of silent unbounded, infinite mind (of the universe) along with dynamic bounded, individual mind is the perfect balance of stillness and movement*

*simultaneously that can create whatever you want. This coexistence of opposites makes you independent of situation, circumstances, people and things.*

As Julia Cameron writes about the results that come out of creativity in *Walking In this World: The Practical Art of Creativity:*

> *Artists:*
>
> 1. *explore the territory of the human heart, braving the dark woods to report to our human tribe that a trail can be found and will survive.*
>
> 2. *report dangers we might wish to ignore*
>
> 3. *record perceptions that feel unbearable to others*
>
> 4. *encapsulate the loneliness of missed connections*
>
> 5. *function out of nerve, daring, stamina, vision, and persistence*

It's exhilarating for me to watch artist clients awaken to their creativity, to own it and begin talking about their particular project. Sometimes we look together at ways they can support themselves with what we affectionately call a "job-job" so they can save most of their energy for their creativity. The "job-job" pays the living costs and takes away the struggle to pay for rent and food that otherwise could erode the creative process.

Many artists do not seem to have marketing and publicity genes, so they have a hard time promoting their work. Hence, society steps in with publishing houses, agents, publicists, and marketing experts. Artists don't want to tell people what they've done or try to sell it. They just want to get on to the next project. Secondarily, they're happy if they can be financially successful, but their primary interest lies in *making a difference* by articulating what needs to be realized.

It's hard to kill an artist's drive, especially when each artist becomes an expert at rising above or ignoring sabotaging remarks, meant to clip their wings in place of useful criticism. With enough encouragement and support, the artist will prevail. Two quotes speak poignantly to this issue.

> *One of life's most exhilarating feelings is to be shot at with no result.*                    **~Winston Churchill**

> *All truth passes through three stages. First, it is ridiculed. Second, it is violently opposed. Third , it is accepted as self-evident.*                    **~Arthur Shopenhauer**

I encourage my clients to listen carefully to their creativity and intuition. When they have the urge to be creative, they're being sent a message from the universe to act. The universe is so much more intelligent than any one human artist that it becomes ridiculous to resist. Only the potent energy of the universe knows the whole picture. The artist merely has to do what is suggested through their creativity. All fear of failure, evaluation, judgment, or rejection of the work has to be sent down the drain of the artist's daily bath or shower. These feelings will only cause writer's block eroding the process of producing valuable works of art for us all.

On March 2, 2009, pianist, Karl Paulnacks's concluded in his welcome address to the freshman class at Boston Conservatory:

> *Frankly, ladies and gentleman, I expect you not only to master music; I expect you to save the planet. If there is a future wave of wellness on this planet, of harmony, of peace, of an end to war, of mutual understanding, of equality, of fairness; I don't expect that it will come from a government, a military force or a corporation. I no longer even expect it to come from the religions of the world, which together seem to have brought us as much war as … peace. If there is a future of peace for humankind … I expect that it will come from artists, because that is what we do."*

Can we even imagine what civilization would be like if just half of the funds that have gone into war, were diverted for education, training, and support of artistic expression. Art would be taught in every school. There would be funding for tickets for live performances so that everyone who was interested would have a chance to attend. Artists would be paid for creating and the development of their art. They would be "honored" instead of "struggling" and "starving." I would have been paid for the hours that went into the writing and editing of this book!

Currently, eighty percent of my clients are artistic. They leave my office when we have worked with all of the above issues and they:

1. understand and respect their particular creative genius
2. have found and accepted their "job-job" when it is needed
3. feel entitled and compelled to use their artistic genes
4. understand the unresolved issues within their own lives and have some artistic way to express them to help others with similar problems
5. have mastered their fears of rejection and are able to create anyway
6. can distinguish between useful constructive criticism to be incorporated, and sabotage based upon threat and jealousy that must to be eliminated

In the final analysis, it is powerful and compelling and hard to be an artist.

## 42

# THERE IS A QUIET WAY TO BE OF SERVICE TO OTHERS

I walked into the waiting room of the dental office and took my place on the couch, waiting for my appointment. *TIME* magazine had a lead article about the interrogation process for the detainees at Guantanamo Bay. My appointment was for a routine teeth cleaning and then a longer session to rebuild a tooth. While waiting, I had read far enough into the article to see that the detainees were facing difficult and painful interrogations if they did not provide information quickly.

I have very sensitive teeth and therefore am not fond of dental appointments. Even though I respect and like my dentist, I'm always glad when the dental task is concluded.

I decided to approach this appointment differently. Both the Guantanamo detainee and I were facing some pain. However, my pain was incredibly minimal compared to the torture he was facing. In my case, I was given a topical anesthetic, a buzzing sensation to hide the Novocain as it was inserted through a needle to numb my tooth, accompanied by kind, gentle, thoughtful care that was going to improve my health. In contrast, the detainee was being mistreated with malice, hate, and total lack of concern for his welfare other than not to break the rules of the Geneva Convention too badly. His situation was so much worse than mine, that my appointment, in my own mind became pleasant rather than painful.

My only problem was that it didn't seem fair. However, a solution for the unfairness made me feel better. **Sitting there for some three hours doing nothing but holding still, I discovered that I could feel more useful by sending my universal energy, or chi, to someone somewhere who was being abused or tortured in some painful way.**

It was the same energy my clients give and receive from others over the years in ways that made a formidable difference in their recovery from loss and illness. It was the vibration energy that told me the exact moment a beloved aunt died three thousand miles away. It was a similar force that made thirty Great Danes in an animal shelter move into total silence while they watched me grapple with a strong but painful insight about my family. A similar force tells a cat or dog the exact moment their master is turning around to return home from wherever he may be, whether he is near or thousands of miles away.

I held on to that action for much of my visit in the dental chair, trusting that the universe would somehow convey my gift precisely where it needed to go, leaving plenty of energy for me to make my way back to my own office for work.

My morning went quickly; and perhaps somewhere, some place, someone else in pain because of abuse felt a little more peace or a little stronger because of my actions. Maybe their abuse stopped. Now that would be a miracle. I was tired when I left, but it was a good tired.

I'll remember what I did, and use it again for any uncomfortable medical procedure in the future. I can share it with any readers who believe that sharing energy can help others. Those who are afraid of going to the dentist might come up with the courage because they can meaningfully distract themselves by imagining a difference in this positive way. Perhaps we can impact a current world that is in need of miracles, compassion and caring every day to combat the actions that plunder people and nature upon our planet.

# 43

# WHATEVER HAPPENED TO RIGHT AND WRONG?

B y the time I decided to write this manuscript, I had been seeing clients for 41 years. There has been one major change that has been disturbing to me over this time. It has crept up on all of us in subtle and not so subtle ways.

When I was a child in the 1950s, I was taught that some things were just plain *wrong*. Doing something *wrong* usually involved hurting someone else. There were also many ways to do things *right*. There was a clear differentiation between the two that was not to be argued. When I did something *wrong*, there was no talking myself or anyone else out of it. However, there was often something I could do to make it *right*.

The clients who have come to see me over the years seem to have the same sense of right and wrong. They raise concerns with me that some of the people they are interfacing with are operating out of the notion, "The end justifies the means," "It's all right to do anything I want as long as I don't get caught," and "It's reasonable to assume that I can get away with not getting caught … so … let's give it a try." Any discussion appears to generate dismissive phrases as, "Whatever … " "Duhhhh … " or "So what." This is especially true for clients that work administratively in the corporate world.

Much of this growing attitude seems to come out of making an initial success. Then the good fortune is maintained indefinitely by sliding into unethical behavior that begins to hurt other people.

For instance, I hear about the specialist in autism that has a two-year waiting list, requires $750 up front for an hour visit with a follow-up interview at the same price. He does not take insurance. There is no sliding scale fee for lower income parents because the specialist knows that parents will spend everything they can to help their child. If he sees five parents a day … you do the math … more than one million in profit over two years. On top of it all, the treatment provided may become so routine that the professional may become arrogant or sloppy at best. The parents stand to PAY $1500 after waiting two years, while nobody cares. These parents of autistic children, who cannot afford these fees, come into my office aghast and completely defeated.

And there is a question about whether the professional is really doing anything wrong? Because others are doing it too… After all "It's the professional standard of care." A potential success meant for everyone becomes a devastating event for all those but the rich who can afford it.

**When there was a clearer sense of right and wrong, I believe that people showed a greater sense of compassion for others, a higher sense of morality and thus benefited from an increased integrity.** Integrity is defined in Webster's dictionary as "the quality or state of being of sound moral principle; uprightness, honesty and sincerity." These are words that rarely show up in our current daily conversations. Greed has become a lousy substitute for taking care of each other well.

In my office, there is a clear sense of right and wrong. It's absolutely not all right to come up with any plan that will purposefully harm, demean, or mislead someone else. I help clients to understand that acting with integrity is richly rewarded with a sense of peace, and satisfaction. When there is integrity, everyone wins. Self-esteem, respect, and confidence come from our ability to do well in our interactions with others. As inherently social beings we need helpful interaction with each other.

Clients who behave unethically often acquire a lot of money or material things, but they rarely seem to be happy or peaceful. They act so self-assured and arrogant that the outside world often turns a blind eye to trying to stop them until they have done incredible damage. The devastation they create for others doesn't help them become happier. It is a total waste of hurt. The wealthy client and I start over from square one, rebuilding an empty, angry, impoverished internal psychic world that has become devoid of love, compassion and meaning.

It is unnerving to discover that our attitude of "do anything you want as long as you don't get caught" has crept all the way to the top of the corporate world, real estate, and even to the White House. We spend billions on destroying others with war out of greed and self importance, while 20,000 people die each day around the world because they are lacking basic necessities. Such behavior sets a very scary example for our youth who are looking to people with prominent lives as models. Unethical behavior creates lack of trust, accompanied by a profound sense of loneliness. My clients are scared, and rightfully so. They may try to talk themselves into grabbing for what they can get as a terribly poor substitute for compassionately caring for each other.

I observe that the animal kingdom and the environment shudder as they perceive mankind to be dishonest with each other and the universe as a whole. The Native Americans believe that the natural calamities that have increased markedly in number during the past years are the universe's way of telling us that we are doing wrong. If we don't correct our dishonest ways, can the universe muster enough force to take humans off the planet altogether? Would global warming accomplish the task? Would our world then become a better place?

Deepak Chopra in *The Seven Spiritual Laws of Success: A Practical Guide to the Fulfillment of Your Dreams* speaks about "ego-based power that is false," and "self power that is permanent."

> *If you have a certain title–if you are the president of the country or the chairman of a corporation–or if you have a lot of money, the power you enjoy goes with the title, with the job, with the money. Ego-based power will last only as long as those things last. As soon as the title, the job, the money goes away, so does the power.*
>
> *Self power, on the other hand, is permanent because it is based upon the knowledge of the self. There are certain characteristics of self power. It draws people to you, and it also draws things that you want. It magnetizes people, situations, and circumstances to support your desires.* (pp. 12-13).

# 44

# WHAT'S HAPPENING ON MY STREET?

My neighbor, Don, knocked on the door. I could tell immediately that he had bad news. He shuffled back and forth with a resigned unhappiness.

"I just thought you might want to know," he said, "The sixty-year old apartment building across the street has been sold and the wonderful new owners have arrived. They've told everybody in the building that there can no longer be any plants in pots by their door or anywhere around the building. The manager is allowed to water, but only occasionally. Got to keep the water bill down. The new owners are going to individually rewire all of the units so that everyone now has to pay for their own utilities. I suppose that's the crude way of getting around rent control. This will effectively raise their rent maybe as much as one third. I just thought you might like to know."

"You've got to be kidding," I muttered under my breath to soften the anger I felt.

He continued, "And, if that isn't enough, the less-than-1000-square-foot house I just sold across the street will now be rented for $3500 a month. The 400-square-foot unit over the garage is being offered for $1700 ... can you believe? That's over twice the amount of the rent I charged!

This time I spoke up, "Damn ... all in the same day!"

Don drove the nail into the coffin by summing it all up.

"There goes our little street into the hands of the wealthy who don't care if they take advantage of the population unable to own a home. I suppose they've finally reached our street." He hopped into his car and took off to run some errands. I sensed his anger by the screeching of his brakes at the bottom of the hill.

Something on the street had substantially shifted. I walked up the steep sidewalk slowly to the "just sold" apartment building, absorbing this news and feeling sorrow about the likely obvious changes for the worse, especially for the elder tenants within the apartment building. Our family has lived on this street for twenty five years. Don has served in the capacity of a local uncle for my daughter, watching her grow from a jump-roping child to a pregnant woman, listening to her life stories, and giving her wise counsel. My office overlooks his home, so I've watched his place for him while I'm talking on the telephone, enough to safely catch the dog that escaped out the door when the repair man came. My husband and Don have done many projects together to clean up the neighborhood, repair damage to nature, and keep it safe for everyone. We've always helped each other. We talk together on the street corner, watching the sun set on the lake.

Coincidently, a friend had just sent me a quote from Haile Selassie by e-mail:

*Throughout history, it has been the inaction of those who could have acted; the indifference of those who should have known better; the silence of the voice of justice when it mattered most that has made it possible for evil to triumph.*

With Selassie's message ringing in my ears, there was only one thing I could think to do about this impending change. I knocked on the door of the apartment manager. He answered quickly.

I reviewed the news I had just heard from Don, and then added, "I know that there are some kind older people who have been here a long time. I know that their plants are important to them. If there is anyone who has to remove a favorite or special outdoor plant that has been growing for a long period of time, please tell them that I would be glad to take the plant into my shady driveway. They could see it from their window, go on taking care of it, and visit it any time they want. I have some garden space, and would also help them plant anything they wish in my garden."

The manager seemed touched and replied, "Thank you so much for stopping by to tell me. Right now we're not moving any plants, because I believe people have a right to have them. However, if we're forced into getting rid of them, I'll tell people what you've said."

I wished that there was something more I could do. Will any exceptions be made for people on a limited income? How many people will have to leave because they can't afford their utilities? Where will they go in this outrageously expensive city? Will anyone become homeless? Will evil triumph on this street slowly and silently?

I didn't know how to fight back and didn't think anyone would understand if I did. The deeper and deeper divide that's occurring between the wealthy and the poor leaves me very concerned.

I can see it now. The building may begin to look run down with dried foliage around it and no potted plant life. Conflict and resentment within its walls may spill out to make an unhappy atmosphere.

Instead the new owners could improve the place, bringing in more content and happy people. They could even **feel good** about what they did in a deeper way than they would ever have by making a lot of money. Perhaps then, they might not **need** so much money. Who knows? Could their obvious improvements and compassion earn them even **more** money?

# 45

# DEAR CEO/CFO

To:    CEOs and CFOs of Large Corporations

Date:  February 22, 2002

From:  A Psychotherapist and Human Beings Sharing This Earth.

First, thank you for taking the time to read this important letter.

It has been said that throughout history the tallest buildings have set standards of behavior for the rest of the people. In the eighteen century, it was the Church. In the nineteenth century, it was the Universities. The twentieth century brought in the Corporations. Therefore, I was especially dismayed to hear about the Enron Scandal because the behavior of those involved sets a bad precedent for all of us. I find it as disturbing as September 11, 2001, because Enron also destroyed the lives of so many families, especially retirees on fixed incomes who were left with nothing.

I am a clinical psychologist, and I have been in private practice for over twenty-three years. I have seen the CEO who comes into my office dressed to "impress." I've watched him sit down and blurt out, "Why do I always want a little more? The man with the most toys doesn't win," and sob his heart out. We start from there to build a new life that has positive meaning well beyond the wealth he has ever acquired. I see a man who has millions on the outside but far too little depth or riches on the inside of his soul to sustain a positive sense of self. This is because he has bankrupted himself by breaking promises, lying, and knowingly hurting others to benefit himself financially.

I've seen many clients who work for corporations. They assure me that what went on in Enron is "Standard practice" … "Nothing new" … "It's been going on for a long time." They feel discouraged from doing well or showing any loyalty to their company because it would be way too devastating if the result was being laid off in under half an hour. Gone, computer locked up, no party, no goodbye, no appreciation, no bonus, no severance, just vacation time left, no letter of reference giving credit for any work well done. Just unadulterated loss for the employee and … more money for somebody at the top.

Every crisis is a danger and an opportunity. It's a chance to build a new and better life for all of us. If we all look the other way and let Enron take the Fifth Amendment, we then silently endorse such unethical and criminal behavior. Our standard of morality will slip another major notch; sowing fertile ground for enraged terrorists and a plundered planet.

Most CEOs and CFOs don't seem to know that something is wrong, so they rarely show up for psychotherapy. However, I have helped some CEOs over the years to rebuild their lives. In place of trying to turn millions into billions, they learn to create a healthier and morally congruent sense of internal self by:

1. Building a sense of loyalty within the company
2. Directing a "family oriented" company with shared jobs, flex time, and onsite day care, paid leave for pregnancy and birth, paid time off to go to children's schools to help out in the classroom and attend a child's performance.

3. Making salaries equitable across all levels of management.

4. Being an outstanding leader

5. Getting to know workers

6. Being available to discuss problems

7. Solving problems

8. Safeguarding retirement

9. Offering counseling

10. Creating a sense of community

11. Dedicating money to worthy causes

12. Offering excellent healthcare benefits, nourishing foods, exercise gyms, and reductions in premiums for good health habits

**For those CEOs who are crying because they have "lost everything," take heart. There is a new, ethical, honest, respectful life for you to start that will bolster you and your family, your employees and community much more securely than multiple millions. There will be respect and admiration from others instead of a shiny new jet. Your company will be solid and stable. You will become rich on the inside as well as the outside. With your compassion, you will feel peaceful and successful.** In one of the tallest buildings, you will set an example for all of us to follow.

We, too, will become more ethical and honest with each other. Our world will become a safer place.

We will thank you and you will feel joy.

Sincerely,

# 46

# A MIDDLEPERSON
# BETWEEN LOW INCOME
# AND THE WEALTHY

An artist, needing to make some extra money, took a job in which she "managed" a large number of unemployed people who were temporarily hired as catering waiters to provide the "set up" and "take down" for a wine tasting and restaurant sampling event over three days in a wealthy city.

The hired temporary workers were given a flat fee per day before they knew that each day lasted from early morning to late night resulting in very little sleep and with pay that was way under minimum wage. They needed to lug wine glasses, wine bottles and food up two flights from a garage below. Each of the three summer days were very hot. Some of them were compromised by heat stroke, dehydration and blisters on their feet. Understandably, they were frustrated and angry, but not daring to take a stand or decline because of an overwhelming need to generate an income.

Upstairs, the persons who attended this event bought $150.00 tickets and walked on the same stairs as the workers, seemingly without noticing the strain the workers were under.

It was a beautiful example of the widening gap between the rich and the poor. Our recent census tells us that the United

States now has the widest gap between the wealthy and the low income of any industrialized nation. Shame on us.

However, this manager/actress positioned herself right in the middle between the workers and the event coordinator. She talked with the workers who were getting exhausted, and also talked with the wealthy people who were likely making a handsome profit from this event. She negotiated with the rich to give the workers a bonus, and allow each worker to invite friends to enter this event on the last day for free.

The very next day, I learned of a very intelligent middle aged actor who had suffered from a stroke and cancer. He had rehabilitated himself to an incredible degree, and was maintaining an income by owning an apartment building. Due to the recession, and loss of rent, he was unable to continue his full mortgage payments. The bank had already sold the building out from under him without informing him. He could not file a "hardship letter" for refinancing because his property was an "Investment." The bank had no interest in his situation.

In this case, there was no middle man to speak up for him.

Finally, there is the city of Bell within Greater Los Angeles with City Managers and staff making unbelievable huge salaries because they financially abused a low income community with unreasonable taxes and parking tickets. There was no middle-man to even begin to understand the number of decisions that were terribly wrong. However, the City Managers have been arrested, and additional communities within the same area are in the process of being assessed and exposed.

We are all here together, yet, when it comes to the wealthy understanding the low income and the poor understanding the rich, it feels like there is no contact and no common ground or language. Of course, there are exceptions, carefully articulated in Bill Clintons' book entitled *Giving, How Each One of Us*

*Can Change the World.* Clinton has carefully researched the for profit companies who are giving to third world countries, and making significant and critical contributions to those in need. Microsoft is a prime example. And, there are countless nonprofit companies who are also addressing those in need.

I can see from the many hours I have spent within the privacy of psychotherapy sessions, that both the wealthy and the financially limited appear to have differing strengths and vulnerabilities. The rich are strong at making money, but seem to put all of their eggs in one basket; striving to look shiny and wealthy on the outside. However, sometimes this coping hides an impoverished internal self, and self-esteem that is lacking in meaningful life goals, concerns, and compassion for others. The poor are often resourceful, resilient, compassionate and persistent at "making ends meet" when the going is really difficult.

As increasing global issues threaten our planet and require our unanimous corrections; both the rich and the less wealthy need, more than ever, to be able to be in respectful contact with each other.

**I propose that we create an advanced Master level or Doctoral degree that is related to study of psychology that would train qualified persons to serve in the capacity of 'Middle person" positioned as the actress/manager was equidistant between the wealthy and the poor. Federal and State government would require these positions within each department, and for profit organizations would make sure "Middleperson" attended all board decision making meetings. This would be important for four reasons:**

1. Those with lower income would be treated in a manner that would give them an increased chance of surviving.

2. Those with many material things would have a chance to be informed, make decisions that would build their self-

esteem in new meaningful ways and benefit those with lower income.

3. All businesses would have an increased chance of flourishing because more people would have some income to spend.

4. We would be in more contact with each other to be able to contribute to the health of the planet.

When each one of us dies and there is a Funeral or Memorial Service, the subject at hand is not what the deceased acquired in material things, but how this person lived life, researched, learned, shared, noticed and participated in helping people, animals and the environment.

# 47

# IT IS TIME TO GIVE ARTISTS A CHANCE TO CHANGE THE WORLD

Richard Bolles said it well in *The Job Hunter's Survival Guide; How to Find Hope and Rewarding Work Even When There Are No Jobs.*

*How did this world get into the economic mess it's currently in? Well, to speak in glittering generalities, far too many of us, (both individuals and nations) spent too much, borrowed too much, lived too high, saved too little, invested with too much risk, and played a Ponzi scheme with nature. When all of this came crashing down, the consequences affected not just ourselves, but others around the world ... You end up with all of us in the same boat. And now what any of us decides to do has consequences for others and not just ourselves ... If I default on my mortgage, it lowers the value of my neighbors' homes. (page ix)*

"Capitalism" and "democracy" should never mean getting whatever you want for yourself with no regard for the negative impact it may have on others.

**I hope that we can learn from the Recession, starting in 2008, that we must replace greed with compassion, generosity, and integrity in a way that markedly reduces the ever widening gap between the rich and the poor. My clients have reminded me that greed does not make anyone happy;**

it only drives each person to aggressively leap for more. Compassion and integrity teach us that we can only be truly happy when we can create and reside in a world where everyone has, at least, the basics. Giving brings more peace, happiness, and contentment than receiving and makes the world safer for all of us. The overall goal towards contentment is achieved through the absence of needless suffering for any person. Relationships are about sharing, within a healthy competitive motivation rather than a greedy survival of the richest. Volunteering brings forth depth and meaning. We can only maintain and truly enjoy nature and the beauty of our earth if we contribute to take care of the planet together.

We have tried to regulate the world with religious beliefs, but fighting over which doctrine is the best has caused more death from religious wars than nature's natural disasters. Too many of our religious leaders have sexually abused members of their congregation. Religion and war together create suicide bombers uncaring about killing themselves and innocent people.

We have tried to win what we want with military aggression, but that solution blows up cities, soldiers and plummets the environment. Sun Tzu in *The Art of War* advocates for deception and harm:

*The Way of War is*
*A Way of Deception*
*When able*
*Feign inability*
*When deploying troops*
*Appear not to be*
*When near*

*Appear far*
*When far*
*Appear near*
*Lure with bait*
*Strike with chaos*
*If the enemy is full*
*Be prepared*
*If strong*
*Avoid him*
*If he is angry*
*Disconnect him*
*If he is weak*
*Stir him to pride*
*If he is relaxed*
*Harry him*
*If his men are harmonious*
*Split them*
*Attack*
*Where he is*
*Unprepared;*
*Appear*
*Where you are unexpected.*

We have elected politicians to run out nations, but they find themselves quickly in a conflict of interest because they have to limit themselves to voting for what will get them financial support on the right committees to be reelected. The movie, *In the Loop,* is an excellent example of this problem.

We have allowed cities, states and nations to go into horrendous debt. We then argue and bail ourselves out by turning a blind eye while cutting services to the poor, disabled, youth, prisoners, and elderly in need for the sake of preserving the bonuses and golden parachutes at the top of our corporations and governments. According to the *Los Angeles Times*, (July 31, 2009) nine banks took 175 billion in taxpayer bailout aid and then rewarded 32 billion of it to pay 5,000 bonuses of a million or more to employers who created and maintained a broken system.

As a culture, we have dismissed our artists as "struggling" and "starving" out of feelings of threat and jealousy. Therefore, we have not considered artists as a powerful independent resource with ideas for the leaders of the cities, states, and nations. Artists solve problems for the collective good of all of us with ideas about the preservation of a rich planet and the best of our cultural heritage.

Why should we give artists a try?

Denise Shekerjian interviewed forty artists who were winners of the MacArthur Foundation Award. She then wrote a book published in 1990 entitled *Uncommon Genius. How Great Ideas Are Born*. She describes many aspects of the Creative Impulse. Some are direct quotes from the artists she interviewed. In summary, these artists have the ability to:

1. "look sideways at problems" p. xvii
2. "produces an effective surprise" p .xvii
3. "look at the same thing as everybody else but see something different" p. xvii
4. "take unremarkable parts to create an unforgettable whole" p. xvii
5. "believe in the importance of living right and being thankful and grateful." p. 28
6. "pay proper heed to the long dance with uncertainty that precedes most creative breakthroughs ... the very soil from

which the creative flower blooms." p. 32

7. refuse to "lust after quick outcomes or definitive bottom lines." p.33

8. have a "lightness of spirit that yields fruits of imagination." pg 33

9. "never accept any form of constraint but immediately move out beyond it.

   ...'can't' simply is not acceptable p.132

10. understand their place in the society, "If I am not for myself, who will I be? If I am only for myself, what am I?" p. 202

11. "when a problem seems intractable, leave it, come back to it, leave it again and again return; invest yourself in the vision, focusing not just on the goal, but on the process." p 209

Artists themselves say:

12. "aim myself true." p. 28

13. "If your mind is right, have things fall into place." p .28

14. "I consciously choose and accept the rejection of being non-mainstream. Instead, I seek a few sustaining words at the right time from a true friend. With a true friend the bruises fade, the wounds heal, and the work can continue." p. 198

15. "I understand living. So, if something difficult happens to me, I try to welcome it, accept it, work with it. I treat it as what is happening now. I don't get too excited by my victories, or too disappointed by my defeats, and in that way I come closer to peace of mind and that deep inner place that creativity comes from." p. 187

16. "Carin' is where it's at ... you got a love for what you're doin' and everythin' else, all the rest of cree-a-tivity stuff you're wonderin' 'bout, baby, it just comes." p. 22

The MacArthur Foundation has been working silently for many years to identify artists and then give them the support, without constraints, that is needed to accomplish their creative goals. Many artists have now received their award. With a seven billion dollar budget, the MacArthur Foundation has also been able to fund many social projects in the United States and around the world that promote equality. Several artists are now serving within United States Cabinet positions.

This culture needs to understand that artists can make a significant contribution to the problems within this nation. Would the current president's administration be willing to invite the MacArthur Foundation to gather some of its interested artists to come together to look at the financial, health, equality and environmental problems we are trying to solve at the present time? Would their input give us new ways to tackle the challenging issues of today?

What would happen if artists and corporate leaders began to talk? Could that ever happen? Both might benefit from learning unknown skills and expertise from each other. Could the present administration restrict bailout funds for bonuses within the corporate world. Instead, more funds would be allocated to remove our artists from the "starving" and "struggling" ranks so that they could also continue to speak out individually and collectively.

# 48

# A PLAN TO RETURN
# A SENSE OF COMMUNITY,
# PURPOSE AND MEANING FOR
# SIXTEEN MILLION UNEMPLOYED

During this long recession and many natural disasters, I am one of the lucky ones who has been able to maintain my work in clinical psychology private practice, with a sliding scale fee, plus added hours of work on weekends. However, my sense of accomplishment has been eroded by the sadness I feel for the sixteen million US citizens who are currently unemployed. It has become evident that the longer they are without work, the harder their chances are of finding a job. I am sure, they are a powerful group as a whole, with many different kinds of expertise to offer a flailing nation. Many of us still working are missing their presence.

Having a job gives most of us much more than a badly needed income. Employment gives us a place to go every day, a structure, a purpose, a sense of satisfaction that the world may be a better place because of what we have ccontributed. Work should give us a chance to interact with honesty and integrity. Doing well in the workplace helps us to define our expertise, maintain a decent self-esteem, feel confidence and belonging within a community.

I wonder how many of the unemployed are home alone, feeling restless and badly about themselves as well as their circumstances? What are they doing to fill their time? I'd hate to be in their shoes. How many are slipping inadvertently into depression with substance abuse or other dysfunctional behaviors? I see their despair in my office "up close and personal." Much of my work revolves around helping those suddenly unemployed **to rediscover their lost dreams and latent talents through self-employment**. This way they can't be laid off … ever again.

My sadness is the fodder for my creativity … allowing the following idea to emerge.

We may not be able to start with salaries for our unemployed right away, but could we, together, create a plan to give the unemployed the other important advantages outlined above regarding going to work?

I am suggesting that the President of the United States would give a series of speeches to the nation to explain clearly a plan that would motivate National, state, and local governments to rally together to offer meeting places for the unemployed across the country. This should be coordinated to take place at the same time. Organizations interested in volunteer and financial help would send representatives to analyze talents and interests of the unemployed. Taking advantage of their findings, the unemployed would restart some of the many projects that have been abandoned because of cutbacks across the country. The talents of the unemployed, already developed from years of working, could be utilized to restore these services. This plan also provides a place to go, meaningful activity, and a sense of community for those unemployed.

Such projects might include:

❀ care for the elderly

❀ restore services that have been cut out of educational programs

❀ assist teachers with crowded classrooms

❀ tutor children with special needs

❀ create after school programs for latch key kids for families working long hours

❀ maintain those foreclosed homes that can be rescued, and demolish the rest

❀ plant community gardens for those short on food

❀ cleanup litter on the same days across the entire country

❀ teach low cost classes to generate creativity, and encourage artists to speak out

❀ continue low-cost community clinics for mental, physical health, and urgent care

❀ keep open and maintain parks for recreation

❀ provide training for prisoners in overcrowded jails

❀ combat Global Warming with green projects, and environmental care

❀ conduct legal investigation into Corporations blatantly contributing to home foreclosures and unemployment

❀ take care of pets abandoned due to foreclosures

Those who are employed would each contribute financially to grants with a "voluntary assessment" that would be completely separate from "taxes." Those working in business could lend equipment, technology and consultation.

As projects became organized and successful, the unemployed could gather together and apply for grants to continue.

They would then be able to pay for expenses and draw a salary for themselves.

The President could run his second term Presidential campaign by going to visit the many projects that will get started throughout the country. He could use some of his millions in campaign funds to pay for travel, televise and award grant money from voluntary assessment for projects getting underway. Since this plan would be part of his campaign, and the "voluntary assessments" from working citizens are in place of taxes; there should be no need to put it through Congress for approval, where it would likely get easily derailed. Might the rich decide to "donate" instead of "being taxed?"

The President would have concrete successful improvements to demonstrate on television, in place of costly TV political demeaning advertisements, to enable his reelection. **Those in need, those unemployed, and those working, would all have a part in the task of rebuilding a nation by restoring equality for the basic necessities of living safely and comfortably within the United States.**

49

# I WONDER WHAT WOULD HAPPEN
# IF ...

**B**IG SUNDAY happened last weekend in Los Angeles. This event started ten years ago with thirty people who decided to volunteer, donate expertise, and materials to non-profit organizations and schools for one day. Ten years later, 50,000 people have become involved and the event now encompasses two days. Volunteer workers have bonded with some of the nonprofit projects and returned during the year to maintain the work they've initiated. The givers and receivers have both benefited from the exchange.

I wonder what would happen if we were able to accomplish the same result with another important issue? With modern technology, we are now able to reach around the globe very quickly to everywhere except the most remote villages. **What if we were to start with one day a year when everyone in the world would refrain from doing any violence of any sort?** This would mean that war would stop, suicide bombers would desist, parents would not abuse their children, siblings would not squabble, gang members would not shoot anyone, robbers would not break into homes and stores, and couples would not engage in domestic violence. Road rage would stop. No one would be raped, murdered, or sexually abused on that day.

Everyone would be fairly warned long ahead of time as to the date and time. Everyone would be ready. Police would have a relaxed, boring day because so much aggression would come to a halt. The naysayers would chime in quickly, "What if some group took advantage of the situation?" If the rest of the world cooperated, they would lose support for whatever damage they did very fast. Police and military would stay on alert.

If we were able to accomplish this for one day, then we could try for two days per year, or one day every six months. If that worked, we could try one day every three months. Perhaps we could work our way to one day every month.

What would such a day be like? As a therapist, I've listened and treated clients with so many stories of aggression and abuse. We've never seen the world without human aggression. Could we unlock our doors, feel the quiet of no police sirens, and walk down the street at night without being on alert for trouble? In place of being aggressive, we could relax our guard against aggression from others. Instead we might become moved to substitute an act of compassion for someone else, an animal, or the environment. Compassion is the opposite of violence. No violence and billions of acts of kindness all on one day could change the world forever.

We could see how we feel without aggression. Would nature reduce violence through hurricanes, earthquakes, flooding, volcanos, tornadoes, heat waves, and droughts on those same days? Would the universe quietly rejoice with beautiful sunrises and sunsets, gorgeous days, and blooming flowers?

Want to try it? Aren't you curious?. Who will come forward to start organizing it? Let me know what you think and what you're willing to do. I'll help. You bet I will.

# 50

# AS A PSYCHOTHERAPIST,
## I WISH THAT...

Everyone in the world would agree to do three kind, loving, and helpful acts for someone else, an animal, a bird, plant or the environment each week. These acts would be above and beyond anything each one of us does in the normal course of a day. Such acts of help do not need to involve money, so that everyone could participate in some way. Every religion, and culture knows what an act of kindness is. Therefore, we don't need to disagree.

What would happen if the radio and television reported people's kind actions and what needs to be done instead of the murders and acts of violence that get on the news each day?

Let's calculate. There would be trillions of acts of kindness each week.

Would that number be enough to overwhelm the acts of violence so much that aggressive acts would reduce in number because they would lose their appeal? We might begin to look at war as useless, inappropriate and even stupid. The environment would be protected, along with the animals and plants.

There would not be so much stress, sorrow, physical illness, mental disorder, death, destruction, and post-traumatic stress. Instead, we might begin to see joy, hope, and gratitude in a much expanded way, not only from the people who receive the acts of kindness, but from the persons who give the acts of kindness. There really is no better way to feel joy and build self-esteem. We would feel more creative and encouraged to come up with new good acts of compassion.

We are all so stymied by the multiple problems in the world each one of us feels that there is little we, as individuals, can do about it. So we trudge onward, taking what we can for ourselves, donating our own small part, often wishing we could make a larger mark on the troubles of the world.

This is such a simple idea, but with such large positive ramifications in so many areas of life.

Would we ever be able to coordinate with each other around the world enough to give it a try? Just for one whole year? Could we use the United Nations and the internet to spread the idea from one country to another? We could do the necessary research to look at the results. The outcome might just be staggering. Is there any viable reason not to give it a try?

# V

## DEFINING MOMENTS FOR CHILDREN

.

# 51

# ANXIETY HELPS

I was skiing with my father in the mountain resort of Stowe, Vermont. It was a cold and windy day, leaving me frozen even though I was fully dressed in a snowsuit, scarf, hat and gloves. I was nine and growing fast. The sleeves of my jacket were getting too short, so the cold snow could slide down my arms. I turned my face towards the sun, trying to break through clouds, for warmth.

We made it down an easy "bunny" slope three times without falling. It had a rope tow to haul me back up the hill. I was feeling a new sense of confidence and control, becoming more graceful on skis. Dad and I went to the coffee shop for a hot chocolate and a chance to warm up. As my hands and toes thawed, they tingled just the way my arm does when I fall asleep on it while reading a book.

My Dad doesn't talk much. He's a smart doctor, but a very reserved man. He works many hours a week, doing stuff I can't understand. I'm a little scared of him. My mother makes him take me skiing; so I can't tell if he really likes to go with me. He talks more easily about science than about feelings.

I was thinking and thinking about asking him if he thought I was old enough to ride the chairlift so that I could go all the way up to the top of the mountain and ski down. I thought I could do it if he would show me the way.

I was a little scared but I decided to ask. "Dad, can I ride the chair today?"

"Sure, I don't see why not."

"Do you think I can ski down okay?"

"I think so."

We were getting hot inside so we bundled up again and went outdoors. We walked over to the single line for the chairlift. There were about fifteen people waiting to get on. I adjusted to the cold again, hoping for the sun to keep me company on my new solo journey to the top of the mountain.

I noticed that the single chairlift came around the corner to pick up each person very fast. I began to get nervous. It looked hard to get in the right place with poles and skis on, and then catch the chair as it came rushing by. What if I fell? What if I didn't get on? Would the man stop the chairlift? Now I was scared. Did that mean I was not ready?

I told my Dad, "That chair is going so fast."

"Not too fast."

"What if I don't get on?"

"Are you nervous?"

"Yes"

What he said next really surprised me because he so rarely talked about feelings.

**"Good for you. It's good to feel anxious when you're doing something for the first time. Being nervous makes you careful. It makes you check things out so that you don't make a mistake."**

"Will you ask the man to slow the chair lift down for me since it's the first time?" I wondered out loud.

**"No, since you're anxious I already know that you'll be careful, and you'll do a good job. I'll be on the chair right behind you."**

Now there were only three people ahead of me. It was getting too late to say 'NO!' I watched how the people in front of me did it. One of them was a kid just a little bigger than me. First, put your head through the hole in a big blanket to keep you warm. Put both poles in the left hand. Line your skis up straight ahead. Turn around and watch the chair coming to swoop you up. Grab the metal pole that holds the chair. Sit down and close the gate in front of you.

My Dad watched. I was anxious. Being nervous made me do it right. Dad winked. The man slowed the chair just a very little bit. How did he know?

I did it! For the first time, I could see out to all of the trails as the chair carried me up the mountain. It was so cold that I had to put the blanket over my face. When we got to the top, my Dad rubbed my cheeks to make sure I did not get frostbite. We skied down to the bottom. I followed him. He fell two times. I fell twelve times. I felt on top of the world.

On the way home, I was proud. We drank hot chocolate together. I told Mom as soon as I got home.

I'll remember always not to feel bad about being nervous anymore, especially when I'm doing something for the first time.

# 52

# OVERLOADED REPORT CARD
# CHILDREN

There are exceptional parents who just plain love their kids. They're able to stand back and watch to see who their kid really is. It doesn't matter whether the child is an athlete, academic, dancer, poet, boxer, blue collar worker, scientist, learning disabled, genius, autistic, or musician. Generally, they are able to support the child's physical, psychological and spiritual growth in a way that allows for the full development of a unique individual. If their child is experiencing difficulty in some area of life, they can speak about it openly and seek consultation that will be of help. The child's problem does little to embarrass the parent or reduce the feeling of love. Instead, the relationship deepens as the problem is addressed, improved and accepted. Parents learn from their children's strengths and vulnerabilities when they are different from their own. In teaching their children, these parents are able to expose themselves, sharing their own vulnerabilities and life story complete with its mistakes and triumphs. These parents also have their own lives to lead, their own successes and vulnerabilities to master, and ways to measure their own self-esteem that are independent from their child's performance.

**In my office, I'm hearing a lot about another group of parents who raise what I have come to call "Report Card" or "Trophy" Children. These children are inadvertently**

or directly given the job of holding up their parents' flagging self-esteem. The child's actions are always seen by the parents as an indication or a report card of how well the parents are parenting. Therefore, the child has to act in a manner that proves to the world that the parent is indeed a good parent. The child has to become the kind of grown up that the parent wants the child to be. If the child steps out of line, the parent becomes extremely anxious. They handle this anxiety by becoming rigidly over-controlling, manipulative or punishing. Some use guilt or financial reward to shape their children's behavior. Others over-protect the child's image by saying that the child can do no wrong. These children "walk on water."

In a word, the parents desperately need the child to behave in a certain way to support their self-esteem as parents, rather than loving the child and watching to see how that child may uniquely develop.

Children who resist this kind of parenting may well face an enormous power struggle that is impossible to win and sometimes results in parental abuse. These children have to bury their own unique selves in order to comply. They tend to be extremely focused on what others want them to do. They know the **right** answer, but they don't know who they are. When I ask them what they are feeling, it is generally hard for them to actually articulate what is troubling.

For example, a mother and father insist that their daughter come home directly after school. One stands behind her chair to make sure that she is studying every minute. If she drifts off or her attention wanders, Dad will start reading aloud to her. She is not allowed to date until she turns thirty. She **will** become an MD. This teenager shows up for counseling at school in tears, wondering how to fight back.

Another female teenager has formed a romantic relationship with another female. Mother and Dad find out. She's no longer allowed to see this friend. Even though it's close to the end of the school year, she's pulled from a girl's parochial school and sent to a coeducational public school in another town just before final exams. How does this teenager cope with the separation and loss, struggle with her sexual identity, pass any exams and fight back?

**These children are difficult to help in psychotherapy because their parents are not interested in understanding and changing their behavior toward their children. Instead they're quick to pull their children out of therapy if they sense that the child is in need of and moving towards more autonomy.** Somehow many of these children make it to adulthood and come into therapy alone when they are old enough to pay for it themselves. The client and I go back and find the interests of the lost child, and grow her up again to become the person she was supposed to be.

Parents of Report Card Children generally don't understand that they've failed to develop their own positive sense of self. Bolstering self-esteem may prove difficult when the job of parenting gives little validation, no pay, and some isolation for stay-at-home-parents. Parents bolster their own self-esteem through their children. The better alternative is for the parents to help the child develop the child's strengths and interests. In this manner the child's self-esteem is built and consequently, so is that of the parents.

Parenting is the hardest job on the planet; yet there is no required training to become a parent. Therefore, the pendulum swings widely back and forth as we try to correct for what we feel went wrong within our own childhoods. Society could reduce the number of Report Card children and adults in need of psychotherapy if educational institutions offered required parenting courses.

# 53

## DEFEATING BULLIES WITHOUT GETTING INTO TROUBLE

"Hey you, what do you think you're doing!?"

Todd almost tripped as he struggled to run fast in his low-slung, wide-legged pants draped over awkward boots. A police car had just parked on the street. The policeman caught up with him and grabbed him by the shoulder so that he had to stop. Todd gulped air to catch his breath.

The policeman was panting too. "Why are you running … away from … middle school?"

"I've just been suspended. If my parents find out, I'm gonna get beat by my dad. I can't go home. I'm running away. Let me go!" Todd tugged against the policeman's grasp. "I can't go to school today. They won't let me be there … and please don't arrest me … I'm too young to go to jail. I didn't do nothin' wrong."

"Hey, slow down there. Let's talk. I bet we can figure out what to do with this situation so you don't get hurt anymore." The policeman put both hands firmly on the boy's shoulders, bringing him to a complete stop. "Come on now. Slow down."

The lump in Todd's throat was too big for him to swallow as his mind flashed on the last time he was beaten by his Dad.

The policeman knelt down so their eyes were level with each other and then said very quietly, "Want to tell me why you got suspended?"

"A boy tripped me in PE, so … I slugged him. I got suspended; he didn't. I'm new at the school. He's been there a long time. They don't like new kids … they bully me every day. I haven't had a chance to make any friends yet. I never have friends because my family is always movin'."

"Let's walk back this way. We'll go back to my police car. While we're walking, I can tell you some of the ways I used to cope with bullies when I was a kid."

"Sure, man, go ahead, but I'll bet no one bullied you, you're a policeman."

"Oh yeah, they did bully me – I wasn't a policeman then."

"There's nothin' I can do."

"Did you know that a bully is someone who feels bad about himself?"

"Nah, they're the tough guys."

"Nooooo … they're pretending to be tough guys. Underneath, they're having a bad day."

"Really?"

"Yeah, try it and you'll see. **Ask them, as they show the first sign of bugging you, 'Are you having a bad day? Want to talk about it?' Sometimes they will. In any case, the question usually stops them in their tracks just long enough for you to slip away. They can't believe that you've asked.**"

Todd stopped crying and was listening intently. "Would Dad be having a bad day when he hits me?"

"Good thinking. It's always a bad day for a parent when a kid gets kicked out of school."

The policeman had shortened his gait so that it matched

that of the boy. They were walking in rhythm together, drawing strength from each other.

The policeman continued, "Want to know something else you can do?"

"There's something else?!" The boy stopped and looked up at the policeman.

'**Yup, you can carry something small and good to eat in your pocket. Start eating it yourself and just silently hand them a piece.**"

"Cool. Anything else?"

"If he turns down these two invitations, then you have no choice but to get physical. **You can trip a bully with your foot carefully and then sit on top of him and pin his wrists to the floor with your hands. He can't hurt you and you can't hurt him. He can't kick you and you can't hit him because your hands are occupied. All he can do is spit, but not high enough to hit your face. You're safe. See? If you don't hurt him, you can't be suspended. Besides, you earn respect from the bully, the other kids, and any teachers who are approaching to intervene. Just pin your bully and say quietly. 'I'll let you up when you calm down and are willing to treat me respectfully.' You just sit there and sit there. The teachers will have no fight to break up … got it?**"

"Yup, got it … but does it really work?"

"When I was your age, one of my best friends was first a bully I had to pin. We talked afterwards and became good friends. He and I were both having "bad days" with the same problems with life. Both of us had parents divorcing. Both of us did not have enough money to buy lunch at school. Both of us missed our dads. Both of us were scared, and wanted to act tough and express our feelings of frustration with a fight. Both of us got suspended."

"Wow. Who taught you this stuff?"

"My grandfather did. He was a policeman, too. He learned it in his training program."

Todd and the policeman walked on in silence, respecting each other. They were approaching Todd's small parochial alternative school.

"Well, we're here. How about we go in and I'll talk with the principal. I'll tell him that I found you on the street. I'll also tell him that I have already talked with you about how to handle a bully and you listened up really well. I'll recommend that you go back to the classroom. If he doesn't agree, then I'll call your parents and make sure that your dad doesn't beat you. That's against the law. He'll listen to me."

"Thanks … so much. Are you a dad? I mean, do you have kids of your own?"

"Yes, I do. I have a boy your age. He's been bullied, too. I tell him the same things. It works for him. It should work for you."

"He's lucky."

"And remember, if your Dad wants to beat you, ask him, 'Are you having a bad day?' Then tell him, 'I'm sorry I'm making you have a bad day. Can we talk, please … instead of you hitting me? A policeman told me that it's against the law for you to beat me.' "

"Ok."

Todd and the policeman just had time to finish their conversation before they were face to face with the principal.

"I found this boy running away from your school." The policeman suddenly sounded official.

"Yes, I've suspended him." interrupted the principal with an irritated voice. He was hurrying on to another meeting.

"I've already talked with him about how to handle kids who might bully him. He listened well. Would you let him go back to class? I'm concerned about his dad's response to his suspension, if you know what I mean?"

The principal paused in spite of his impatience and said, "Well, boy, what did you learn from the policeman?"

"I learned the right question to ask and how to control someone without hurting him or letting him hurt me," said Todd looking the principal in the eye.

"I'll send you back to class this time. You better show me what you learned if there's trouble next time."

"Yes, sir." Todd stood up straight.

The policeman winked, squeezed Todd on the shoulder, and slipped out the door saying too quietly for anyone else to hear but Todd, "I'll just bet I'll never see you running down this street again. Go for it."

Todd's eyes filled with tears, so he ducked his head, brushed his face with his hand, then straightened up as tall as he could and lumbered shyly back to his classroom.

Four days later, the principal was walking through the school yard. He noticed a crowd of children and two teachers. He went over to see what was going on. Todd sat on top of a kid the principal knew well to be a bully. Todd's hands pinned the bully's wrists. There was no fight to break up. As the principal reached the circle of onlookers, Todd got up and brushed himself off. The bully rose more slowly, stunned. Todd touched the bully's shoulder briefly but respectfully. Then Todd held his head high and walked right toward the principal.

"What's going on?" the principal asked as the small crowd dispersed.

"Just doin' like the policeman taught me." Todd muttered under his breath.

# 54

# HOW TO HELP MORE DIFFICULT CHILDREN

I attended a seminar by Robert Brooks from Harvard that was entitled, *Children with Attention Deficit/Hyperactivity Disorder or Learning Difficulties: Strategies for Building Motivation, Self-Esteem, Hope and Resilience*. Dr. Brooks spoke of his personal journey through 30 years of work with these children. He has a son, now in his thirties, with learning difficulties. He feels that he almost lost his relationship with his son because he would come in the door every night and the first words out of his mouth were "Have you done your homework?" For four years, this child did no homework. Now his son is designing and maintaining Dr. Brooks' website (www.drrobertbrooks. com). Dr Brooks spoke for six hours. I pass on to my clients the following points that were very useful from his seminar:

It is an obvious fact, but we often forget that children are born different. Within three months after birth, they fit into one of three categories.

**The Easy Child:** These children act in ways that say, "I'm going to make you look like a great parent." They are truly easy children to raise. The parents of these kids have a lot of good advice for the parents of the other two kinds of kids.

**The Slow-to-Warm-Up Child:** These children are born shy, but with support become more outgoing by the age of 12.

**The Difficult Child**: These children feel that life is not fair. They see the world as not providing adequately for them. Some of them have Learning Difficulties (LD) and/ or Attention Deficit Hyperactivity Disorder (ADHD). They tend to be insatiable, wanting to "suck you dry" leaving you feeling like an inadequate parent. They may be hypersensitive to touch and to noise. They often experience you as yelling when you are not. A towel can feel like sandpaper to them. They lack organization and consistency in their behavior.

Brooks advised us, **"Never judge a parent unless you have walked in their shoes."** There are terrific parents out there not evident from their kids' behaviors. Few people understand just how worried these children are about being loved and being successful when they grow up. They don't feel intelligent. Their self-esteem is extremely low. They don't like compliments because they don't believe in them. They often believe that the praise they receive is manipulative to force a certain behavior, and is therefore false. Many of these kids have lost hope. They say, "What's the use." The feelings of loneliness are very profound, especially when they have finished their formal education.

We cannot expect these children to change unless we're willing to change the way we treat them. It does not help to punish, reject, isolate, or take away the activities in which they are interested and do well. These kids have three basic needs:

❀ The need to belong, to feel connected, to feel welcome

❀ The need for self-determination

❀ The need to feel competent

Many difficult kids are doing well in other areas of their lives. Therefore, these children often display conflicting beliefs about themselves. Each child assesses both their special talents and difficulties as Carol Wren and Jay Eihorn express in *Hanging By a Twig: Understanding and Counseling Adults with Learning Disabilities and ADD.*:

"I want it/ I fear it"

"I'm proud of myself / I'm ashamed"

"I feel confident in myself / I have no confidence."

"I'm smart / I'm dumb"

"I'm lazy / I'm trying as hard as I can"

"I'm rational / I'm losing my mind"

Be sure to help your child recognize and build on their strengths so that they can feel competent. Focus on their skills. Therefore, speak of your child as not a "LD child" but a "child with LD."

**Never say, "Try harder." or " If you did another hour of work, life would be all right."** Difficult kids hear this all the time from parents and teachers. There is no test for trying harder. We don't know what it is like to walk in their shoes. We do not know if they are not trying as hard as they can. Instead say, "I think that you are really trying."

**Don't get into an argument with these children, they will always find a loophole. Validate them instead. Do not try to discuss something while your kid is arguing with you. Try not to say what you don't want said to you. If you get frustrated, you can take a "time out" instead of the child. In your darkest moments, try to keep your sense of humor.**

**Empathy is a key feeling that works well with these children,** and all children in general. It is "the capacity to put yourself inside of someone else's shoes and see the world through their eyes." It is not sympathy or feeling sorry for them. Therefore, it's important to ask these kids just how they see you at the moment. Have them draw, write, or give you a description so you can see your relationship with them through their eyes. Empathy means saying, "I know that what you are trying to do is not easy. It is not easy for a lot of kids. Maybe we can figure out a way to handle this together. It gets easier over time."

If you wish to tell a child something, preface it with: "I have something to say to you. If you feel criticized, will you please tell me?" When they tell you something, say, "Thank you so much for letting me know." When interacting with these kids, ask yourself, "How can I say this so that we both problem-solve?" Is what I'm doing going to develop hope in this child? Being fair is not treating these kids the same way as other kids. Being fair is giving them what they need.

Children love to help and to make a difference, and come up with a solution. Give these kids choices. "You can choose to do three out of six problems." However, it is always wise to have a backup plan that will aid in being successful. These kids have some excellent ideas. When they come up with a good idea, tell them, "That was a great idea! Can I share it with others?"

Fifteen hundred difficult kids reported their most positive memories of school. Their memories involved being noticed or recognized or being asked to help out. The most negative memories involved public humiliation for not understanding. Our schools need to provide a curriculum for caring in addition to academics. These children have learned not to have a good day because it will be held against them for the rest of their lives. For example, parents and teachers have said, "You were able to do it last week, why can't you do it now?" Instead, focus on what they were able to do to make it a good day.

**The most important key to success for a difficult child is to have "one person who stood by this child and believed in him/her or a charismatic person from whom this**

**child gathers strength**." Try consciously to minimize the fear of making mistakes, by letting these children know that mistakes are a normal and necessary part of learning. Adults make them too. Engage your entire family in a community service project that your difficult child can handle well.

In a study done by Raskind, M; Goldberg, R; Higgins, E; and Herman, K, entitled *Children with Learning Disability Grow Up: Results of a Twenty Year Longitudinal Study,* the researchers found that the following "Success Attributes" determined whether these students did well in adult life. These attributes were:

- ❊ Self-Awareness and acceptance of LD
- ❊ General Self-awareness of all strengths and weaknesses apart from LD
- ❊ Pro activity
- ❊ Perseverance
- ❊ Emotional stability
- ❊ Appropriate goal setting and self-directedness
- ❊ Presence and use of an effective support system.

The participants in this study said that they had been profoundly affected by their LD diagnosis. Many said that they lived in fear of their LD every day. They felt beat up by the constant tutoring and remediation.

The recommendations in this essay encourage achieving these "success attributes." They are healthy recommendations for raising all children, but are essential for the more difficult child.

# 55

# UNDERSTANDING ADOPTEE'S
# LOSS OF FAMILY

I was standing in the Dulles Airport in Washington DC. My seven year old daughter, Kendall, was holding my hand tightly.

Kendall is an adoptee. Because she had been relinquished by the two people who were supposed to love and take care of her, she never seemed completely sure that I would not relinquish her also. Therefore, when traveling, she made sure to never let go of my hand during a long trip. My words did nothing to reassure her. My deep love for her was apparently never quite enough to quell the attachment trauma within her heart of losing her birth parents at birth. She did not trust the words "I love you." Her life experience had already told her love likely meant, "Please go away." Therefore, it appeared scary for her to say "I love you" to me.

Sometimes I became weary or impatient about her need for reassurance. It had been hard for me to fully understand until, on this day, I looked up at the airport monitors to locate the gate and the plane that would take us both back to Los Angeles. We had been visiting an aunt and uncle who had stepped into the role of grandparents for my daughter. We had a great time.

The monitor showed the flights that were going to Burlington, Vermont. That is where my parents live. They had disinherited me because I had written and published another book that they hated. There was no contact with them by phone, letter or direct meeting. I had not heard from them for six months. I felt a deep pain. Suddenly, I could begin to feel what it is like to be an adoptee in a closed adoption because I had a biological family "out there," but I was no longer invited and I did not "belong."

Finally, I got it. As the tears silently ran down my face, I understood, at gut level, what it felt like to be Kendall. Hallelujah! ... not intellectually the way the books on adoption gave it to me, but at a wrenching feeling level. I could understand why my daughter was so difficult to please during the holidays. **There was a family out there who had relinquished her and was celebrating without her. No other family can really substitute.** It didn't matter how hard my husband and I tried to meet her needs; it's just not the same. I could begin to forgive myself for never being the right parent for my daughter, and understand better why she reacted the way she did.

I looked down at Kendall. She was gazing somewhere else and did not notice that I was crying. I knelt down and put my arm around her shoulder, located where to board the plane for Los Angeles, stood up again, and started walking with her while holding hands, towards the gate. There was no way to tell her, at her young age, what I had just learned.

# 56

# WHEN "I LOVE YOU" MEANS "PLEASE GO AWAY"

Anne, an adult adoptee, and I had been working in psychotherapy together for a few months. She started her hour with me abruptly. "I was looking at my birth certificate and discovered that my name was spelled wrong, although who knows what the wrong spelling is anyway. It's only wrong if I think I know who I am … when I was a child, I used to stare into the mirror for hours, and I never knew why. Perhaps I was trying to figure out who I was. It was confusing because I knew I was adopted, but everyone said I had the body type of my adoptive mother and I acted like my adopted father. Of course, I can't really know who I am because I don't know my birth father. I also have two different names for him on my birth certificate. One of them is listed in our local phone book."

"What you describe sounds very difficult."

"Well, I'll tell you something else. I hope you don't think I'm crazy, but I hate the words 'I love you.' "

"Do you know why?"

"Absolutely. My adoptive mother always told me that my birth mother loved me, but she couldn't take care of me."

"What did that mean to you?"

"It's really simple. **My life story tells me that if someone** 'loves you,' that means they 'give you away.' Who in the hell wants that? Whenever I hear 'I love you.' it makes me really uncomfortable."

"Now I understand ... Did your adoptive Mom and Dad say 'I love you'?"

"Yup, they did and I liked it, but they're not the same as me, even though they're relatives in my extended family. So 'I love you' from them means 'mismatch.' That makes me uncomfortable in a different way. I can't look to them to see who I am."

Anne paused in thought for a few minutes. "There's one more thing to say. I think that I'll only feel safe within my family when I have my own child. Then I can say and hear 'I love you' without feeling uncomfortable. I want to get married and have a family more than anything else in the world. But it's hard, because it scares me to hear 'I love you' from a date. I just want to run away. So ... how can I ever get married to have a child?"

"I hope that it's helpful for you to talk about this with someone. You've really helped me to understand. It makes good sense to me. Perhaps your understanding about what you've discovered will make it easier for you to dare to fall in love."

"You're right, I would never have gotten so far with my new relationship if I'd not been able to talk with you this way ... Perhaps that's why I treat life so casually. Sometimes, I take risks I shouldn't ... it's as if I don't care if I do die ... maybe it's because life feels not much fun without love in it somewhere, where it does feel comfortable."

I wished she could see herself through my eyes. Therefore, I ventured, "You're a beautiful, thoughtful person. You deserve to be loved and to love without fear. You and I are working on that issue until we get there. Remember you are adult now and will never be "relinquished" again. That word is for children who need a home. Your birth mother placed you because she was afraid that she could not manage to take care of you. It wasn't because she didn't like you."

"We're getting there. I feel different after we talk about it."

Later that day, I spoke with another adoptee on the telephone. She'd married and had adopted two children. She's a good friend, so I asked her how she felt about hearing the phrase, "I love you." She responded immediately the same way Anne did, as if she'd overheard our psychotherapy dialogue. "Oh, that means 'please go away.' "

The next morning, my adopted daughter, Kendall, came home after one week in the hospital after an emergency C-section to deliver her baby five weeks early. The baby was still in the hospital. Kendall had created the new family with matching genes that Anne longed to have so she could feel love safely for the first time. When Kendall arrived, she walked into the nursery and missed her baby terribly.

I'd missed Kendall while she was in the hospital, and had cleaned the house and put up a welcome sign. However, Kendall felt no joy at her homecoming. In addition to missing her baby, she probably could only feel the disappointment of our natural ongoing genetic mismatch. She was rude to me as she tried to cope with her pain. I could not say anything right. But this time, I understood that there was no place for the 'I love you' I wanted to say.

The next day, I overheard Kendall speaking kindly about me to someone on the telephone, reminding me that her affection for me was present as long as it was not stated in the form of "I love you."

One day later, another adoptee failed to come for a psychotherapy appointment designed to help her cope with an impending court hearing for committing a felony. Her frantic adoptive mother was wondering why her adoptee was not focusing on the court hearing.

I responded as gently as I could, "Your adoptee might get a year in prison and will, therefore, have to relinquish her one-year-old son to the care of her extended adoptive family. Perhaps she cannot bear to think about another relinquishment. Therefore, she's simply blocking it out."

How does the universe organize the same defining moment from four adoptees within two days? How could I miss understanding?

# 57

# ADOPTEE CONTRADICTION

I was editing this manuscript. Out of the silence came a panicked call from a new client, Angie. "I'm calling to ask you to see me as soon as possible. I'm having panic attacks and can't handle staying at work. I have no idea why this is happening."

We made an appointment that same day. The initial evaluation revealed that she had fallen in love with a boyfriend, and he had expressed the same feelings towards her. Then the boyfriend suddenly and unexpectedly announced that he would be "moving to Philadelphia across the country to find himself." He had abruptly departed two days later.

I asked my client, "How do you feel about his departure?"

Angie responded, "I feel abandoned … cold, sad and worthless."

We talked for some time about Angie's life story. I learned that she was adopted. Her birth mother was a graduate student and "needed to leave the country to go on a fellowship to Japan to find her career." Her birth father entered the military. She was relinquished to a "really nice adoptive couple, and had a good childhood." School went well. She has talent as an artist. She'd taken some community college classes and worked as a preschool teacher.

As her story unfolded, I began to understand why she was likely having anxiety and panic attacks. Towards the end of the hour, I explained to her, "Do you see a parallel between your story thirty years ago, and the relationship you just lost?"

"Ohhhhhhh," Angie responded. She shifted position abruptly.

"I wonder if you're having the feelings that you had when you were a baby, just born. Your birth mother probably had to leave you at the hospital, and you were alone until you reached your adoptive family."

"Oh, noooo."

"Yes," I suggested. "You suddenly lost everything you knew about your birth mother ... the music she listened to, the TV programs she watched, the food she ate, the position she slept in ... You knew this lady and loved her. She was suddenly gone. Both your birth mother and your boyfriend left you to "find themselves."

"But why would I feel so worthless. My parents told me that I was 'special.' They had 'chosen' me and brought me home. They picked me over other kids. They love me."

"Indeed, you are 'special' to them. However, when you are an adoptee, unfortunately you have to be 'unchosen' before you can become 'chosen.' "

"I see ... sort of."

"Your infant brain was very young. It takes thirty years for all of the brain to reach full maturity. Your infant brain could only see that grownups are 'all powerful and all perfect.' Therefore, if anything goes wrong, it is unquestionably the infant's fault."

"I feel as if the breakup with my boyfriend is all my fault now, too."

"Well, if I were in your shoes, I would feel terribly confused."

"Why?"

"Because, your infant brain says 'relinquishment was all your fault' while your adoptive parents say your were 'special' and 'chosen.' Which is right?"

Angie engaged with me while moving to the edge of her chair. "Maybe that's why I feel so uneasy, I flip back and forth between the two contradictory feelings. I thought being 'special' made me better than other kids. But I was also 'abandoned' by the one person who was supposed to love me."

"Perhaps those are the feelings that made you feel panicky enough to call me today."

"Yeah, the voice of panic confirms I've been left and I deserve it … I guess it was also hard to feel that my adoptive family brought me "home" because I grew up in a family where no one was like me in any way … I just didn't fit in … Nothing was the same, not the voice, the eyes, they way we laughed. It was all so different. I couldn't be like them even when I tried. Boy, did I try."

"Did you feel that your difference made you feel 'less than' the rest of your adoptive family?"

"Yes … and I couldn't really get a handle on who I was because I had no information from my biological family. I wanted to be like them, but I didn't know who they were."

"Are you saying that it's hard to value and love yourself when you don't know who you are?"

"And that makes it my fault that my boyfriend left town. He couldn't see who I was … because even I didn't know. **So it is all my fault** … get it? Obviously, he didn't love me."

"It must be so hard to have those feelings. Have you considered that perhaps your boyfriend had some problems of his own that made it hard for him to make a commitment to someone he loved?"

"Nooooo … I guess I just blamed me … like the little baby … I haven't dated much. I've always felt safer being alone, then no one can leave. I should have let it stay that way. Keep the walls up and no one can see that I don't know who I am. When I let the walls down, that little baby you described cries out that I deserve to be abandoned again because it **is** all my fault. She's so loud and constant it makes me crazy and keeps me up at night. "

"This time we can make it different. You also have a grown-up part of you that called me up and understands that you have made a life for yourself that you can honor and respect. This grown up part can begin to calm the little infant."

"What can I say to the baby?"

**"You can tell your baby that your relinquishment was not her fault. You see ... I have never met a birth mother who wanted to give up her baby or thought something was wrong with her baby. Every birth mother I've met is afraid that they won't be able to be a good enough parent, and that an adoptive couple can do a better job. A birth mother doesn't have a clue as to how psychologically hard it will be for you, the birth father, her and the adoptive family. Birth mothers grieve the loss of their child every year for about thirty years. Many of them report thinking about their relinquished child every day."**

"Yeah ... that's what my birth mother said when I finally met her two years ago. I could hardly believe it ... But, the infant still says, 'It's my fault.' "

"Well the infant is wrong. Relinquishment is **never** the infant's fault."

Angie sat quietly for a time absorbing what we had said. I could see her body begin to relax. Tears of pain and relief slowly rolled down her cheeks.

"So, if you like, you and I might need to meet together for a while to decide what to do with all of these contradictory feelings. We need to decide which are the ones that are going to take you through the rest of your life."

"I'd love to feel as if it were all right for me to want and deserve love, a home, and a family of my very own. I hope I can believe that someday."

**"Believing it has a lot to do with its actually happening. I can see that you have many fine qualities. Perhaps it will be both disappointing and relieving for me to say that you are neither "special" nor "worthless." Instead, you're a person with your own unique strengths and vulnerabilities, like all the rest of us. You're equal to those who are not adopted. You will come to know and appreciate who you are as we talk this through."**

"Well, I feel tired now ... but thank you so much for making sense of what's going on in my head. I didn't get it, not one bit. So I had no idea what to do. I couldn't sleep last night. That's so scary ... I feel more settled now. Can I come back and talk to you again?"

"Of course. I would be honored to talk with you further. I have a lot of respect for the feelings you've shared today. You should also know that your feelings are normal and shared by all of the adoptees I've counseled. Your feelings are not crazy, but are natural to your unique life experience of adoption. Next time you come in for your appointment, perhaps I can begin to learn more about your adoptive and birth families."

"Yeah, there's a lot to say. They were good people even though they were different from me. I've appreciated what they have given to me."

"Let's stop for today, and we'll meet again next week when we can have more time."

# 58

# A LETTER OF TRIBUTE TO PARENTS
# OF SPECIAL NEEDS CHILDREN

You come into my office, unsure. Maybe something is not quite right with your child. Your little boy is not progressing the way your friends' children are. While you notice the difference out loud, your friends are strangely quiet.

I encourage you. "Yes, it's time to have your child evaluated by a specialist. It's time to make the call."

The news brings contradictory feelings flooding your mind. You're relieved, on the one hand, that there's a reason why things don't feel right. At the same time, you're devastated. Suddenly you have to acquire knowledge about something for which you may know little or nothing. What did you do wrong to make this happen? Is there something you can do to fix it? And, you don't want your child to see how confused you feel. But how do you hide these feelings without pretending to an absurd degree?

Maybe the diagnosis is Birth Trauma, Down's Syndrome, or Spina Bifida, Attention Deficit Disorder (ADD), Attention Deficit Hyperactive Disorder (ADHD), Learning Difficulty (LD), Asperger's Syndrome, Autism, Obsessive Compulsive Disorder, genetic addiction genes, perhaps combined with Highly Sensitive Person (HSP), physical or medical problem such as Mitro Valve Prolapse, Diabetes, or Cancer. Perhaps your child is a foster or an adoptee with a traumatic history. Many adoptees frequently have learning difficulties and ADD.

I listen carefully, give you support and a chance to express your emerging feelings.

You will see that there are three kinds of children out there. The first kind of child is **easy**. Easy children are born with a good gene package; they mostly raise themselves. Their parents feel pride in their successful parenting. The second kind of child is **shy**. They may cling to parents, needing extra support, but usually outgrow their shyness by the age of twelve. **The third kind of child is a difficult child with special needs. They require extraordinary parenting and the right kind of genuine support. The love that develops is important and deep.**

You go to bed and cry quietly. You begin to feel the first twinges of aloneness, as if you're stepping into a foreign land, and no current friend has learned the language that you'll have to learn to speak.

You have only two choices. If you have plenty of money, you may choose to handle your situation by hiring full time nannies to do everything your child needs but can't do for himself. You can find tutors, and after school programs to manage homework. Both turn the child's special needs over for training outside of the family.

**Or**

**you can enter the world of extraordinary parenting. You will mentor your special needs child while your special needs child will simultaneously become your mentor. You'll learn facts you thought you never needed to know.** Your sense of humility will grow tremendously, while any arrogant or demeaning attitude you may have had fades as you begin to see the world through your child's eyes. You will step out of your own narrower easier space to broaden your horizons. You will come to understand that the diagnosis is not your fault.

There may be confusion and conflict in your marriage if one parent wants the Nanny and the other one wants to do extraordinary parenting. I can encourage some marital counseling to assign responsibility, reach a compromise, or decide which way to proceed.

As you go out into the world with your child, you will interact with all of the people who don't comprehend. Sometimes it's hard to remember that they lack understanding just as you did before the diagnosis for your child arrived.

Parents of easy kids may stare at you and your child in public places. From their perspective, they're wondering what's going wrong and why on earth you're not able to fix it. They may even look annoyed. They do not have the information or experience to respond differently. Their parenting is much easier than yours; they believe you're doing something wrong, while they know how to do it right. Their children walk away with the awards in school assemblies, while you and your family have earned none for your extraordinary efforts.

Parents of kids without special needs have no idea what kind of support you need for you and your child. Therefore, you're on your own until you find a friend who is able to understand and may silently give support. You have to hold up your own and your family's self-esteem. Validation from the outside world is rare. However, I can help you to see yourself clearly and respect the honest efforts you've made.

Perhaps you have holiday celebrations with friends who have children. Your child may not behave in an acceptable manner because of his special difficulty or related psychological feelings. You may have to take a "time out" from the gathering, or leave the party early. Next year, you may find that you're no longer invited because your child's behavior "does not set a good example for the other children." You will grieve quietly, and I will be there to comfort you. Your current social life may feel as if it's sliding away.

I will encourage you to seek new friends who also have challenging children. They will become your best friends because they already understand. They're able to listen. They will support you because they're on the same journey with their children. They may replace some of the parents of easier children, because they're seeking the same depth in living life that you are. They're the ones to understand the days that are heartbreaking, wonderful and frustrating beyond belief.

Look carefully, because your child may have special needs, but is also likely to be very talented in some area of living life. Nurture and support her talent, letting it flower in a way that carries her out into the world, in spite of other difficulties. You'll learn to notice what goes right. There will be magical moments, inconsequential to others, when your child masters some task that has previously been difficult or even impossible. You'll scream a silent, "Yeah." Notice the depth that your child has acquired in the mastery of her difficulty. Make sure your compliments are genuine validation, and not manipulations to make your child behave in a particular way. Otherwise, your child will come to hate the very compliments we all need to get on with life.

There will be days when you're very discouraged and will perhaps want to give up; but you know that you can't. You may burn out with a child, who needs to test your limits by doing something bad to see if you'll kick him out, fail to do what you expect because he simply can't. He may seek negative attention because it feels louder and stronger than positive attention. You may try to talk with a parent of a child without special needs who may impatiently say, "When you decide to stop all of this, your life will change for the better." They'll say this because they don't understand that there's no way out without abandoning your child. That, you know, is totally unacceptable.

Your commitment to this child is ongoing ... as long as it takes ... much longer than is needed for 'easy' and 'shy' children. You'll be on deck advocating for assessments and special services, and on the lookout for professionals who can really help. Generally, you'll also have to constantly evaluate that you're not spoiling, rescuing, or enabling. You strive to reliably articulate positive, narratives of moments when your child did well, rather than criticism, because it's the only interaction that really helps your child to feel some sense of competence, belonging and self-determination. During these times, I can walk with you as needed through this journey, having made it myself.

**There will be defining moments in which you realize that mentoring this child has given you a richer gift than you ever thought possible. It has given you direction, a sense of purpose, opened a door you would not have seen, and has allowed you to make a difference in a way that you never imagined.** Perhaps you will be a candidate to write an article, a book, a script, to serve on a board, start an organization, raise money for a cause, or teach a seminar, sharing who you have become with other parents who can gain from your insights. You have become accustomed to persevering while riding the waves of criticism. Your life will not be easy but it will have been worthwhile. That counts for a lot.

Your child may never be able to tell you how much she loves the help and belief in her that you have given. Instead, she believes in her relationship with you enough to show you her most discouraged feelings. She stays connected and tells you what's important in her life.

I have seen parents of special needs children walk into my office devastated by a diagnosis and muster the courage to go ahead with a love that's passionate, dramatic at times, and deep. These parents discover the unique inescapable beauty of their child no diagnosis can erase. They eventually leave my office, after our work is concluded, with their heads held high, and with a purpose that was totally unknown when they first arrived.

**I salute you all. You have taught me so much.**

# VI

## MORE DEFINING MOMENTS WITH NATURE

# 59

# RESOLVE AND STAYING POWER

I arrived at a neighborhood party on time. The hostess appeared frazzled but declined my offer to help. She still needed some time to get ready, so I asked permission to wander out onto the back patio.

Another guest arrived and I heard our hostess say something about "hosing down the patio." She had "sprayed the trees with water and a baby bird **might** have fallen out of its nest?"

The patio was indeed clean, except for one small spot. I thought it was just a dirty leaf. I walked closer to discover that it was instead a tiny bird no more than two inches in height in soft colors of wet gray and brown. She was standing straight and completely still on her tiny feet, underneath a table, looking wet, and utterly alone. I saw what appeared to be a baby humming bird, almost ready to fly.

The guest and I began a search for the bird's nest. We were unable to find anything resembling a home for this little creature. We knew that if we touched her feathers with our hands, her mother would later reject the bird.

There were cats in the neighborhood and a ten week old puppy inside the house. Therefore, we decided to coax the bird gently onto a folded piece of cardboard without touching it. We moved her to a planter on higher ground more secluded and less in harm's way. She fluttered her wings briefly, confirming that she was alive and accepting of our help.

This tiny bird continued with the same total stillness in the new location. Her eyes were closed, I couldn't see her breathe, but she was still standing on tiny legs and feet.

The party had started with drinks and appetizers in the living room. An hour passed while dinner was cooking on the grill. We talked together and played with the puppy.

Before we sat down to dinner, I wandered out into the garden to check on the bird. She was still in the planter, but had managed to rotate her body so that she was facing in the opposite direction. She was, once again, perfectly still with features that were now beginning to dry out.

Dinner was served. I helped to clear the plates in preparation for dessert, so I could sneak out once again from the kitchen to see my little friend. The bird was still there, but this time her beady, intensely black eyes had opened. I could see her blink.

After dessert, I did some dishes for the hostess, and thereby earned another chance to slip out of the kitchen to check just one more time before dark. No bird was there in the planter or anywhere around on the ground. I could only imagine that the feathers had dried enough for the bird to fly ... perhaps a maiden voyage. As the sun set, I heard one lone bird singing a joyful song. Was it the mother? Had the bird found its way back to the nest?

**So much of what we have to do in life requires "staying power." This bird attracted my attention because she knew exactly what she had to do to survive, even though she was so very young. Nothing could throw this bird off course. We were able to protect her for a time until she reached her goal of survival. I believe that she succeeded.**

A suicidal client came for a psychotherapy hour just after I finished writing this essay. I told her about the bird. She came to understand that she had to choose whether to flap her wings helplessly, vulnerable to who might come along to help or hurt her; or stand up by herself, like the little bird, and attract the aid she might need to take flight for the rest of her life. The story of the little bird gave her hope, and a concrete decision to make before the end of the hour.

When I have "staying power," and a sensitivity to my feelings, I attract help from the universe to achieve my life's work. Whenever I worry, get lazy, or let someone talk me out of what I still have to do, the bird's intense blinking black eye comes into my vision from the inside of my soul, urging me to stay on my own individual course … always onward.

# 60

# BECOMING WELL

It was a nasty virus. A tight cough, no fever, but a feeling of lethargy. I just wanted to lie quietly and look at the ceiling. It seemed to go on for several days. I worked half-days and rested whenever I could. But still, the virus seemed lodged within me. Liquids, protein, extra sleep, immune builders, good music, a great book; cats and dogs curled up by my side; nothing seemed to help. I felt alone, with not enough energy to interact with others. It felt strange because I hadn't been sick for years.

Finally I decided to go outside. The rains had been heavy this year, leaving behind an enormous burst of growth of flowers, succulents, cacti, and a huge variety of weeds. I did not feel strong enough to stand for long. However, I was able to sit in the middle of the flowers to pull some weeds. Sitting made me the same height as the flowers. I could see them vividly because they were so close to me at eye level. The birds I fed every day were chirping constantly. Each weed that came loose felt like a piece of the virus lodged but breaking out of my body.

**I had found a way to feel connected to the energy of the universe. Being amidst nature, at its own height, made me feel better and not so alone.** The virus loosened but still lingered for one more day, forcing me to quiet myself and think more deeply about my life. The virus had decked me for a reason.

Nature told me to give more respect and free time to myself, and that I had become burnt out in helping others to get back onto their feet. It told me to ask others for what I needed and trust each one to respond. I did not feel so isolated because I knew that I could go back into my back yard and sit with all that grows so respectfully and courageously. I knew that energy would return me to health.

# 61

# DEPLETION BLOOMS

Jason hobbled into the house using a walker, and sank into the warm water of our hot tub hoping that it would erase the constant pain in his lower back and leg. He stayed for only a few minutes because the water was not providing any relief. Angela, his girlfriend, was constantly by his side, taking superb care of him. She had brought their two miniature dogs, now chasing each other around the backyard with an astonishing abandon in marked contrast to Jason's painful constriction. Angela did not have time to get all the way into the hot tub herself before Jason asked for help in getting out. He slowly edged his way back into our home.

I offered him some homemade turkey soup before he left to go back to bed in his apartment. He was hungry so he tried to stay by standing, sitting, and then went to lying down on the couch. I could hear his quiet but audible moan. His only sentence was, "I'd amputate this leg if I could." Too pained to wait for soup; he was already out the door climbing into their truck to lay down in back of the cab, crying quietly. I watched helplessly. His only comfort came from snuggling the two little dogs. Angela drove him home swiftly.

My heart reverberated his pain.

Jason was suffering from a back injury that had occurred twenty years ago and had never been treated with proper med-

ical care due to lack of family support and insurance. Therefore, he'd handled the pain by taking too many illegal pain
medications. However, he had insisted upon going off his pain
pills without any medical supervision. On the sixth day, he had
a seizure that shook his whole body, making his damaged back
much worse. He was in the hospital for nine days, only to be
dismissed still in pain.

Laid off at the end of a grocery store strike, Jason had no
insurance. Reputable physicians would not evaluate him further
even when offered payment up front. County hospitals were
closing down because of deficit budgets. The wait to see a county physician was eight to ten hours with no place to lie down.

Jason's parents and siblings had cut him off, psychologically
and financially because they insisted that he attend a particular
drug treatment program. It was obvious that he could not
stand, sit, or walk enough to make it to the mandatory daily
meetings. We had to fix the pain before he could truly face his
addiction. I'd already talked with his family to no avail. The
pain had been this way for weeks; yet he was valiantly holding
to his commitment to stay away from drugs.

It was true that he had "messed up" with his life and hurt
others in the process; but was that an adequate justification to
ignore his physical pain?

What can I do to help? I cared about what happened to
him because his girlfriend was a special person in my life. She
was patiently determined not to abandon him. His illness and
previous drug addiction had hurt her and us and was now
holding back the forward progress she now must make to
support him.

In an attempt to sort out my feelings, I went walking in the
high trails of Griffith Park in the middle of Los Angeles where
steep hills create a huge bowl of nature that makes me feel
cradled by the universe. Below is the bustling city. For fifteen

years, I've done some of my most insightful, creative thinking in that location. It's my time, with three dogs, before the work day begins, to think about how to conduct myself during the day. Therefore, I hesitantly asked the universe for a miracle for Jason and Angela.

On the dirt road was a stem with buds for a number of small violet flowers. Someone had probably plucked it and then decided to discard it. I lifted it up. There were eight tiny blossoms and only two of them had come into bloom. The flower was badly dehydrated. The stem was still hydrated enough to hold it straight up, but the flowers bobbed aimlessly at the top.

Perhaps bringing it home would save it. However, it took another half hour to return, and the flower was further squashed in my hand twice in leashing the dogs. At my house, I cut the stem to half its length, put the flower in water, and wondered what would happen. There was nothing else to do to help except to handle it and speak to it softly.

Within two hours the flower began to lift its head. After half a day, it stood straight and tall. The blossoms were still closed except for two. This tiny little flower was sending a message about Jason and Angela.

The following day, I came back to my office to see how my little piece of nature was faring. The flower was on the sidewalk outside of my window, once more without water and crushed again. The cleaning lady had thrown it out, believing it was not important.

I picked it up and returned it to its vase. Again, it revived.

The next morning, five of the remaining blossoms had opened, revealing tiny intricate central stamens in white, yellow, and pale violet.

I was happy to be able to help, and content because a miracle of the universe was encapsulated within the flower. I was moved to see that the miracle came in the form of a lesson. **I could bring the flower home, give it water, and speak to it encouragingly. That was all; the rest lay in the stem and buds of the flower. It was not my job. Trying to help in any other way would have forced the process of blooming and destroyed the flower. The same miracle of health lies within each one of us, but we cannot command someone else to make it happen.**

The five remaining blossoms lasted for four days. I searched for this kind of flower in the park for many years. It was nowhere to be seen.

Jason's girlfriend called to say that a chiropractor and an AA sponsor had both offered to help Jason. The chiropractor was willing to see him for free. I could help by talking with Jason, giving him encouragement to endure his pain and do what he could to recover. We visited and talked by telephone. I could also pay for acupuncture.

I could only do what I did for the flower. I told Jason about it.

Jason reminds me of other flowers in my garden that have broken stems. It's hard to simply throw them away. Instead, I clip off the dead parts that are draining it of survival, and put the live parts in water. They become flower bouquets for my office. Sometimes they bloom, sometimes they don't. Our help can be lifesaving; but too much help can kill, even if it is done with the right spirit.

I visited my own garden and saw the flowers bursting forth with all of the energy of spring. Walking by the river presented the same energy in the racing water, the swallows dive bombing the waterfalls and the ducks tending their new broods.

That energy was just waiting there for Jason and his girlfriend to grab it in a way that made them feel better. If they claimed it, they could reach their own new goal, because they wanted it more than any drugs, leaving them with a feeling of accomplishment and confidence. There would be no leftover guilt to drown with the next drug. They could tell others how they helped themselves and have the pleasure of sharing what they decided. They would earn money and not spend it on illegal drugs. People like myself could notice and decide to contribute.

I had relearned once again from the flower that I could also take pleasure from being generous and caring, receiving back the biggest gift of all, that of giving. I had to quell the need to do more.

Angela and Jason took hold of the energy just as the flower chose to lift its head and open its blossoms. Jason's girlfriend continued to take care of him, but decided to go back to school so she could find a job that would earn a higher wage. He's sixty per cent better now and can sit up and take steps on his own. When I showed him this essay, he read it and wept. Perhaps he felt heard and supported. That opened the door further to understanding new options.

Within six months, my husband was able to acquire, at a cost we could afford, the right eight-hour surgery to fix his back and leg. Jason and Angela gave birth nine months after surgery to a baby girl. Jason got back out into the world as a fitness trainer, with an expertise in helping people with back problems. Their love for this little girl has centered them and far surpasses any lingering wish for drugs.

Thank you, little flower, for your brave gift to us all.

# VII

## CLIENTS SPEAK OUT

# 62

# THIRTEEN WISHES TO REBUILD
# A NATION

## FROM THE CLIENTS OF A PSYCHOTHERAPY PRACTICE

### PREFACE

I have listened to the fearful palpitations of the citizens of the United States in the inner sanctum of my private office as each client, whether child, adolescent, adult, or elderly, teaches me about their psychological discomfort, what is missing and what needs to change for their lives to work well. They have taught me about the survival skills that kept them going through life even when they were unable to acquire the support they needed.

The psychotherapy process becomes more difficult when I realize that some of my clients' concerns reach beyond the ability of a single therapist. **They're speaking about societal changes that need to be made.** I hear the same themes coming up over and over again until they have carved deep synaptic connections within my brain. Some clients have encouraged me to express their collective feelings by writing the final section of this book. Some of these desires are put forth by children without the complex psychological defenses that sometimes mask the truth. Our youngsters are honest in their requests and insistently patient with me until I get it right.

I was raised in the1950s and 1960s in the small university town of Burlington, Vermont. I look back on my childhood longingly because it seemed so simple in contrast to the world my daughter and granddaughter live in now. I know that I'm as guilty as the next older person in not being able to accept what's happening for the next generation, but I also fear that some aspects of our current lives have gone astray.

As a child and adolescent, I lived in the country. Nobody ever locked their cars or their homes. I spent my afternoons after school and weekends skating on the pond in my backyard, skiing on the hills and mountains, sailing a small and larger boat on Lake Champlain, exploring farms and forests, playing card and board games with friends, taking care of my younger brother, working in the garden, reading, playing with the pet duck and family dogs who ran freely throughout the neighborhood. Television did not enter our home until I was in 7th grade.

As a teenager, the only responsibilities I had were to be a careful teenager sexually and to drive safely in the snow. There was some alcohol, but no drugs, gangs, graffiti, or drive-by shootings. Life was free of computer games, computer viruses, internet pornography, or term papers to steal and plagiarize off the internet. School was safe, with no metal detector tests and no shootings. I was not afraid to walk the streets at night and I could see the stars, the Milky Way, and the Aurora Borealis. I knew nature intimately. I was comfortable within the world I inhabited.

My father worked long hours as a physician and a researcher. My mother was a full-time Mom, regarding her parenting as an honorable profession. She also served her community avidly with volunteer work. She was always in the kitchen when I came home from school ready to serve me something to eat, talk with me about my day, and teach me how to maintain a home. She shopped for clothes with me at an unhurried pace. We had time together to teach me how to become a woman. We all ate dinner as a family in the evening and shared time together on the weekends. We took vacations on the family sailboat when I was not at summer camp.

I have been fortunate to be married to the same responsible, kind and honest man for forty-three years. I loved the mixture of working with clients and parenting my daughter. Although my husband and I both worked full time, we were able to replicate my mother's parenting style by working a staggered work schedule. My office is the second floor of my home where I can flexibly organize both my professional work and parenting time on a weekly basis. My commute is, therefore, fifteen steps. My husband and I have had time to spend together with my daughter, dogs, cats and horses. However, even this privileged lifestyle sometimes felt hurried, stressful and overwhelming.

I observed my daughter understandably afraid to walk to the grocery store even though we live in a decent city neighborhood. She, too, has found her way to nature with horseback riding. Her talents have kept her outdoors with the discipline and responsibility inherent in the total care of two horses. We did not buy her any computer games. We monitored her use of the TV, computer and internet so that she could gain from its great research benefits but would be shielded from viruses, aggression, addiction and pornography. She often disliked school because it was large, impersonal and unable to meet her more individualized academic needs.

In forty-one years of seeing clients, I have witnessed three major societal changes.

**First, women are having babies in their late thirties instead of their early twenties in order to fit in the time to train and start a career.** As the cost of living escalates at an alarming rate, full time moms are disappearing into the workforce. Mothering is no longer regarded by society as the honorable profession it used to be. The super-mom is "in" yet the by-product is often emotional and physical exhaustion. She and her husband are often gone up to fifty-five hours a week to manage the average workweek of forty-seven hours and a half-hour commute each way with only a few weeks of vacation time. Children are farmed out to day care, after school programs, or structured activities they may or may not want. Others are lonely latch-key kids locked in their homes because it's not safe to go outside. Too many children are cooking their own microwave dinners alone. Many parents return to their house too exhausted to meet their children's needs for attention. These super-moms are working sixty hours a week to maintain job, parenting and housework. Single parents have an even harder time with a staggering amount to manage.

To counteract this problem, new Moms are taking six years off before launching their children in school and then returning to work. However, they appear to be having a hard time getting back into the workplace.

**The second change is the dramatically increasing amount of aggression and dysfunctional sexuality that children are exposed to on a daily basis through television, computer games and the internet.**

**The third change is a shift in the concept of morality.** I remember as a child, a clear sense of right and wrong. Now, morality is "anything you want to do as long as you don't get caught." If you get caught, then "Oh, well" and "whatever," is the attitude used to withhold or obliterate evidence to save one's neck. Large institutions exhibiting corporate greed, and religious organizations covering up sexual abuse seem to lead the way in defining this lack of morality. Integrity is a fading concept, thought to slow down the fast-track need to propel oneself up the corporate ladder. American children and adolescents appear to show less respect for parents, mentors and teachers than children in many other countries.

Although technology has given us tremendous advantages in communicating with each other and sharing information; life is, at the same time, harder. In the spring 2002, I was astounded to read the following statistics in a Newsletter from *Touch the Future*. Their article entitled *Home Alone America* confirms and validates my concerns over the past 30 years.

1. The teen suicide rate has increased three-fold from 1960-1990. The suicide rate rose 27 percent for girls and 71 percent for boys from 1979-1988.

2. There is a marked upswing of behavior problems in children.

3. The number of substantiated cases of sexual abuse rose from 13,000 in 1975 to 130,000 in 1986

4. Between 1965 and the late 1980s the amount of time the average American child spent interacting with a parent dropped by 43 percent from around 30 hours a week to around seventeen.

5. Most estimates of the number of latch-key kids ranges from five to fifteen million.

6. August 19, 2002 data from a national survey of *Family Growth* shows that 11 percent of girls under the age of fifteen had intercourse.

7. *Newsweek* (October 7, 2002) states three million teens are depressed.

I see children who are both lonely and very confused about what is right and wrong and who is really there to help them grow up. They present themselves to me as angry about this state of affairs. They want me to do something to help. We've had this information for nine years. What, collectively, are we doing about it?

Most of the time, I can help my clients fulfill their individual needs. However, my job becomes more difficult when my clients' wishes involve change at the societal level. Here I feel limited. I can validate wishes as they are expressed by my clients, support their good thinking, inform them that others feel the same way, and encourage them to act with integrity to make grassroots changes within their own homes, schools and communities. It is my hope that I can impact these issues in a larger way by passing them on to our society through this book.

The following wishes have been completely disguised and generalized to reflect a composite of many clients.

I am also aware that there are many ethical, responsible, conscientious, caring individuals who are "out there" in the world doing what they feel is best for themselves, others, and for society with much integrity. Many of these people are truly making a difference in a very definitive and public way. Unfortunately, the news media does not highlight these actions as much as they could. We need to hear about them for the purpose of generating good ideas, feeding compassion, and demonstrating integrity. Instead, the news tends to report problems and wrongdoing.

**My clients and I see the heart of the problem as this: We have stopped taking care of each other as a tribe used to take care of its individual members. We seem to have lost the ability to put the heart back into our interactions with each other. My clients express repeatedly that they are hungry for this lost caring. These issues regularly pop up easily within a psychotherapy hour.**

**Therefore, since we are hungry for a kind of caring we are not receiving, we have slipped into thinking that we are justified in becoming greedy. Somehow it is all right for us to grab whatever we can in terms of money and possessions, even if it means hurting others financially, as in steal-**

ing from 401Ks; laying people off, scamming the already disadvantaged, and abusing children sexually or physically. We can do this as long as we don't get caught. Often, when we do get caught, there is no punishment because those who are supposed to punish us are not responsible themselves. We have lost our trust in authority because of the lack of accountability.

Our immorality breeds rage, which is acted out with violent TV programs, aggressive computer games, road rage, and pornography that is damaging, especially to children. Those who watch pornography regularly become addicted to virtual world relationships. This activity appears to lower self-esteem and increases feelings of loneliness, isolation and worthlessness.

As a nation, we have the ability to read more deeply the meaning of our rage and loneliness. Instead of acting it out, we can use our negative reactions wisely to direct us to make changes so that we all receive more care, concern and help from each other.

In Mary Pipher's book, *The Middle of Everywhere,* she describes her interviews with some of the four-and-one-half million refugees who have come to America and lived in Lincoln, Nebraska. She describes how we help these refugees and also make them suffer needlessly. Our refugees who thought they were coming to the land of their dreams, speak of US citizens as:

> *"dismally ignorant about the rest of the world,"*
>
> *"having an enormous sense of entitlement,"*
>
> *"spoiled children in a world of hurting people."*
>
> *" take too much for granted."*
>
> *"born on third base and think that we have hit triples."*
>
> *"everyone has to be some place all of the time."*
>
> *"never slow down and talk with someone."*

My clients have articulated the following thirteen wishes. Their wishes are many. Stay with your frustration in reading them until you see the suggestions my clients and I have made at the end of this essay. Then, see which one turns your frustration into involvement.

## HOME

**WISH ONE: from a ten-year-old boy: "Dr Mac, could you help Mom and Dad about how to be parents? They fight a lot with each other about what to do with me. Mom wants to be nice to me; Dad wants to punish me. I don't think they know how to treat me. Sometimes I wonder if I should just go away 'cause if I weren't around they wouldn't fight."**

I believe that loving parenting and education are the two most important cornerstones of society. Good parenting leads to the development of responsible, honorable young adults. It's the hardest job on the planet. The only model we have is the parenting we've received. Sometimes that's not a very good model. Since it's such a formidable job, it would make sense to provide parenting education to everyone who wishes to become a parent. We must offer mandatory courses in high school and/or college that provide basic information regarding child development, attachment and what children need from their parents throughout the process of growing up. Since parents must provide a car seat before an infant can leave the hospital; can we require parents also to have completed a course in parenting and child development? We should train parents in positive, constructive ways to discipline their children.

When parents don't know what to do with their children, sometimes they "lose it." These are the times when we need instant information that must be made available through hot lines on the telephones and in chat rooms on the internet. Such support might significantly cut down on child physical and verbal abuse.

WISH TWO: from an eight-year-old girl: "I want to play with my parents. I don't get to see my Mom very much anymore. She's always working, and when she comes home, she's mostly too tired to talk with me. She still has to do the laundry and the housework. My Dad gets home late, reads the paper and goes on the internet. They're exhausted by the weekends so we don't get to do anything fun any more"

or:

"Dr Mac, you've talked to my teacher. Can you talk with my Mom's boss?"

"Why? What do you need?" I asked curiously.

"Well ... you see ... I didn't do so good the other day in the school play." Tears began to stream down her cheeks. "I let everybody down. I ran off stage instead of singing my song."

"What happened? I remember that you had practiced a lot and knew your part well."

"Well ... you see, I never should have noticed the audience because it looked like everyone had their Mom or Dad there but me. My Mom's boss wouldn't let her come to my play even when she said she would bring her work home. I got a lump in my throat that was too big to breathe. I ran off the stage so people would not see me cry. Doesn't Mom's boss know that kids need Mom or Dad to be there for a school play in the middle of the day just sometimes?"

Could employers give fifty hours a year for parents to take paid time off to do volunteer work in the classroom and be present for our children's school shows, sports, demonstrations, music performances, assemblies and plays? I have seen so many children who were devastated that their parents were unable to leave work to attend these events. Strengthening family time makes happier employees, resulting in less sick time, and thereby builds loyalty within the workplace. Everybody wins.

Most of the families within my practice have both parents working very hard earning an income to meet the expenses of living and owning a home. The average commute in Los Angeles is a half-hour each way. Many jobs allow only three weeks of vacation time. We work much longer hours and take less time off than most European nations. Our lunch hours are nonexistent or short while the European nations frequently close down business for two hours each day. Those with a longer commute to afford cheaper housing in outlying areas, and those working in the corporate world, often are away from home longer. Our latch-key kids get lonely.

My work with families has taught me that children need up to six hours of parenting time daily to be able to grow up in a psychologically healthy way.

The only way to achieve this is for this nation to return to a shorter work week, and establish a staggered work schedule. Then, parents can go to work at different times of the day so that children could be guaranteed at least one parent in the home before they leave for school in the morning and when they come home from school in the afternoon. It seems feasible to create work shifts that go from 6-2, 7-3, 8-4, 9-5, 10-6, 11-7 with staff meeting or a longer lunch hour sometime between 11 and 2. There would be wonderful additional benefits. Parents would not have to sneak so much time away from work to call or e-mail their children who are home alone.

The commute might take a shorter time since the congestion would be spread out over a ten-hour period of time daily. Road rage would likely be reduced as well.

**WISH THREE: from a teenage girl: "I don't want any more technology I just want to have some fun with my parents. I want them not to be so harried. I want to do something that makes us laugh."**

and

From a mom: "I want our society to stop teaching kids poor behavior through technology. I came home from work and discovered my son was playing a computer game in which he was being taught how to steal a car and murder a lady. Why are we making such games for our kids? How did my kid get a hold of this? How can I stop it? Will you please talk to him? This is just not Ok!"

and

Another mom: "My daughter is only seven. She was on the internet looking at a Barbie Doll site. She pressed the wrong key and suddenly porn was on the screen! How can that happen? What can I do to block this garbage from getting through to her? Do I have to take the computer away completely? I was so furious, poor kid, she thought I was angry with her! I don't know enough about computers to know what to do to protect her from porn."

and

From a father: "I just learned that my wife's nephew sexually abused a niece. He's a very talented, bright boy. At first, we couldn't imagine why he would want to do something like that. Then we learned that he's alone much of the afternoon after school and that he has been into pornography. His parents didn't know because, unfortunately, the computer was unsupervised in his room. The parents of both kids are working together with a therapist to understand what happened."

There are so many ways to develop games for children that teach them to do something useful, to do something well, to acquire mastery in something productive. Games can be created to teach children to skateboard, ride bikes on the streets, go out on a date, build things solidly, and choose the best moral decision. Why are we teaching our children to be thieves, robbers, murderers, and sexual voyeurs? We should be able, as a society, to make the virtual world a safer, richer place for our children?

Deep down, our children are fed up with technology as parental substitutes. Many of them are afraid to talk about it. Instead they're "acting out" about it. That is, they're doing something that their parents don't like in the hopes of gaining their attention. Aggressive TV shows, and computer games are ways of experiencing the anger they feel at the lack of parental time. Pornography and chat rooms, where people can pretend to be someone else, become the false virtual world companions at the end of the day. Access to pornography has predisposed some children to sexually molest another member of their extended family. They tell me that they do it because they're so lonely. They're missing the experience of playing safely in the neighborhood with other kids.

A last resort is gang activity for teens who have little or no time with family. Although the rituals that hold this group together are aggressive, destructive, and dysfunctional; there's a strong sense of belonging. It's amazing to me just how persistent the graffiti is on the LA River. Over and over, we paint it out and the gangs deliver more art the very next day. Is there not a strong message here? But it's written in a language that we can't easily understand. I believe gang members are pleading for the family time needed to raise responsible children to adulthood.

In Mary Pipher's book *The Middle of Everywhere,* a Mexican immigrant father saw his son in a T-shirt that said, "More f. . . . ing blood." The father said, "America is the best country in the world, the richest, the freest. Why do you make things like this for children?"

There are some senior citizen groups who are coming together to provide supervision, conversation, tutoring, and transportation to after school activities for children who have parents who cannot return home before six in the evening. For instance In Los Angeles, Deborah Constance, a high school dropout and a victim of childhood abuse, alcoholism, three divorces and cancer, opened **A Place Called Home** in 1993. This is an after-school residence where children can get a snack, stay away from drugs and get their homework done. By the year 2000, it has grown to 4,800 members.

I believe that we could help the super mom by offering employment that can be done at home or during the hours their children are in school. We also need to offer these mothers shared jobs where two mothers assume the responsibility for one full-time job, working out the hours that work best for their children's schedule.

## EDUCATION

**WISH FOUR:** from a middle school boy: "I hate school, do I have to go? Please help me tell Mom that I won't go anymore."

"What don't you like?"

"There are so many kids. The building looks terrible. The teachers don't really want to teach. We don't have any books, we don't get homework some of the time. The teachers don't know my name. I can get a bathroom pass at the beginning of class and no one notices that I don't come back. I want to go to a small school where someone cares about me and can help me accomplish something."

and

A generally somber, quiet, older female science teacher came for her appointment with me after her first week of teaching middle school in the fall. She had an obvious smile on her face.

I asked, "How are you? How was your first week of school?"

She responded, "It was really great. I have only 26 students in my class. I used to have 35. It makes such a difference. I have two tables in the back of the room that can now be used for experiments instead of being filled with talking students. I can pick out the trouble makers, and I have already had a chance to talk with them. I couldn't believe it, but they came up to me at the end of the day and said, 'Thank you.' I will be able to get to know each student well. I've already learned all of their names. I hope, hope, hope it stays this way. I'm going to have my best teaching year ever ... but, tell me, why did the trouble makers say 'thank you?'"

"You already know who the potential troublemakers are. They don't want to be bad. They just think they have to do that to get recognized. You told them you have already recognized them in a positive way. They want to be on your side. You've already invited them. Any kid can tell whether they have a good teacher in the first fifteen minutes of class. It sounds like they are very relieved that you are a good teacher. It's really awful to get a bad teacher for the whole year."

"I guess so ... I didn't dare believe the administrators when they told me that they wanted to have a smaller class size. It makes such a difference."

"If only all schools could do as well as yours ... a lot of kids would be happier."

Teaching, parenting, and child care are three of our most important jobs on the planet because these jobs are the most influential in creating psychologically healthy, educated, moral citizens. Home provides a foundation while school is the second cornerstone of society. Many children spend more time with their teachers and child care workers than they do with their parents. We can have a strong society if we are willing to educate our child-care workers and teachers well, provide them with colorful, attractive, well stocked schools, and then pay them **very well.**

For some reason, teaching and parenting have fallen out of favor in terms of being "honorable" professions. I've met wonderful parents and teachers within my practice who keep on doing their work despite the ongoing fact that their labors often go unrecognized. Since these are two of the hardest jobs, we need to reward those who care for children with our highest respect, encouragement, support, and excellent pay because their job is so challenging and critically important. Then we would be able to fill many of the vacancies in teaching positions within our schools and day care centers. I have seen so many students capable of achieving a high school diploma want to drop out because school was not meeting their most basic needs.

As we claim to have a shortage in funds for education, especially in California, we have cut back on the very courses and services that our children need to be able to express their emotional, physical and creative energies. These courses are physical education, where stress can be released through exercise, dance, art, poetry, creative writing, music and drama. These are the classes where emotions can be expressed and understood. Many a suicidal student has been identified, not a moment too soon, through creative writing classes.

I have supervised Master and Doctoral level interns who go into the Catholic schools and offer counseling to the students. These students who come in are self-referred (with parental approval) for counseling that is free. My interns' caseloads fill quickly with students eager to come and return every week for as long as they can. They are hungry for time to talk about their growing up and the problems within the lives of their significant others. In the public schools, most of the counseling has been eliminated, or the caseload is so huge that it's impossible for student and counselor to get to know each other well. Can we ask collectively to increase this basic service to our students?

I believe that there is only one way to make a school safe for all of our students and teachers. Metal detectors can only catch a destructive plan that has already been made. The only way we can protect everyone is to meet our children's needs in a way that lets them know clearly that they are important to us both at home, and at school; and that their educational, social and moral development are a top priority. Then we can reduce the kind of rage that is out of control enough to kill others.

I dream about richly-funded day care centers and small elementary schools within larger businesses, universities, banks and corporations so that parents could visit their children during their work day and have time with them in the car during their commute. These larger organizations have the capability of funding rich educational projects in place of giving excessive salaries and 'golden parachutes' to high level corporate leaders. Such a project would be an excellent way to attract and keep qualified employees. Families involved within the school could feel a heightened sense of community because they share both school and work. Families with children of the same age would get to know each other even though the employees may work on different floors, professional levels or departments.

**WISH FIVE: from a twenty-two-year-old woman, who came into therapy to confront shopping addiction and consequent debt: "I wish that companies with catalogues and stores would stop advertising buying with no payments for six to twelve months. Although this is allegedly presented as a gift, it really hurts us by encouraging us to spend money that we don't have, to increase our debt load, and not be accountable. This philosophy takes advantage**

of people who are still figuring out how to handle their finances. We would do better to buy only what we can pay for, avoiding completely high interest payments that I can now see are for the benefit of others."

When I request a financial form be filled out for a reduced fee, I ask each client to list their basic expenses so that we can see what income remains to pay for therapy. Often the credit card debt is very high. They didn't seem to know that spending money they do not have is not all right. Paying later makes the item they purchased cost much more.

## CORPORATIONS

**WISH SIX: from a forty-year-old man: "I wish I worked for a company that appreciated my loyalty and good work, and wanted to give loyalty back to me. I wish that I liked the CEO of my company and that he would talk with me. I deserve job security as long as I continue to do responsible work. I'm afraid all the time that my CEO will find a way to take away my job as a means of making more money for himself."**

A neighbor worked for Amtrak. The federal government had been holding back on providing the full funding needed to keep the trains in operation. Every worker was waiting to see if they would lose their jobs. One person could, if laid off, come up short one day of the thirty years needed to get her retirement benefits. Everyone was worried for her. Would this corporation truly let her leave without any benefits? A new CEO was hired. His name is David Gunn. The employees liked him so much that they wrote him a memo saying that they would work for free to keep Amtrak in operation if necessary. My neighbor's signature was number 87!

I asked him, "What was this leader doing to generate this loyalty?"

My neighbor responded without hesitation, "First of all, he's honest. Second, and equally important, he's right there with us. He rides the trains, and asks everyone questions about their work. He seeks our opinion and our help instead of talking down to us. He tells us when he thinks we're not doing as much as we could. He fired two people who were asleep on the job, and a man who swore during a public meeting. He stays in touch with us in person and in memos. When a memo didn't come for two weeks, we got worried. He responded right away. We're beginning to laugh again. The guys on the trains paid for their own tee shirts that say. 'We like to ride under the Gunn.' They show their shirts to him when he rides the trains. I guess you could say we have hope. Hey, I'll bring you some of the memos so that you can see them for yourself."

Look at what David Gunn achieved within two months through the simple act of caring for his workers. The rewards he gained far exceed the money so many corporate CEOs allegedly earn or steal. He achieved richness on the inside crafted from having a purpose in life that gave satisfaction for others and consequently himself.

Unfortunately he was asked to resign after three years. When he refused, he was fired.

## COMMUNITY

**WISH SEVEN: from a young woman: "I wish I could come to your office without seeing a single piece of trash. It would make me feel like the people around me cared. How can I ever teach my kids to be neat when the outside world is so messy and dirty?"**

and

**A young man arrived a few minutes late slightly out of breath. I asked, "Did you just finish a walk around the lake?"**

"No," he huffed. "I stopped to pick up about two hundred pieces of newspaper that were blowing away at the intersection down the street. It only took me ten minutes to pick them up after they blew all over the place. Several hundred cars must have passed by me. People were waiting near by at the bus stop. No one offered to help, smiled, or gestured to thank me. They must have noticed me because they did not run over me as I darted across the intersection several times. It was as if what I was doing was invisible. No one seemed to care about the mess or the cleanup. I felt so separate and alone. Tell me, am I crazy, or addicted to validation, or do people truly not care anymore?"

"You're not crazy in your observation, nor addicted to validation. Sometimes we have to step away from the crowd to do what we think is right, or to make a difference. I respect you for what you did. I drive through that intersection several times a day, and will appreciate that it's clean, remembering your contribution. "

It seems as if everywhere we go there is trash. We fling it out of cars, dump it on the paths where we walk in the park, drop it on the sidewalk as we walk along, or leave it three feet from a trash can in a public place. We dump large items such as sofas and old washing machines on back dirt roads. Why do we insist upon continuing to trash our own universe? It feels like such a blatant statement of anger and not caring about each other.

Some states, like Oregon, have come up with effective no litter laws. Everyone participates. In a meeting, the trash is collected in the middle of the table. Everyone helps make the environment a beautiful place.

**Would it be possible for all of us to agree to do some community service for an hour or two once a week until we have completely cleaned up our neighborhoods?** Ideally it would be at the same time each week so that we could socialize as we work together to clean up our world. Communities could designate particular areas with the mutual agreement that the area would stay clean. Our drives and walks would then feel more peaceful, decreasing road rage. We would have a vivid visual sense of supporting each other.

At this time, the only people, besides our garbage collectors and park workers, who are actively cleaning up and recycling, are the homeless to earn money for food. In Los Angeles, I see many of them working very hard with grocery carts as their only means of transportation.

**WISH EIGHT: from a client with a chronic illness: "I want all of us to have an equal amount of universal medical insurance. We would pay some and the government would pay some. I want to be able to choose my doctor and to be able to talk with him/her for more than three minutes. I'd like my doctor to care about me and have some bedside manner like doctors used to in the old days when they made house calls. I want my insurance claims to be accepted promptly rather than denied, lost or thrown away."**

and

**From a middle aged woman: "When my lab results came back saying nothing was wrong with me, I was not allowed to talk with my doctor. He's too busy and doesn't remember my case. I still had questions to ask. My insurance company doesn't care either."**

Medical insurance breeds rage among both clients and fellow clinicians. Their rage comes into the clients' psychotherapy hours. This anger is about the claims that have been "lost," the call to the company where you can't ever get through to the person you've talked to before, or being put on hold for 45 minutes listening to the same speech over and over about how wonderful the insurance company is. Then there is the call where there is some new reason why coverage can't be granted after you have filed the claims twice and talked to them eight times. Many clients simply give up while the insurance company gets away with not paying. Many qualified clinicians drop off of panels of "Mangled" (instead of managed) Health Care in total frustration, leaving too few doctors to provide the necessary service.

I think we all have to admit that we have not been able to solve the health crisis in this nation. I see clients, at reduced fees, who cannot afford to go to a doctor. Routine preventative tests are being passed up as prohibitive. People without insurance will only see a doctor when they feel really ill. Then the cost is astronomically higher and sometimes it is too late to really be of help. The death rate is much higher for people without insurance. No one should have to go without health care. The fees for medications, physician, and psychotherapy visits have all become too high. Clients without insurance in Los Angeles are going across the border to Tijuana where they can see doctors at a reasonable cost, have the time to talk with them, and can receive follow-up calls. The elderly in the northern part of the country are taking bus trips to Canada to get prescriptions filled at a more reasonable price. The AARP Bulletin, September 2002, reported that 12-14 per cent of elderly with insurance and 25-31 percent without insurance cannot afford medicines for congestive heart failure, diabetes, and high blood pressure.

With Managed Care Companies trying to manage us out of existence, doctors have lost sight of the notion that our work is to do **what is best for the client.** We have been forced into a position of looking at our interactions with clients from the vantage point of "What can I get out of this for me?" This is not a successful way to approach client care.

Other countries are doing a better job with health care.

We must take a closer look at what they are doing and see if we can set up a new system that provides equal basic insurance coverage for all of us so that we can get on with the business of providing quality care. If other countries can do it, we can too.

**WISH NINE: From a frustrated art teacher: "I wish that a portion of the money that goes into defense could be made available to fund the work of qualified creative artists. We need to provide funding for both children and adults. Artists speak louder than guns. We are in the unique position of having to do our creative work before we might get paid. Artists are in need of outside funding just to pay our most basic expenses while we work. Artists (musicians, poets, actors, dancers, painters, sculptors, authors, potters, gardeners, script writers) tell us what is beautiful, and what changes need to be made. Artists hear the pulse of the nation and pass it back to each one of us. We cannot afford to go without their guidance."**

I have worked with many artists over the years. Most of them worry about being able to pay for their basic expenses. This kind of worry can keep the creative process from unfolding properly. The unstable income artists make erodes a confident self-esteem needed to perform or realize their art. Many of them have reduced this worry, by having a second job that pays the rent, can be done during odd hours, may take little intelligence, keeps them in contact with people, and/or uses their creativity and strength in a different way. This important wish has been elaborated in Section IV, Chapter 41 – "Artists and Society" and Chapter 47 – "It Is Time to Give Artists a Chance to Change the World."

**WISH TEN: From a single mom: "I wish I could afford to go out to dinner more often. As a single parent, I'm often tired when I come home from work. I don't want my children to eat fast food. When I do go out, I find**

that the food is too expensive for me to afford and there is too much food on my plate. The size of the helping is more than I serve my family of three for dinner. I wish that I could order and pay less for a half or even a quarter portion. Then I could afford it and my children could select a meal of their choice to eat."

Countless numbers of research studies and news photographs demonstrate that a staggering number of Americans are overweight and obese. Our children are gaining weight at an alarming rate and exercising too little. Our latch-key kids who have to stay inside until parents return home, are spending their time on the internet and playing computer games. Only their fingers get exercise.

Our restaurants are setting a poor example by presenting a plate that has too much food. Often, I will bring home extra food from a restaurant meal enough for two additional lunches. Restaurants could offer half portions with a simple sticker added to any present menu. Our fast food industry is insufficiently interested in serving food that is conducive to losing weight or unclogging our arteries. Fast food restaurants have even made their way into hospitals and schools. We can now make more informed choices since restaurants are required to list ingredients and the total number of calories for each meal. I was staggered to discover that so many meals are over 1500 calories.

**WISH ELEVEN: From an elderly client.**" My husband has died and my children have relocated to faraway parts of the country. They're too busy with their own children and their work. I need to find a place to live that has people my age and emergency medical care, should I need it. I'm afraid that there are not enough affordable planned community retirement facilities for all of us who are growing older. We need retirement communities with well developed resources to connect us with nature, pets, and our communities instead of being shut away to die. I want an organized program where I can work with children who do not have grandparents nearby."

I believe that our elderly deserve our best and kindest care, free from abuse, neglect and with adequate insured medical care. Many of our elderly have a rich wisdom and expertise to share with the rest of our culture. They have the time to be altruistic, volunteer and support community projects. They can be a generous resource for our children when we take care of them well.

To nourish constricted lives, our Board and Care Homes for the elderly need to have a rich array of plants, visiting cats and dogs, fish tanks, and rich landscaping that can be viewed from inside windows.

WISH TWELVE: From an eight year old boy: "Dr Mac, I gave my allowance to a homeless person today. My Mom said that I shouldn't because he will probably spend it on cigarettes or booze."

"How much is your allowance?"

"Two dollars."

"Was there a special reason you decided to give it to him today?"

"Yes, it's raining. I don't want him to be wet. He doesn't have the money to rent an apartment, but he could go to the thrift store next door and buy a used umbrella. Maybe his dog could fit underneath it too."

"I see your point. I really appreciate your kind thoughts towards this person. Have you seen him before?"

"Oh yes, we see him often. Sometimes he's outside of the grocery store and I bring him a treat for his dog. He always says 'Thank you.' He's very shy. He doesn't have shoes, only sandals, but I don't have enough money to buy them for him. I'm not scared of him. Kids and grownups and dogs should be able to have a home"

"You do a lot of sensible thinking."

Our homeless are a constant source of pain for all of us as they stand on exits to freeways and street corners asking for help. Some of them are truly homeless and others are manipulating us to take an easy buck. Homelessness increased when we dumped psychiatric patients out of our Mental Institutions. We have become accustomed to seeing our homeless instead of providing the resources to help them out. Their requirements for shelter are simple and many often have a useful skill to offer society in return.

**WISH THIRTEEN: From an outraged daughter of an elderly parent: "We have to stop ripping each other off. We are setting a terrible example for the next generation. I refuse to do it. I feel very discouraged about stopping it. Am I paranoid or something, or do I see it the way it really is?"**

National Public Radio reported a company that was making calls to the elderly to protect them from scams. The company itself was a scam!

A test reported in the *Journal of the American Nutritional Association* showed that only 16 percent of alternative medicine companies making medications for arthritis actually delivered the medicine they claimed on the label.

Our economy has declined in part because equity loans are being advertised and sold to homeowners who are not able to afford them so that the company can earn broker's fees, despite later foreclosures.

As I was making the final corrections to this manuscript, a company that wanted me to purchase their virus control software kept interrupting my work. The virus warning notice they put on my screen was a scam.

The ultimate example of our rage is terrorism. This appears to be a blind anger acted out on randomly selected innocent strangers. Terrorism is the end result of our global community that sanctions hurting members of our own tribe. Our wars now extend way beyond the battlefield. We are all soldiers with no training on how to fight back. As a global community, we are perched on the edge of uncertainty as we wonder what to do with terrorism. We are mesmerized by destructive leaders who manage to side-step our every attempt to invite them to deal with the rest of the world squarely.

We have responded to terrorism with banners and flags that say 'United We Stand." We, as citizens, have bought the flags and put on the tee shirts but, in my opinion, have taken little action. We can take the opportunity to do so much more than we have done. With the balance between giving and taking lopsided, we worry about what we might not have and have lost sight of what we can generate by giving.

The gap widens between those who have and those who don't. More health clinics are closing, and soup kitchen lines are much longer. During this recession, twenty percent of Californians are receiving some form of welfare. The price of housing is finally beginning to drop. The only way we can close the gap is for the "haves" to give much more to the "have nots." We can rent an apartment to a tenant at less than the going rate, and offer some of our services pro bono or at lower cost. In the process we forge new relationships of value. As we help each other, we will be more able to utilize laughter, calm, the beauty of nature, caring for people, consistent routines, music, touch, dancing, food and prayer as a means to support growth.

My clients are representatives of the general population. They are people who have taken the chance with me to figure out what they truly believe and to say it without hesitation. I respect the wishes they have collectively stated over and over again. I feel privileged to share these wishes with anyone who wants to join the fight to make this society a more equitable and loving place. Any collective progress makes it more possible for us to achieve a negotiated settlement in place of aggression.

It doesn't take a congressional hearing or even any funding for ALL of us to :

- ❀ slow down

- ❀ talk within your workplace about cutting back on work hours

- ❀ treat each other well

- ❀ eat smaller portions at restaurants

- ❀ pick up the trash

- ❀ reinstate loyalty and integrity in the workplace

- ❀ limit aggressive and pornographic entertainment available to children

- ❀ have one day a week when all entertainment technology is turned off for family time

- ❀ make sure to have a meal together daily as a family without the television on

- ❀ return parent time to our children

- ❀ provide professional services on a sliding scale

- ❀ reach out to an artist

- ❀ engage the expertise of an elderly person

It only takes belief. If, at a grass roots level, we speak our minds loudly enough, we increase the chances that we can acquire both governmental and corporate funding and expertise to:

- ❀ make a school or a daycare center on one floor of a

corporate building by reducing excessive salaries and bonuses

❁ give our homeless persons shelter at night and activity in the daytime

❁ build affordable, enriching retirement communities with medical care and community service opportunities on site

❁ create equal medical insurance for every American child to adult with an emphasis on preventative care

❁ rebuild attractive schools with current books and technology with smaller class sizes and higher salaries for teachers

❁ provide education in parenting for all students in high school and college

❁ allow parents to take paid time off to volunteer and witness their children activities at school and in the community

Ralph Waldo Emerson advises, "Do not go where the path leads. Go instead where there is no path and leave a trail."

Each one of these wishes contains something we, as individuals, can contribute to our society that is nurturing for all of us. Are we ready to begin? Change will take all of us, not just some of us.

I ask you, myself and the ones I love, and you, and you. Which wish do you want to come alive? What are you willing to do? How many wishes can we make come true?

# VIII

## CONCLUSION

# 63

# JAPAN ON MARCH 11, 2011

In my lifetime, I have never heard of a tragedy of such magnitude. The 9.0 earthquake and generated tsunami rattled over the land treating people, animals, nature, cars, homes and boats as toy match box items to be flung about until completely destroyed. Well over 10,000 dead, and 190,000 people living in temporary shelters three weeks later. There were aftershocks every day for weeks deepening the PTSD response for everyone. People were working in the nuclear reactors absorbing radiation, giving their lives to save countless others. They were a population of survivors showing unbelievable restraint as they stayed away from looting and vandalizing what little was left. Children are without parents, pets and grandparents; parents are without children and extended family. Will the radiation contamination cause cancer for years to come in those that survived? And … how about the people in Japan who are old enough to have lived through Hiroshima in the beginning of their lives, and this disaster towards the end of a lifetime. Is it possible to integrate both devastations?

How could this happen? I don't know what other people felt. I personally experienced it as the universe screaming at humanity. "Damn you. You have to do better, with everything … your deficits, your integrity, your morality, your obesity, your care of the planet, your wars, your settling for incompetence, and your greediness. If you don't improve, this is just a little example, believe me, of what I can do to take you off the planet completely. Look up and listen, feel, then act."

Those of us in Los Angeles, 5,000 miles away across the ocean, took note that we live in a part of the world where a **similar** earthquake is way overdo. And ... we have a nuclear power plant 60 miles away that we **know** is not working properly.

How do we handle such a reality? What can we do to care for the people left in Japan? What can we learn from this experience to care for everyone on the planet? How can we come together? What will happen if we don't? Is it merely accidental that we are responding to this tragedy by turning the bloody violence within Libya into a new war involving many nations?

My heart hurts daily for those who are alive in Japan and have lost their loved ones, homes, possessions, assets, and jobs within one short horrible few moments. There must be more we can all do besides give money to the Red Cross. However, we don't share a common language and every country, and many individual families in the world appear to be struggling with a deficit.

My clients have been addressing these questions. We have added one more. **What would you do with your life if you could know that a devastating earthquake and tsunami would take you out four years from now?**

Here are some of the concerns that came up and were addressed in the process of answering this one big question:

❖ Would I give up now?

❖ How has my life been?

❖ Do I experience gratitude about what I have?

❀ What would I change if I could do my life over?

❀ What would I want to accomplish within the next four years?

❀ How big are my present problems in the larger scheme of events?

❀ Have I done anything wrong for which I still need to make amends?

❀ Do I treat my significant relationships well?

❀ Do I have aggressive/competitive behaviors I need to curtail?

❀ Do I take charge of holding up my own self-esteem, or expect others to do it for me?

❀ Am I bored? If so, what can I do to change it?

❀ How would I handle an earthquake or tsunami if I was indulging in my addiction (alcohol, drugs). Would I be able to take care of myself/ or my family? Am I prepared?

❀ Do I bother to notice how beautiful the universe is in a way that allows me to reach out to appreciation, new insights and goals?

❀ Do I help others less fortunate enough with generosity, positive verbal support, donations and/or volunteer work?

❀ How can I directly contribute to leaving a positive imprint on the planet before I die?

If everyone could answer these questions in a positive way, what would happen to the changes needed on this planet? One client, who has power to share energy with others, said, "If everyone on the planet could put aside our differences, our separateness and our oppositions, stop what they are doing and hold hands together for the same ten minutes, the vibrational energy generated would do much to heal the damage."

If we can't do that, I still believe that each and every individual's change in a positive way anywhere does register and make a difference. Many people out there are already doing their job. They know it gives meaning and richness to life.

Take a deep breath. I dare you not to miss this opportunity. What will you personally offer? Will the universe notice and offer us a less destructive more peaceful world? Can we bother to find out?

# 64

# WHEN PAIN FROM THE PAST BECOMES A STRENGTH

Clients first come into my office to confront a painful circumstance from the past or a knockdown in the present. They can feel hit, hurt, demeaned, rejected, angry, guilty, embarrassed, confused, anxious, panicky, lost and/or ashamed. Their misconceptions fuel these feelings, leaving a sense of discouragement and failure. They may even wonder if they should kill themselves. Their initial hours are often heavy ones.

As our work progresses together, clarification of the unresolved issues, and related misconceptions leads to taking charge of life again in a meaningful way. Each hour builds hope.

I have the highest respect for the work each client undertakes. Out of the pain, unfolds, like a miracle,

- ❀ a foundation of strength,
- ❀ a new character that understands both past and future survival,
- ❀ a new known purpose in how to lead life,
- ❀ and a sense of confidence, security, and protection about how to handle inevitable future knockdowns.

They sometimes enter bent over, and leave my office at the end of their last hour with their head held high. When they have "got it," they earn the respect from others because they have a depth of character that recognizes and articulates compassion for others' adversity.

# 65

# SO HOW DO ALL THESE THOUGHTS ADD UP ANYWAY?

Most clients **do** go on to lead a successful life. It is an awesome responsibility and a privilege to be a human being instead of a mosquito or slug. Our bodies are the most beautiful gift we will ever be given.

Deepak Chopra in *The Seven Spiritual Laws of Success* claims: *"A single cell in the human body is doing about six trillion things per second, and it has to know what every other cell is doing at the same time." p.71 "The internal dialogue of every cell in the human body is, 'How can I help?'"(p.108)*

Therefore, it makes ultimate sense to take exquisite care of your mental and physical being regardless of what may have happened to you in the past. If you do so, as a result of reading each chapter, you will inevitably be able to:

1. Achieve a reasonable balance of working, loving, playing, resting and eating.

2. Read signals from your body when medical care may be needed. Check it out promptly. Use regular checkups and preventative care.

3. Exercise and stretch daily to release stress, oxygenate your brain, generate new ideas, burn calories to maintain an ideal weight, and remain limber.

4. Spend time alone in nature with stillness and meditation to discover what you desire and release your goals into the universe.

5. Eat cave man food (fruits, "veggies," nuts, grains and fish), not heavily processed junk food.

6. Read your negative and positive feelings quickly, and take constructive action if a correction needs to be made.

7. Find a way to talk through any unresolved issues with a therapist or knowledgeable supportive significant other for the purpose of integrating/ resolving any hidden parts of yourself, in place of being condemned to repeat what you do not understand.

8. Resolve the past enough to let it go to "back burner" while you make plans for the future that compensate for whatever you didn't receive.

9. Love and respect you both for yourself, and to present a model of how you want others to treat you.

10. Believe that you deserve to give and receive intimacy.

11. Allow yourself time with powerful supportive mentors. They will become a memory you can consult with forever.

12. Never put yourself down because it only weakens you. Instead, recognize what you don't like and change it. Then, forgive yourself and let it go.

13. Acknowledge your strengths and let them work for you in a way that gives you meaning, pleasure, and "makes a difference" for the planet and/or those who inhabit earth.

14. Forever fight/ignore any fear that whatever goal you want to reach won't happen. Substitute persistence in place of worry and avoidance.

15. Be honest with yourself and others.

16. Never purposefully plan to hurt anyone else blatantly physically, emotionally or financially.

17. Apologize or make amends when you hurt someone unintentionally or intentionally.

18. Share any good fortune. By giving generously, you achieve richness on the inside which is more powerful and fulfilling than extraordinary richness on the outside.

19. Know that we are not intelligent enough to understand all of the ways of the universe. There never has been, nor will there be a duplicate of you. What happens to you in your unique life story may not make sense for a long time.

20. Expect knockdowns, loss and pain as a necessary and expected part of life instead of demeaning yourself. Use adversities as opportunities to grow, learn new coping and/ or retrieve forgotten dreams.

21. Remember that life does not go on forever. Don't deny your unknown time of death. Use every day as a gift.

22. Take time to realize what you are thankful for each day.

23. Be alert regarding danger, (such as fires, floods, earthquakes, tornadoes, drunk drivers, scams) but not preoccupied by it. Instead, make sensible survival plans.

24. Set reasonable boundaries; instead of trying to control others.

25. Balance use of technology with time in nature. Technology gives us contact with friends and information, while nature shows us survival, growth, and renewal.

26. Get a pet. If you give him/her a secure life, s/he will become a most faithful and loving companion.

27. Eat dark chocolate, sunflower seeds, walnuts, and ginger as potent natural anti-depressants.

28. Never expect any addiction to make you happy. Generate happiness from within yourself by doing these twenty eight actions.

Take a look. How many of these are you already doing? What changes need to be made? Remember, no one will ever know you as well as you do. Therefore, you are the most qualified to take care of you and you will do the best job. As you set the example of taking care of you well, good people will decide it is worth their while to lend you a helping hand, and the bad guys are more likely to pass you by as too great a risk. Also, when you take care of yourself well, you will then have more to give to others effectively.

Don't just read this list and skip reading the book. The details within the text are important to making changes happen. We all know how we are supposed to behave, from church services, parents and teachers, but we often struggle with the knowledge, reasons, and means to do it.

Always remember that having a psychologically "painful" or a "bad" day is often also a very "special" day because that is when feelings, insights, and depth of learning creates richness inside and guides you onwards in a new way.

After you have absorbed this book, and what is already inside of you to recall, you may just end up feeling "happy," "peaceful" or "content." These are some of the many meaningful messages from the mind, that say that life is, indeed, going well.

If everyone everywhere were privileged to take these twenty-eight actions perhaps we would get much closer to what religion likes to call "heaven." here on this planet.

Finally, we can all throw in a handsome dose of GOOD LUCK!

# 66

# MY PERSONAL "MAKING A DIFFERENCE"

Two final questions remain: What do all of these essays have to say in terms of a central theme? How do I activate the way in which I have chosen, or been assigned the task by the universe, of making a meaningful difference during the time that I have been on this planet?

All of these essays have the **central theme of understanding and "being" in a caring way.** My life's work is invisible in that it takes place in the privacy of my office in a confidentiality that prohibits sharing with others. Clients stay as long as they feel a need and then say "goodbye," often never to return. Sometimes, they come back for additional help, call, or send a card, but most often, I don't get to see what happens to the rest of their lives. I grieve each loss.

We are social beings and we all crave compassionate giving, love, validation, honesty, and constructive confrontation with each other. I believe that we slip into greed, abuse, power struggles, materialism, crime, drugs, porn, and scams only when we don't believe we deserve, or give up on acquiring what we truly need to flourish.

I can only hope that each client and I have been able to meet together in a truly productive way that will last for the rest of their lifetime. Our goal is to see each individual's suffering and to transform it into compassion, peace, laughter, even some joy, in an assertive meaningful way to go on with the rest of life. In the process, we have moved away from indulging in despair alone. We have learned that anger, hate, retaliation, or passive aggressive behavior never defeats the anger and hate that has personally visited us, and resides on this planet. We have let go of resentment, straightened out misconceptions, and replaced both with as much forgiveness as possible.

Even though there will always be challenges and difficulties that lie ahead, we can move towards the inherent goodness that still lies behind each struggle with a stolid intelligence, courage, persistence, and stability. Each client has learned from our relationship that compassionate listening reduces suffering for both themselves, loved ones, friends and professional relationships. From this vantage point they can come to others in peace, building a sense of safety, confidence and caring.

The hours that I have spent with brave clients struggling with their difficult lives and in writing this book have brought to me a richness that is greater than any money I've earned or possessions I've acquired. My reduced-fee clients often present the most enlightening hours because the struggles they have been through have left them rich on the inside. I've watched many clients go on to make their own unique difference in an effective and compassionate way.

I listen carefully to what I say to clients, making sure that I follow my own remarks, remembering to act in a kindly way that strengthens both myself and others. Too often, I still slip and fall, but get back up to try again. However, I pray that the work and writing I have done, in the final analysis, has been strong enough to contribute to making this planet survive and become a better place for us all of us to live.

For those of you who cannot or have chosen not to do psychotherapy, I hope that the dialogues, stories and essays you have read will help you in finding and reaching your own unique goals.

# BIBLIOGRAPHY

## BOOKS THAT HAVE INFLUENCED THE WRITING OF *DEFINING MOMENTS*

Anonymous. *Through the Eyes of a Child: Parenting in the 21st Century*. New York: Popular Publishing Company. 2002.

Averill, James and Nunley, Elma. *Voyages of the Heart: Living an Emotionally Creative Life*. New York: The Free Press. 1992.

Bolles, Richard. *The Job-Hunter's Survival Guide: How to Find Hope and Rewarding Work Even When "There Are No Jobs."* Berkeley: Ten Speed Press. 2009.

Cameron, Julie. *The Artist's Way*. New York: Jeremy Tarcher/ Putnam. 2002.

Cameron, Julie. *Walking in this World: The Practical Art of Creativity*. New York: Jeremy Tarcher/Putnam. 2002.

Chopra, Deepak. *The Seven Spiritual Laws of Success: A Practical Guide to the Fulfillment of Your Dreams*. San Rafael, Ca.: Amber-Allen Publishing and New World Library. 1994.

Clinton, Bill. *Giving: How Each of Us Can Change the World*. New York: Alfred A. Knopf. 2007.

Clinton, Hillary Rodham. *It Takes a Village: And Other Lessons Children Teach Us*. New York: Simon and Schuster. 1996.

Colby, Anne, and Damon, William. *Some Do Care*. New York: Free Press. 1992.

Crenshaw, David. *Bereavement: Counseling the Grieving Throughout the Life Cycle*. New York: Continuum Publishing Company. 1990.

Edelman, Marian Wright. *The Measure of Our Success. A Letter to My Children and Yours*. Boston: Beacon Press. 1992.

Fassel, Diane. *Working Ourselves to Death; The High Cost of Workalcoholism and the Rewards of Recovery*. San Francisco: Harper. 1990.

Foster, Rose Marie; Moskowitz, Michael; Javier, Rafael. *Reaching Across Boundaries of Culture and Class: Widening the Scope of Psychotherapy*. Northvale, New Jersey: Jason Aronson. 1996.

Fitzgerald, Helen. *The Mourning Handbook*. New York: Simon and Schuster. 1994.

Gladwell, Malcolm. *Outliers: The Story of Success*. New York: Little Brown and Company. 2008.

Glasser, Howard, and Easley, Jennifer. *Transforming the Difficult Child*. Tucson, AZ: The Center for Difficult Child Publications. 1998.

Goleman, Daniel. *Social Intelligence: The New Science of Human Relationships*. New York: Bantum Books. 2006.

Goleman, Daniel. *Emotional Intelligence: Why It Can Matter More Than IQ*. New York: Bantum. 1995.

Hawkins, David. *Power Vs. Force: The Hidden Determinants of Human Behavior*. Carlsbad, CA: Hay House Inc. 2002.

Hill, Napolean. *Think and Grow Rich*. Hollywood: Melvin Powers Wilshire Book Company. 1966.

Hyatt, Carole. *Shifting Gears. How To Master Career Change and Find the Work that's Right For You*. New York: Simon and Schuster. 1990.

Katie, Byron with Mitchell, Stephen. *A Thousand Names for Joy. Living in Harmony with the Way Things Are*. New York: Harmony Books. 2007.

Kozol, Jonathan. *Amazing Grace: The Lives of Children and the Conscience of a Nation*. New York: Crown Publishers Inc. 1995.

James, John, and Cherry, Frank. *The Grief Recovey Book: A Step-by-Step Program for Moving Beyond Loss*. New York: Harper and Row. 1988.

Loab, Paul. *The Impossible will Take a Little While*. New York: Basic Books. 2004.

Myss, Caroline. *Invisible Acts of Power: Personal Choices That Create Miracles*. New York: Free Press. 2004.

Pipher, Mary. *The Middle of Everywhere: The World's Refugees Come to Our Town*. New York: Harcourt, Inc. 2002.

Pipher, Mary. *Another Country*. New York: Riverhead Press. 1999.

Pipher, Mary. *The Shelter of Each Other: Rebuilding our Families*. New York: Ballantine Books. 1996.

Remen, Rachael Naomi. My *Grandfather's Blessings: Stories of Strength, Refuge and Belonging*. New York: Riverhead Books. 2000.

Remen, Rachael Naomi. *Kitchen Table Wisdom*. New York: Riverhead Books. 1996.

Shekerjian, Denise. *Uncommon Genius: Tracing the Creative Impulse with Forty Winners of the McArthur Award*. New York: Viking. 1990.

Starhawk. *The Fifth Sacred Thing*. New York: Bantum Press. 1993.

Tzu, Sun. *The Art of War.* New York: Oxford University Press

Weiss, Robert. *Staying the Course; The Emotional and Social Lives of Men Who Do Well at Work*. New York: The Free Press. 1990.

# INDEX

## A

AARP Bulletin 289
ACA (Adult Children of Alcholics) 59
Actions to fight depression naturally 55 - 58
Acts of kindness 216
Addict 39
Addiction 36
  genes 40
A Dog's Purpose (poem) 128
Adoptees
  adult 239 - 242
  contradiction 243
  understanding their loss of family 237
Adult children of alcoholics 59
Affair
  definition 150
Affairs
  statistics 150
  the backside of 149
Altruistic Work Personality 74, 75, 76
Animal Rescue 12
Anxiety attack 47
  and medication 48
  can be helpful 221
Approval 67
  from others 26
Artist Personality 77
Artists
  abilities 207
  and society 181
  encouragement or lack of encouragement 181
  self-esteem 183
  serving in United States Cabinet positions 208

two conditions that contribute to becoming successful 184
Asperger's Syndrome 248
Attention Deficit Disorder (ADD) 248
Attention Deficit Hyperactive Disorder (ADHD) 248
Attraction
  of mutual strengths 172
  three kinds of 171
Autism 248
Autistic children 191

## B

Becoming well 260
Behavior problems in children marked upswing of 273
Bell, city of
  city managers, arrested 201
Benefiting from the wrongs done to you 144
Big Sunday
  volunteers 214
Bipolar depression 100
Birth 139
  and war 139
  the man's role in helping the woman 140
  trauma 248
Blogging 73
Bolles, Richard
  *The Job Hunter's Survival Guide: How to Find Hope and Rewarding Work Even When There Are No Jobs* 204
Boston Conservatory 184, 186
Brooks, Roberts
  *Children with Attention Deficit/ Hyperactivity Disorder or Learning Difficulties:*

*Strategies for Building
Motivation, Self-Esteem, Hope
and Resilience*  232, 233
Bullies, defeating them  227

## C

Calcium and sleep  33
Cameron, Julia
*Walking in this World: The
Practical Art of Creativity*
144, 185
Cancer  248
Capitalism  204
Career
drugs  37, 39
Care-taking role  60
Cats in the psychotherapy process
111 - 115
Cave man  155 - 158
CEOs and CFOs of large
corporations  197
Chelsey  125
Childbirth (*Also see* Birth)  140
Children
three categories of  232, 249
with learning disabilities
success attributes of  236
*Children with Learning Disability
Grow Up: Results of a Twenty Year
Longitudinal Study*  236
Children's wisdom  50, 51
Chi or universal energy  189
Chopra, Deepak
*The Seven Spiritual Laws of Success:
A Practical Guide to the
Fulfillment of Your Dreams*
138, 184, 193, 305
Churchill, Winston (quote)  186
Circadian rhythm  33
Clients
speak out  267
two parts of  50

Clinton, Bill  137
*Giving, How Each One of Us Can
Change the World*  201, 202
Commitment
to a child with special needs  252
Community service  suggestions
287
Communicate
ways to  70 - 73
Companies
wish six  285
wish five  284
Compassion  204, 205, 215
Compassionate
giving  309
listening  310
Computer games created to teach
children to do something useful
wish three  279
Conflict of interest
politians  206
Confrontation
the highest form of support  87
constructive  309
Connect with nature, pets, and our
communities
wish eleven  292
Conversation
how to get one going at home
83
with a deceased loved one  96
Creative Impulse  207
Creativity  24, 184
and drugs  36, 37, 40
Crisis
as an opportunity  146 - 148

## D

Deer, wounded  7
Defining Moments
for children  219

from nature 5, 255
in taking care of yourself 19
with furry associates 107 - 116
with handling life 131
Democracy 204
Department of Child and Family
Protective Services 164, 169
Depletion blooms 262
Depression
and unemployment 211
fighting it the natural way 55 -
58
Despair 99
Diabetes 248
*Diary of Anne Frank, The* 73
Difficult Child 233
their three basic needs 233
Dogs in the psychotherapy process
117 - 120, 124 - 129
Down's Syndrome 248
Dramatic increase in the amount
of aggression and dysfunctional
sexuality 272
Drugs 36
false sense of security 38
loss of career opportunities 39
poor judgment 41
Ducks, abandoned 10

E

Earthquake 300
Easy Child 232
Education improvement
wish four 283
Ego-based power 193
Emerson, Ralph Waldo 296
Emotions
translating into reasonable
constructive language 44
Empathy
and children with learning
disabilities 234

Enron scandal 197
Exercise
fight depression 55
reduce stress 57
Extraordinary parenting 249

F

FaceBook 70
Family growth (survey data) 273
Family-oriented company 198
Feelings, your 43
looking at and describing them
143
Flower, growing through a cactus
16
Foods that contribute to lifting
depression 55 - 58
Forgiveness 142
Four actions to help you when you
feel you are losing control 44 -
46
Four basic types of individuals
in the work force 74
Freud, Sigmund 162
Friendships 177 - 180

G

Gap between haves and have nots
widens 294
Gates, Bill and Melinda 137
Genetic addiction genes 248
Geneva Convention 188
Gentleness 88
Givers 59
Global issues threaten our planet
202
Goldberg, R.
*Children with Learning Disability
Grow Up: Results of a Twenty
Year Longitudinal Study*
236
Golden parachutes 207
Greed 191, 204

when it takes away your job
133 - 136
Grief support group 95
Grieving 89
and the elderly 94
Guantanamo Bay detainees 188

## H

Happiness 22
Health food stores 33
Health, the miracle of
within each of us 265
Heather 114, 115, 116, 117, 122,
127
Help yourself 63
Herman, K.
*Children with Learning Disability
Grow Up: Results of a
Twenty Year Longitudinal
Study* 236
Higgins, E.
*Children with Learning Disability
Grow Up: Results of a
Twenty Year Longitudinal
Study* 236
Highly Sensitive Person (HSP)
100, 183, 248
Hill, Naposeon
*Think and Grow Rich* 147
Hiroshima 299
History Channel 141
Honesty 309
Honeymoon period 176
Hurricanes Hanna and Ike 146
Hysterical Personality 162

## I

Immorality breeds rage 275
Independent Psychotherapy
Network 104
Insight 17
Integration process
of child self and adult self 51

Integrity 191, 205
maintain self esteem and peace
of mind 135
Introject 31, 95, 98
definition 28

## J

Japan
March 11, 2011 299
Jefferson Airplane 174
Job-job 80, 185
Journal of the American
Nutritional Association 293

## K

Kendall 114, 115, 237, 238, 241
Klonopin 48

## L

Lack of sleep 32
Lamaze 139
Latch-key kids 273
Learning Difficulty (LD) 248
Lehman Brothers 146
Letting go, in grieving 93
Life, Begins After Work
Personality 76
Life is not fair 64
Life's Two Most Important and
Privileged Questions 78
Long-term monogamous love
requirements for both husband
and wife 175
Los Angeles Humane Society
award to dog 115
Los Angeles River 10, 13, 56
*Los Angeles Times* 207
Love 309
when it means "please go away"
239, 241
Luke 125, 126, 127

# M

MacArthur Foundation 208
  award 207
Magnetic attraction 172
Major societal changes 271 - 272
Making a difference 309
Managed Care Companies 289
Marijuana 36
Master level or Doctoral degree
  202
Materialistic Work Personality 75,
  76
Meaning in life 9
Melatonin, and sleep 33
Memorial 91
Mental health clinic
  suicide 99
Metro link-Freight train crash in
  Los Angeles 146
Middleperson 202
  between low income and the
    wealthy 200
Mitro Valve Prolapse 248
Modern technology
  and communicating 70
Money put to better use
  wish nine 290
Morford, Mark
  *San Francisco Gate Columnist* 25
Mutual strengths attraction 172
MySpace 70
Myss, Caroline
  *Invisible Acts of Power: Personal
    Choices that Create Miracles* 15

# N

Nanna 121
National Public Radio 293
Native Americans 192
Natural medication from a holistic
  doctor 100
Needs

fear of expressing 60
Negative feelings 39
  trust them 44
*Newsweek* 273
Nicholas 111, 112, 113, 114, 115,
  119, 120, 122

# O

Obsessive Compulsive Disorder
  (OCD) 248
Opportunities to give to others 15
Order food at a restaurant and pay
  less for smaller portions
  wish ten 291
Over-protective parents 225

# P

Pain
  when it becomes a strength 303
Parenting 226
  extraordinary 249
  wish one 276
Parents
  exceptional 224
Paulnack, Karl (pianist) 184, 186
Peace Corps 65
Perfection
  impossible 27
Perpetrators of sexual abuse
  and low self-esteem 167
Pets, to reduce depression 57
Pet Assisted Therapy 109
Physical attraction 171
Pipher, Mary
  *The Middle of Everywhere* 275,
    280
  *Writing to Change the World* 22
Poor judgment
  and drugs 41
Post Traumatic Stress Disorder
  141
Pot 37

Power struggle
  between parent and child  225
Pregnancy  140, 158
President  213
  of the United States  211
Projects, to help the unemployed
  211
Provide the resources to help the
  homeless
  wish twelve  293
Psychiatric medication  100
Psychic pain  56
Psychology Examining Committee
  and Pet Assisted Therapy  109
Psychotherapist
  finding the right one  101
    office procedures  103
    professional background  103
    recommendations as to
      options  103
    rules of confidentiality  103
  underlying philosophy of this
    21
Psychotherapy  28
  a journey  142
  children in  226
  process  269
  session, successful  30
  when you have been hurt  142
Psychotherapy Network  165
*Psychotherapy Networker*
  article by Bessel Van Der Kolk
    "In the Eye of the Storm"
    160
PTSD (Post Traumatic Stress
  Disorder)  299

R

Rachael  127
Rage  275
Rascals  121, 122, 123, 127
Raskind, M.

*Children with Learning Disability
Grow Up: Results of a
Twenty Year Longitudinal
Study*  236
Reading, and sleep  34
Recession of 2008-2011  204
Red Cross  300
  shelters  147
Reduced fee  105
  don't be afraid to ask for  104
Reduced-fee clients  310
Relationships  205
Religion  23
Religious wars
  death toll from  205
Relinquishment  246
  and the adoptee  243
Report Card Children  224 - 226
Repressed memories  143
Resolve  257
Results of taking care of your
  mental and physical being  305
  - 308
Retaliation never really works  64
Retaliation vs. confrontation  169
Rich and the poor
  widening gap between  200,
    204, 294
Right and wrong  191
  whatever happened to it  190
Ripple effect  145
Romantic attraction
  three kinds  171 - 173
Romantic love
  what makes it last  174

S

Santa Ana winds  146
Sarton, May
  quote  144
Sasha  117, 118, 119, 124
Scams, perpetrated on elderly  293

Second adolescence 97
Second adulthood 97
Selassie, Haile (quote) 195
Self
  integrating lost parts of 50 - 54
Self-esteem 88
  building 86
  struggle for 66
Self power 193
Self-worth
  feeling of 68
Sense of loyalty within a company
  198
Serotonin
  lack of 100
Services to the poor and elderly
  207
Sexual abuse
  from family 161
  family and societal response to
    victim 163
  victim response 162
  number of cases rose 273
  religious leaders 205
  the therapist's responsibilities to
    the victim 164
Sexual abuser
  punish or help 166
Sexual abuse victims
  protecting 160
  why they are easy to dismiss or
    abuse again 160
Sexual identity 226
Sexual relationship 33
Sexually abusive behavior 163
Sheehy, Gail
  *New Passages* 97
Shekerjian, Denise
  *Uncommon Genius. How Great
    Ideas Are Born* 207
Shift in the concept of morality,
  272

Shopenhauer, Arthur (quote) 186
Sleep
  and calcium 33
  and melatonin 33
  and reading 34
  not enough 32
    and technology 32
  six actions to help you 33
Sliding-fee scale 104
Slow-to-Warm-Up Child 232
Special needs children 250
  commitment to 252
  letter of tribute to the parents of
    248
  mentoring
    defining moment 252
  talented 251
Spina Bifida 248
Squeaker 121, 122, 123
Staying power 257 - 259
Stop ripping each other off 293
Stowe, Vermont, skiing 221
Strengthening family time
  wish two 277
Substance abuse
  and unemployment 211
Success attributes of children with
  learning disabilities 236
Suicidal thoughts, a cry for help
  99
Suicide
  is first degree murder 99
  psychotheray 99
Suicide bombers 205
Super-mom 156, 157, 158
Support
  highest form of confrontation 87
  in building self-esteem 86
  understanding what it is 86
  understanding what it is not 87

## T

Take care of yourself 64
Takers 59
Taxpayer bailout 207
Teaching English in a Foreign
    Land (TEFL) 65
Technology 273
    and sleep 32
    suggestions to preserve its
        importance but keep it
        from running our lives 72
Teddy 124, 125, 126, 127
Teen suicide rate 273
Terrorism 294
Texting 70
Thinking of things you are
    thankful for and sleep 34
Thirteen wishes to rebuild a nation
    269 - 296
Three Most Important Questions
    for Your Significant Others 83
*TIME* magazine 188
Torture 188
*Touch the Future* (Newsletter)
    "Home Alone America" 273
Trader Joe's 33
Trophy children 224
Tsunami 300
Twelve-Step AA Program 40, 123
Two opposite positive forces
    within each person 24
Two parts of a client 50
Tzu, Sun
    *The Art of War* 205

## U

Unconscious, the 48
Understanding 309
    one way to love someone 154
Unemployed
    return a sense of community and
        purpose 210

Unemployment
    and depression 211
    and substance abuse 211
Unethical behavior 191
    in clients 192
Universal energy or chi 189
Universal medical insurance
    wish eight 288
Universe
    energy within 31
Unresolved conflict 142

## V

Validation 69, 309
Valium 48
Van Der Kolk, Bessel
    "In the Eye of the Storm" 160
Virtual world 71
Voluntary assessment 212

## W

War and birth 140
When someone hurts you 142
Wildlife Rescue Organization 12,
    13
Wisdom
    children's 50, 51
Working couples
    and splitting the chores 158
    statistics regarding 155
Wren, Carol and Eihorn, Jay
    *Hanging by a Twig:*
        *Understanding and*
        *Counseling Adults with*
        *Learning Disabilities and*
        *ADD* 234

## X

Xanax 48

## Y

You Tube 70

# ACKNOWLEDGMENTS

My first acknowledgment is to the clients who have taken the responsibility and courage to come and talk with me. I have the highest respect for the hard work they have done, the emotions they have shared, and the responsibility they have taken for making their lives run successfully. Questions that have been asked many times constitute many of the titles of the following essays and dialogues. This book would not exist without my ongoing work with each client. They are my teachers and mentors, sharing with me "defining moments." No psychotherapy is a good one unless both of us learn something new.

Secondly, I would like to thank my husband, David McArthur PhD as my computer expert with his immediate availability to help me format this manuscript into a presentable document, bail me out from computer errors, and keep ongoing backups of this manuscript at his work location. I thank my family for giving me time to write when it was not always convenient for them.

I would like to thank Connie Hood, Charlotte Fletcher PhD, Steven McNicholl, Ruth Ridenour, Barbara Mullens-Geier, Gohar Chivichyan, Portia Artunian, Jennie Redner, MAI, and Linda Simmons for reading and supplying editing suggestions for many of the essays. Linda Simmons and I shared a joint experience of writing a book at the same time, giving each other encouragement and support. My special thanks go to Thomas Howell, PhD, to Bernard Liebman PhD, ABPP for reading the entire manuscript and offering suggestions and an endorsement, and to Suzanne Arms for her Foreword, reading, encouragement and help with publication.

Writing a book is the easy part for an author. This book would never have seen the light of day without the guidance and support from One-On-One Book Production and Marketing with Carolyn Porter and Alan Gadney.

# ABOUT THE AUTHOR

**Dorothea McArthur, PhD, ABPP** is a Diplomate Clinical Psychologist maintaining a private psychotherapy practice for the past thirty-four years. She is also a wife, mother, grandmother, artist, choral singer, and author of four other books.

*Photograph by Susan Harper Slate*

Dr. McArthur acquired a BA from the University of Rochester in English Literature. She then attended Columbia University and the Art Students League in New York City to acquire the qualifications for her to achieve a Master of Arts in Teaching at the Rhode Island School of Design in sculpture and drawing.

Dorothea married and moved to Southern California to pursue advanced degrees in psychology. She acquired a M.Ed. in Counseling Psychology from the University of California in Santa Barbara, and a PhD in Clinical Psychology from the California School of Professional Psychology in Los Angeles.

After seven years at the Verdugo Mental Health Center in Glendale, California, as Head of Adult Services and their training program for graduate students, Dorothea transitioned into full-time private practice. She sees individuals, couples and families, with a specialization in crisis intervention, adoption, sexual abuse, borderline personality, learning difficulties, marital issues, and surviving as a working artist. She has always maintained a sliding scale fee, believing that psychotherapy should be available for all people at all socioeconomic levels.

Dorothea and her husband adopted Kendall at birth, and began a Cooperative adoption in which their daughter visited periodically with her birth family. Kendall is in ongoing present contact while both birth and adoptive mothers came to know and respect each other. Kendall and her daughter, Kaitlyn, now constitute a three generational family

During this time, Dr. McArthur became a Diplomate Clinical Psychologist of the American Board of Professional Psychology, and served on their board from 1987-1993. She was one of the authors for the *Revised Clinical Diplomate Oral Examination Manual for Examiner and Examinee.*

In 1994, McArthur created the Independent Psychotherapy Network, a group of 15 psychotherapists meeting monthly to share information for the purpose of maintaining clinical practice at the highest level of quality. She has been elected their president for the past seventeen years.

Dorothea's artistic talent migrated from sculpture and drawing into writing. She authored, with Dr. Glen Roberts, the director of the Verdugo Mental Health Center, the *Roberts Apperception Test for Children (RATC),* a projective test for children. By 1988 she had published one of the few books on the borderline patient, written specifically for the educated lay public, clients and therapists, entitled *Birth of a Self in Adulthood.*

Two other books, besides *Defining Moments,* are being completed for publication. The first is *Love Beyond Love,* a memoir of Dorothea's family's journey through open, closed and cooperative adoption, and all of the learning that took place for everyone. In this book, Dorothea has also shared the disguised experience she gained from assisting many members of the adoption triangle (adoptees, birth parents and adoptive parents) within her private practice.

*Tomorrow's Child* has been written with the help of award winning author Suzanne Arms. This book contains a Parent-Child Checklist and a set of Children Rights, with ways to actualize those needs and rights. Responsibilties of parents and teachers are presented within the home and the community through specific case examples.

Dr. McArthur has done many presentations over the years on adoption, parenting, borderline patient, crisis intervention and short-term psychotherapy. Throughout the years, she has supervised many interns working with special needs kids and K-12 students in the parochial schools through a project entitled Outreach Concerns. She has done training psychotherapies for many master and doctoral level students from Alliant University.

Dorothea continues her private practice in Los Angeles. In her spare time, she does gardening with succulents and takes expeditions into nature. She and her husband have enjoyed thirty years of choral singing, resulting in performances at the Los Angeles Olympics opening ceremony, Hollywood Bowl, and Los Angeles Philharmonic. Together, they rescue and care for many dogs and cats who have lived in their home over the forty-three years of marriage.

Additional copies of *Defining Moments*
are available through your favorite
book dealer or from the publisher:

Cove Press
2632 Cove Avenue
Los Angeles, CA 90039-3123
323-666-3598
Fax: 323-666-3598
Website: www.CovePressBooks.com
E-mail: Cove.Books.Publishing@gmail.com

*Defining Moments*
ISBN Softbound: 978-0-9847735-0-3, $19.95
ISBN Hardbound: 978-0-9847735-1-0, $24.95
Add $5.50 shipping for first copy
($2.00 each additional copy)
plus sales tax for CA orders.

If you wish to contact
Dorothea S. McArthur, PhD. ABPP
her E-mail address is
DorotheaMcArthur@gmail.com
Phone number is 323-663-2340
Website: www.DorotheaMcArthur.com